What Would

G000153489

Lyndsay Brown

What Would Love Do?

Parenting a child through the first year
of gender transition

For my precious Stirling and Olivia,
from whom I have learnt so much:

'Do not be dismayed by the brokenness of the world.
All things break. And all things can be mended.
Not with time, as they say, but with intention.
So go. Love intentionally, extravagantly, unconditionally.
The broken world waits in darkness for the light that is you.'
L.R. Knost

*What Would Love Do?: Parenting a child through the first year
of gender transition*
ISBN 978 1 76041 864 9
Copyright © Lyndsay Brown 2020
Cover photographs by Wendy Williams

First published 2020 by
GINNINDERRA PRESS
PO Box 3461 Port Adelaide 5015
www.ginninderrapress.com.au

Contents

Maybe the journey isn't so much about becoming anything.
Maybe it's about unbecoming everything that isn't really you so that
you can be who you were meant to be in the first place.

– Paulo Coelho

Preface

Every story has a beginning, if not an end. But where does this story start? Does it start with my connection with my husband as our love was forged in the crucible of student politics and our passion to change the world? Does it start with the endless visits to fertility specialists, the painful operations and procedures I endured in my longing to become a parent? Does it start in a petri dish as sperm and eggs fused to form my beloved twin boys? Or perhaps it started on 20 March 2004 as they were handed to me from the belly of our surrogate, Brigitte, my heart already swollen with love for them.

My journey as a parent could be said to have begun at any of these moments in time: it was a slow and meandering start. But my journey as the parent of a transgender child started on 25 October at about eight-fifteen p.m. It was abrupt and shocking, with no prior contemplations or parental imaginings to pave the way. It was the birth of a daughter I had absolutely not anticipated even for a single moment in my life until then.

Most names and identifying features have been changed in order to protect the identities of those who may not want to be identified. Where I have referenced the stories of other trans parents, I have created amlagamated characters in order to protect their anonymity.

I wrote this book using notes that I made in my daily diary. The book, thus, is a reord of my own transitioning as a new trans parent just as much as it is my reflections on my daughter's early journey.

1

The tiger in the psychiatrist's room

In my dream, I was in a doctor's consulting room with my two boys and there was a tiger in the room with us: a giant, orange, striped, soft and furry tiger. We were seeing a paediatrician who was checking out my boys and this was her pet tiger. The tiger seemed to be hostile only towards me, gently threatening to attack me, clearly smelling my fear. I was absolutely terrified of it. The doctor was impatient with me for my fears. She just ignored the tiger, stepping around it as she checked my boys. I had no way of controlling my fear. I had a very visceral reaction to the beast. Everywhere we went, so did the tiger. My boys were entirely unfazed by it, cuddling it and playing with it.

The day that our lives changed fundamentally and forever – Wednesday 25 October 2017 – Angus was away working in Singapore and the boys and I were at home in Manly on the northern beaches of Sydney. Angus being away meant that we were having pasta for dinner – again. When Angus is at home in Sydney, we have a balanced meal for dinner: meat, carbohydrates and at least three vegetables. When he is away, the boys ask if we can have pasta every night, and most often I agree because it is so easy to make pasta and because I am always reluctant to be in the kitchen for long. That night, I had cooked spag bol, the outright favourite pasta meal for both boys, and also one that allows me to get maximum vegetables into them.

When they had eaten two or three giant bowls each, it was

Orlando's turn to take the dogs out for an evening walk, and Stirling's turn to help me tidy up the kitchen.

As always when I cooked, I had created extensive chaos in the kitchen and a significant clean-up was required. While I was washing the many pots and pans I had managed to use, and Stirling was packing the dishwasher, he asked me a seemingly ordinary question, 'Mum, you know how Orlando and I like to play Would You Rather…?'

Of course, I knew this word game of impossible dilemmas. Would you rather be born blind or deaf? Would you rather climb Mount Everest or go on a spaceship to the moon?. I had heard them playing it with each other for months. That is one of the joys of being a twin: usually going through the same phase/interest/game at the same time.

'Yep,' I said, only half listening because I was absorbed in watching how badly Stirling was stacking the dishwasher, with all the plates pushing up against each other so that they had no prospect of being properly cleaned. I also knew that, as a thirteen-year-old, he was hypersensitive to criticism, so I was thinking about how to ask him to do a better job while still keeping him cheerful and willing to pack the dishwasher again.

'Well, the other day when Orlando and I were walking the dogs to Graham Reserve, he asked me, "Would you rather win a million bucks or wake up as a woman?" and so, of course, I said, "Win a million bucks," and he said, "Well, I would rather wake up as a woman." I said OK, then he said, "I'm not straight, you know."'

'What did you say then?' I asked.

'I said, "Cool, cool, cool." Then the next day, when we were walking the dogs along the beachfront, he asked me, "Would you rather be an ugly man or a beautiful woman?" and I didn't answer. But he did. He said, "I would rather be a beautiful woman."'

As Stirling said this, a seismic shock ran through me, leaving me with a disassociated, out-of-body feeling. I had never ever considered the possibility of Orlando being transgender, but at a fundamental level, this secret rang true and seemed absolutely possible as an explanation for his deeply depressed state of mind.

I was aware of Stirling looking intensely and anxiously at me, clearly overwhelmed by this secret and completely conscious that he was revealing something loaded with significance about his brother. From the time that he was very young, it had been apparent to me that Stirling is powerfully socially attuned, instinctively able to identify what is really going on in an interpersonal interaction or social situation. But he also needs to be the good guy, and he eschews conflict, so he wasn't prepared to be identified as the source of this revelation: he made it very clear to me that I couldn't tell Orlando that he had told me the story because, he said, it would be a trust-breaker between the two of them.

Like many twins, Orlando and Stirling's relationship is complex, competitive and connected. They live their lives contingently, always in relation to each other, always conscious of where their twin is and what he is doing, jealously observing whether their brother might have more of anything (love, attention, lollies, money, presents, access to technology and so on), mostly wanting to be with him, and often needing space from him too. Stirling knew that his being the source of this revelation to me about his brother would impact, probably negatively, on his relationship with Orlando, so I had to reassure him that I would not tell his brother that he had spoken to me about it.

Consequently, on that very auspicious evening, despite being in a state of profound shock, I continued with the preparations for bedtime as though it was business as usual, all the while my thoughts racing in every direction and my stomach churning in the way that it always does when my anxiety levels are sky-high. As I cajoled both boys into the shower, one after the other, and then into bed to read, I could only think about Stirling's revelation, and how it potentially explained what had been going on with Orlando over the last year or two.

I thought about how, a year or more before, Orlando had been diagnosed with depression by a psychiatrist and he was on antidepressants that seemed to be making no difference to his state of mind. I also reflected on how much he had hated being in an all-boys selective high school (even though he had thrived academically and had chosen to go to that school himself), and how, even when we moved him to Stirling's nurturing co-educational high school, he was still suicidally unhappy.

For years, Angus and I had been lost and desperate because we could not understand *why* Orlando was so despairing. Yes, we had emigrated from Durban to Sydney six years before and emigration had been very tough on all of us but we were relatively settled in Manly by this stage and Orlando lived in a happy home full of love and compassion, with parents who loved each other and a brother with whom he had a lot of fun. We lived in a gorgeous little house close to North Steyne beach, the children went to enriching and well-resourced schools, and we had friends and family around us with whom we had positive social connections. We had a good life. Yet, despite all this, and despite Orlando's visits to a psychiatrist and a psychologist, we were no closer to understanding the source of his profound depression and what seemed to me his sense of inherent alienation in and from the world. Perhaps, I thought to myself on that fateful night while I haphazardly folded the clean washing, we might finally have solved the mystery of what had been making Orlando so profoundly, mournfully sad.

I was so distracted by these thoughts that I didn't really notice what was going on around me, and so the boys took much longer getting to bed than usual. When, finally, Orlando was ready to sleep, I went to into his room to say goodnight and I lay down in his bed to chat and lightly scratch his back.

Most nights I tried to make time to be with my boys at bedtime: it encourages them to open up and talk about what is going on for them, and I love the closeness that it generates between us. Orlando is less able to talk about what is in his heart, always keener to talk about what is happening in his head, what he is thinking about at that time – usually something about the material world that he has observed and is pondering. That night, though, I was hoping desperately that he would tell me the monumental news about himself, but he didn't.

He did say to me, again, 'Mom, I just don't fit in at school because I'm so different.'

When I asked him how he was different, he couldn't, or wouldn't, say. He just said that he was feeling very demotivated at school. This was very unusual for him because, no matter how miserable he had felt in the past, he had continued to work diligently. Then he told me that he was worried that he was going to harm himself and that he was still having suicidal thoughts. This wasn't the first time he had said this to me, but that night it frightened me more than usual; that night, my fear was right off the scale.

I felt hopeless and helpless as I tried, in vain, to instil hope in him. 'Dad and I love you so much, babe. You're a very special human being. I know you're feeling sad now but it won't always be that way. We'll make more time for you to talk to Joy [his psychiatrist] about how much you're struggling.' And on and on. As I tried to reassure him in this way, I knew I was just talking for the sake of talking and connecing, being present with him so that he knew that I loved him. I never had the sense that what I said at times like this significantly altered his sense that life wasn't worth living. However, as his parent, I had to try everything to stave of this psychological emptiness and darkness.

'OK,' he said, 'you know that I'm too close to you to talk to you, so it'll be good if I can chat to Joy.'

When eventually Orlando settled and was near sleep, I went to Stirling's room to lie with him in his bed for a while. He is a very tactile and affectionate child and, most nights, he asks Angus or me to lie with him, and he will snuggle up close and chat for hours if we stay there.

'What are we going to do, Mum?' he asked, as though, somehow, I might know.

'I don't know, babe, but it will be OK.' I really had no idea if this was true but I felt I had to reassure him – and me. I hugged him tightly and, for once, we didn't say much.

Stirling is such a strong extrovert, his energy levels so completely determined by his interaction with others, that he can't actually fall asleep with me there. So eventually, I kissed him goodnight, patted Serena and Archimedes, already asleep in their soft dog baskets next to his bed, and headed for the study to email Angus about Stirling's revelation to me.

As I sat down in our very small study, I was deeply still for the first time in a few hours, my heart racing so hard that I could barely breathe. I am not someone who can contain big news and sit with it on my own. I needed to talk to Angus about this development but, oddly enough, I felt conflicted about telling him: part of me believed that if I didn't write down in an email what I had learnt from Stirling, then perhaps it would not be true. At the same time, though, I was overwhelmed and scared, and I simply could not contain myself and had to talk. So I wrote to Angus with all the details.

Hey babe, I don't even know how or where to start this heavy email. It's been an incredibly hectic night. It's all mixed up but essentially what happened is that Stirling told me – very confidentially – that Orlando came out to him a few weeks ago as gay, and then he told Stirling that he would rather be a beautiful woman than a handsome man and that he wishes I would let him wear make-up. He told me I couldn't tell Orlando that he had said all this. He also said that Orlando doesn't realise how his sadness makes us all sad and how hard it is for all of us to cope with his sadness.

Then, at bedtime, Orlando was telling me he doesn't fit in at school because he's different but he wouldn't say why and he told me that he worries he'll harm himself and he feels demotivated at school.

God, Angus, I feel overwhelmed and terrified and I so wish that you were here. This all feels so heavy that I don't even know how to send this email to you. I feel as though if I don't send it, that it may all not be true. Not sure how I'll sleep tonight.

Love you L

When he got my email, Angus Facetimed me immediately. He was on the way to dinner. Sitting in a taxi in Singapore, the telecommunications poor at best, Angus wasn't able to say much, except to register his caution in response to my garbled and tearful commentary that our baby was probably transgender.

'Sweetie, I hear that you're upset but let's not jump to conclusions here. It's pretty shocking what Stirling told you but he may have it all wrong and maybe it was just part of their word games or maybe Stirling misheard what Orlando said. You know he's like you and he can get a bit carried away.'

Angus's response reflected how much he is used to my rather melodramatic, impulsive, emotional and intense approach to life, an approach which is the absolute antithesis of his rational, calm and understated approach. Unlike me, he won't accept anything at face value or without significant evidence. I guess it was inevitable that, in this situation, I would immediately overreact and he would, correspondingly, underreact.

The taxi arrived at the restaurant where Angus was due to meet his friend, so he said he would call me later when he got back to his hotel. I sat at my desk for a few more hours in my fug, thinking chaotically about everything and nothing.

I had lived through a childhood where the things that I most feared usually did happen. For example, when I was eight, I feared my mother would leave my father and move in with the violent alcoholic with whom she was having an affair, and that did indeed occur. After years of my childhood fears materialising in this way, I learnt to assume the worst and was therefore inherently, as an adult, rather pessimistic and prone to catastrophise.

Because of this tendency, my mind kept wondering to the worst possible scenarios for Orlando, including living a troubled life as a transgender outsider, regarded by society as odd and different and hence marginalised and ostracised, never able to love and work in the way that I had imagined and anticipated for him. As far as I knew at that time, being transgender would mean a lifetime of social isolation and rejection, limited opportunities, painful medical procedures and endless hormone treatments. It seemed, quite possibly, the most difficult life that a person could lead. My heart ached for our darling child.

As I sat there ruminating, slumped in my desk chair, I remembered an older transgender woman whom I had met recently, the aunt of a friend, who had transitioned in her sixties and who looked so gaudy with her excessive make-up and denim miniskirt and very low-cut tops, someone who didn't fit into any of my preconceived ideas of what was male or female. I regard myself as someone who is open-minded and progressive and even I was alienated from this woman, regarding her as a misfit, observing her from a distance at the barbecue where we met her, talking awkwardly to her because I saw her as different and unfamiliar. I knew from my friend that his aunt was alienated from much of her family, who refused to accommodate her gender transition, and so she wandered around the world looking for a place to belong, not welcomed into most of society,forced into doing menial work because she wasn't acceptable in mainstream society, and living her life largely alone.

I could not bear the idea that this might be the life that my darling child might lead one day. Orlando is a bright and academic youngster and I realised, as I sat staring blankly at my computer screen, that my long-term dreams for him included him doing very well at university, working as a scientist or engineer in an area where he was able to have a significant influence and having a happy long-term relationship with a life partner, and maybe even a few children. And now, it seemed to me, those dreams were impossible to achieve, given the way the way that transgender people seemed to be excluded from mainstream society, rejected and isolated, and therefore never able to actualise their potential.

I was still at my desk when Angus called and we talked about this immense and overwhelming development. It was apparent from our disjointed conversation that both of us were entirely blindsided by the possibility of having a transgender child and what it would mean for his future life.

'Perhaps it's a phase,' Angus suggested, not very hopefully.

'I don't know,' I said. 'Being transgender really would explain why Orlando has been so depressed and suicidal for years. He's been living with this massive secret. And think about all the transgender teen novels we've seen him reading on his Kindle in the last year. And how he wants to do ballet, when he seems a very unlikely candidate for a ballet class.'

'And,' added Angus, 'this sheds a whole new light on his comment to me the other day when you dropped us at the Kiss and Ride at the Manly Wharf. Remember I said something about picking up his bag and he said to me, "You guys should not assume my gender." At that time, we all laughed at his joke but now I realise maybe he wasn't joking, maybe he was trying to tell us something.'

It seemed that perhaps Orlando had been leaving us clues, maybe unconsciously, hoping that we would work out his secret. As Angus and I spoke, it became clearer and clearer to me that this secret that Orlando was keeping – that he felt that he was a girl/woman – was very likely the basis for his deep and dark soul-sadness.

I said to Angus, 'I'll keep him home tomorrow and take him to see Joy to get a different antidepressant, although probably that isn't going to help if he's depressed because he's transgender. Maybe he's ready to talk to Joy about this now.'

When I ended the call, I realised that it was Angus's birthday – 25 October – and that I hadn't even asked him whether he had had any celebrations. It was apparent that Angus hadn't told the friend with whom he had dinner the big news about our Orlando. I wasn't surprised. Angus is an intensely private person and, unlike me, a key coping strategy for him in times of emotional turmoil is to withdraw into himself, thinking and reflecting and analysing until he feels that he has fully understood what is troubling him. Then he might talk to one or two other people, sharing, maybe even only partially, his clearly formulated thoughts about the subject. In addition, it would also have been difficult for him to talk to his friend about the dramatic news because it was so new and unreal to him and there were, as yet, no words for him to express it.

As I continued to sit, inertly, in front of my flickering screen, I thought about how we would always remember the date that our lives changed forever. 25 October. Angus's birthday.

Slowly, while sitting there, I felt my familiar need to engage with the people I am close to in order to survive any kind of emotional turmoil. I opened up my Gmail and starting typing an email to my very good friend Jacqui, who lived nearby. Jacqui and I have similar histories: we are both English teachers who retrained as psychologists at the Pietermaritzburg campus of the University of Natal in South Africa, and we both place a high value on relationships, home life, reading, open conversations, holidays, equality and social justice. We also love to email and text each other about what is going on in our everyday lives, and to support each other in tough times. This was definitely a moment for this kind of reaching out. I couldn't write it all again, so I simply cut and pasted the core of my earlier email to Angus and sent that on to Jacqui as a way of telling her my news.

Like me, Jacqui and her phone are rarely separated and so, within a few minutes, she had replied to my email, a response that immediately helped me to feel heard and understood.

Lynds, I can only imagine how freaked out you are about Orlando. I know that you would be fine with him being gay, but the gender stuff and suicidality are another thing altogether.

Jacs suggested we meet for coffee the next day but, before I could commit to it, I had to see when I would be able to book an appointment with Joy. I needed her help, as I felt totally overwhelmed and had no way of dealing with this on my own.

Eventually I went to bed and, unsurprisingly, I really struggled to fall asleep and stay asleep. When I did finally manage to sleep, I woke up pretty quickly and, as I came to consciousness, I found myself wondering why something felt so utterly, utterly wrong in my life. Then I remembered that my enormous, nearly six-foot boy believed himself to be a girl; that he felt that he was born a girl. As I remembered this, I felt shock waves coursing through my body. Again and again, my fears about Orlando's future overwhelmed me. What kind of life was my child going to have in this world that had only just started to accept and welcome people who were gay and lesbian? How would my child be able to cope with it all? Would he ever be happy now? Who would love him? Would he be able to have children? How would Angus and I cope? What about Stirling, who might be about to lose a twin brother and acquire a twin sister? Was any semblance of normality possible ever again for our family?

As I lay in bed tossing and turning, I was entirely and absolutely at sea in wild and uncharted waters, waves crashing around me, no direction, no sense of safety, unable to make sense of it. I think my traumatised state of being was, to a certain extent, a consequence of the news being completely and absolutely unexpected. In retrospect, it was probably also tough for me to process the news because I didn't really know any transgender person living a happy and successful life, and so I couldn't conceptualise Orlando ever living a happy and successful life if he was transgender.

At one point, I got tired of my racing, chaotic thoughts and I went down to the kitchen in search of comfort food. I made myself porridge, took more Panadol, and eventually went back to bed, desperate for the obliteration and escape that sleep offered.

In one of the brief periods when I was sleeping, I had a dream that woke me in a sweat, dizzy and breathless. I was too terrified to sleep again in case I returned to the dream so I got up to email the details of the dream to my Durban friend Fawn, someone with whom I have always shared my dream life. Fawn is a psychologist with a strong interest in the psychic power of dreams to help us to understand ourselves in our waking world. She had been my informal supervisor when I was doing my internship as a psychologist in Durban in the mid-1990s. Within a few weeks of our first meeting, she and I had bonded closely over our mutually dysfunctional childhoods and our shared belief that the unexamined life was not worth living. Our friendship had deepened from there, and we had spent many evenings together, over many years, exploring Durban's restaurants together, drinking gin and tonic and talking, talking, talking. Indeed, when Angus and I emigrated from

Durban to live in Sydney, leaving Fawn was one of the very hardest losses for me in the move. Over the years since the emigration, we had managed to keep up a long-distance friendship via email, sharing the stories of our lives as openly and honestly as ever. I wrote to her, knowing she would hear me and understand me.

> Hi. Fawn. I woke up a few minutes ago unable to sleep because of a dream where I was in a doctor's consulting room with my two boys and there was a tiger in there with us: a giant, orange, striped, soft and furry tiger. We were seeing a paediatrician who was checking out my boys and this was her pet tiger. This tiger seemed to be hostile only towards me, gently threatening to attack me, clearly smelling my fear. I was absolutely terrified of it. The doctor was impatient with me for my fears. She just ignored the tiger, stepping around it as she checked my boys. I had no way of controlling my fear, I had a very visceral reaction to this beast. Everywhere we went, so did the tiger. My boys were entirely unfazed by it, even cuddling and playing with it.

As I typed up the dream to Fawn, I knew that the day residue – the reference in my waking life that gave content/plot to the dream – was the kelpie dog that Joy had in her room during her sessions. She recently had to send it to live on a farm because it had begun to growl at young patients. And, of course, the meaning of the dream was fairly self-evident, highlighting my terror as I tried to process the new life-changing, completely unanticipated information about Orlando. What was interesting was that the doctor and the children were completely unafraid of this tiger; the children were even happy to play with it.

After writing to Fawn, I went back to bed, lying there exhausted and eventually falling into a troubled sleep. When the alarm on my phone went off at six, I was groggy and, initially, confused about why I was so exhausted. As it dawned on me that Orlando was probably transgender, I was instantly wide awake and shaky, immediately aware of the threatening tiger in my life. I am *skrikwakker*, I thought to myself, a very apt Afrikaans expression meaning wide awake with shock and fear.

I slowly got up, freezing cold in the way that I always am when I haven't slept enough. I wrapped myself tightly in my velour men's winter gown and threaded my feet into my slippers. As I brushed my teeth, my reflection in the mirror was barely recognisable and seemed miles away. I was conscious of the feeling of the tiger still being nearby. The dogs were jumping energetically around my feet, working hard to get me downstairs to feed them. They are so cheerful, I thought to myself, because they have no idea at all how radically our lives might have changed; they have no idea of the tiger in our presence.

I shut Orlando's door so that the morning noise didn't disturb him. He wasn't going to school that day, so he could sleep in a bit. Then I went downstairs, fed the dogs, made coffee and porridge, concentrating really hard on what I was doing because I was so distracted. I felt queasy and could not imagine eating or drinking anything at all ever again, but I craved the familiarity of my morning routine and so I just kept moving forward and preparing the food. The warm porridge curled down inside of me, seeking to fight off the tiger within.

At six-thirty, I opened the blinds and windows in Stirling's room, reminding him that it was Thursday and that he had cricket training after school so he needed to take his cricket gear with him to school. He is a very reluctant waker in the mornings – unless there is sport during or after school – so I knew that reminding him about cricket training was a way to get him up and going without coaxing.

'Orlando isn't going to school. I'm taking him to the psychiatrist to get him a new antidepressant because the one he's on isn't working.'

His revelation about Orlando hung in the air between us, unspoken but very loud. He got ready without any further prompting, putting on yesterday's crumpled school uniform, eating his cereal – while catching up on Instagram, of course.

While Stirling was eating, Orlando woke up on his own and came downstairs, asking me crossly, 'Why didn't you wake me, Mum? You know I need a lot of time to get ready in the morning.'

I told him that he wasn't going to school that day as he needed to see

Joy to discuss his medication. He didn't argue but, while eating his giant pile of gluten-free toast and eggs, he did ask me, completely out of the blue, 'Will you and Dad love me no matter what?'

'Of course, babe, we will always always absolutely love you and accept you for who you are.'

'Will Joy judge me?'

'Of course not. That's her job: to be unconditionally accepting and supportive and to help you with whatever you need help.'

After I had dropped Stirling at the wharf so that he could get the ferry and train to his school in the city, Orlando and I set off to walk the dogs. Walking the dogs is a powerful ritual for him and me, one which has, most often, been a connected and chatty experience. There is something about us walking side by side together that inspires Orlando to talk, sometimes even monologue for hours, in a way that reminds me of Aristotle's peripatetic walking and talking learning methodology that I had used in a research project so many years ago. Usually my conversations with Orlando are about how the world works, in big and small ways, and sometimes, only sometimes, we talk about personal matters of the heart.

On this day, however, I didn't wait for him to initiate the conversation as I usually did. I could not contain myself. As soon as we were around the corner from home, I asked Orlando the big question: 'I've put together your joke about how we shouldn't assume your gender with your interest in reading transgender teen novels, and your depression, and I'm wondering if you're struggling with your gender identity?'

His head jerked backwards and he looked shocked. He kept walking, not looking at me, absolutely silent.

'Is that right, Orlando?'

'Yes. I'm gender-dysphoric.'

And there it was. Out in the open. True. Our son was, in fact, quite likely our daughter. Amidst all of the intense trauma of this moment, I consciously acknowledged to myself that, for each of us in our family, our lives had changed irrevocably. After a few moments of walking in a mutually shocked silence, I asked Orlando a series of questions which he, very reluctantly, answered.

'How long has this been troubling you, Orlando?'

'About a year, maybe longer.'

'How long have you been thinking about it?'

'I don't know. At first, I assumed I was gay and then I thought I was bisexual and then, when I read all those transgender books, I realised I was like them. But I've always known that I'm different in some big way.'

'Who have you talked to about this?'

'Nobody.'

I realised that for Orlando, who had always struggled to recognise nuances in interpersonal communication, the Would You Rather…? game that he had played with Stirling the previous week did not, for him, actually constitute telling Stirling that he was gender-dysphoric. He had no idea that Stirling had read between the lines and recognised that Orlando was suggesting to him that he was potentially transgender.

I could see that Orlando was furious with me. He told me, with his eyes tight and furious, 'I wanted to tell you in my own time, Mum, when I was ready.' He wouldn't say anything else about the subject.

I told him – a few times – that Angus and I would love him and support him no matter what. He ignored me and walked slightly ahead of me, talking about anything other than gender dysphoria. And thus we walked and we talked: about dogs he had seen on the ferry, assessments that he had to do for school, whether newspapers would still be printed in five years' time, and many other mundane things, with me really only able to think about the monumental issue in our lives.

During our many silences, I berated myself over and over. How could Orlando have been so alone with these struggles for so long? How could I not have worked out what was going on for him? How could I have missed it all? I had trained as a psychologist and prided myself on my ability to know what was going on in situations like this. In addition, as a child of a dysfunctional childhood, I was usually acutely sensitive to the details of people's psychological pain. I was shocked that, despite my sense of having been enmeshed with Orlando, I not been able to recognise the name and nature of my child's trauma, that he had not felt able to tell me about his gender struggles. No wonder he had been so deeply and profoundly depressed. This mother-guilt stayed with me for months.

Later in our journey, I learnt from a psychologist who specialised in gender dysphoria that this is a very common experience for parents: the feeling of guilt at not having intuited at all that their child was struggling with something so significant as gender identity. This psychologist had been very gentle with me, explaining that the lack of knowing on my part was partly a reflection of the child's own confusion about what was really going on for her or him.

When Orlando and I finally got home from our walk that morning, the dogs were exhausted because we had walked further than usual – I had kept walking, hoping in vain that Orlando would talk to me about his secrets. I realise, in retrospect, that he didn't yet have the language to talk to me about his gender dysphoria, but at the time I wanted to know everything and was really struggling with his silence.

On the dot of nine a.m., I phoned Joy's receptionist and booked an afternoon appointment for us to see her.

I noticed that there was a brief WhatsApp message from Angus on my phone:

I hope you managed to sleep, sweetie. I've been awake since 3 worrying about our boy (?). I love you. A

I sent a few well-used emojis in reply. I didn't know what to say.

The previous evening, I had emailed my sister, Fiona to tell her about Stirling's revelation and when I finally looked at my phone, there were numerous missed messages asking me to call her. I finally did so, even though I didn't feel able to talk. Fiona lives on the northern beaches with her daughter and her partner. She works as a psychologist in a private psychiatric hospital in Sydney, running group therapy for inpatients and outpatients, so she is extremely adept at asking open-ended questions that get people talking. Despite her gentle, probing questions, I could not find ways to talk about this new development. I felt so intensely wordless, a most bizarre and unusual experience for me.

By then, I was late for work so I showered very quickly and rushed off to the supported playgroup that I co-facilitate as part of my community psychology job at a local community organisation.

When I arrived at work, my lovely co-workers asked me, 'How are you doing?' in their usual friendly and warm way.

I did not know what to say in response, given that there was only one thing on my mind. Of course, I didn't tell them what was really going on for me – I wouldn't have even known what words to use. Perhaps they thought I was being oddly and unusually distant that day. I don't know. I just worked on like an automaton, letting them make all the decisions about what play stations we would set up that day, following them around and trying to be helpful, even though I felt as though I wasn't present with them at all.

When the babies and toddlers arrived with their mothers, I looked at the youngsters intently, wondering if, someday, one of them might rock their parents' world with a massive revelation that changed everything about the past, present and future. Everything I saw and experienced was filtered through my new framework as a mother with a gender-dysphoric child. I saw the tiger everywhere I looked.

Somehow, I got through to lunchtime. During breaks, I phoned Orlando a few times to check that he was OK, pretending to him that I was phoning to see if he had eaten, or what he was watching on TV when really, I just needed to check that he was OK. And alive.

When I got home to him at lunchtime, I wrote an email to Nonnie, my friend and the deputy manager at the community organisation where I worked. I needed to let her know that I couldn't be at work that afternoon. I told her that I had discovered that the source of Orlando's depression was that he was gender-dysphoric and felt that probably he was, in fact, a she. It was so shocking to see this in printed text but what else could be said? There was no way to convey the information easily or lightly. Nonnie replied instantly and, as usual, she helped me to gain perspective.

> Poor Orlando. Whether this is real or not, in the long term, he has to be heard and allowed to process it all. Damn bloody hard. You will get through it. At least you now have a heads up that he's in pain and you can deal with it and him as a troubled alive child, not the awful alternative. Just let him know how much you love him regardless of anything else. This is big-picture stuff – none of it matters as long as he survives the process and you have your child.

As I read her email, I was reminded that Nonnie, a social worker who works largely with domestic violence survivors, has seen and heard more tales of heartache than most people. It is partly what makes her so able to see the big picture in moments of crisis.

In the car on the way to the appointment with Joy, I asked Orlando how he wanted to structure the session. He asked if I would go in first and tell Joy the story and then he would go in on his own and talk to her. I agreed, and then took the opportunity to see how he framed his revelation.

'What shall I tell Joy, Orlando?'

'Tell her that I'm gender-dysphoric and that I've read everything there is to read on the internet about being transgender. I've watched endless YouTube videos of parents of transgender kids talking about how devastated they are at losing the child they know and love because he or she is becoming someone else. Tell her that I've listened and watched many transgender people talking about their experiences and, even though I don't identify with any particular story, I do identify with parts of all of them.'

'OK.'

When we walked through Joy's red door, I was conscious again of how intensely I was moving through life at that time: the doorbell seemed so loud, the door seemed so red, the classical music in the waiting room seemed so melancholic, the bohemian receptionist so gentle and kind.

When Joy called us up to her room, I went on my own, leaving Orlando scrolling through his phone in the reception area. I almost fell into Joy's deep chair. I started immediately to explain the new developments.

She listened and listened, and then set out to contextualise, and to contain me. 'Lyndsay, you shouldn't take it for granted that Orlando is transgender – it's unusual for people to be transgender if they haven't shown, from a very young age, a hatred of their gender physicality and body, and a desire to embody the other gender in dress and activities. Also, a temporary attachment to gender dysphoria is common in people who, like Orlando, have Asperger's syndrome, as they feel so different in their world and hence latch on to gender dysphoria as a way of making sense of it. I've seen a number of teens with these issues but many of them have passed through this as a stage and, ultimately, identified as gay. But, of course, it is possible that he is, in fact, gender-dysphoric. We need to affirm Orlando's struggles and his need to work through the issues with a therapist, all the while trying to keep his mind open to all possibilities.'

As she spoke, I felt myself growing slightly hopeful that Orlando would not need to lead the tortured life of someone who felt themselves to be in the 'wrong body': perhaps Orlando was indeed, as Angus said, going through a phase, and he was not transgender but gay.

Then Joy told me something that immediately obliterated this hope. 'Recent research studies show that people with Asperger's are seven times more likely to be gender-dysphoric than those with no traits of Asperger's. I think it's time to tell Orlando that he has some traits of those with Asperger's. What do you think?'

I agreed that she could tell him. She gave me a script for a new antidepressant, Effexor, and another stronger drug to facilitate sleep and lessen anxiety. Then she called him in for his session with her. He told me afterwards that she had told him that he had some traits of Asperger's and explained to him what it meant.

Angus and I had known that Orlando was on the Asperger's

spectrum since he was six years old, at the same time that we emigrated to Sydney. Orlando's reaction to this massive change was extreme: he would have emotional outbursts and major meltdowns a number of times a day and he was fearful, anxious and clingy, refusing to separate from me or from Angus. By evening, he would turn on the shower and sit, holding his knees, folded into the corner of the blue and green mosaiced shower space, and shout over and over, 'I want to go home' and then, after a while, sob as though his little six-year-old heart was breaking. It was traumatic for all of us, especially as we were all struggling with the extensive loss and changes that emigrants have to process all day, every day. When I took him and Stirling to school in the morning, Orlando would cling to me like a baby vervet monkey, and his teacher would have to prise him off me and forcibly take him to class, leaving me tied into an emotional knot, anxious and troubled until I could fetch him in the afternoon.

After a few months of this trauma, Angus and I took Orlando to see a child psychologist, Amanda, who explained to us that the shock of emigration had activated a latent series of traits in Orlando which were very much associated with being on the Asperger's spectrum. We didn't know much about Asperger's then and did a lot of reading and research about it. Amanda tried to do play therapy with Orlando, working hard to get him to process his struggles while he played, but he barely spoke to her, instead finding much to fascinate him in Amanda's complex mechanical play-therapy toys. Amanda spent less and less time with Orlando and more and more time with me, teaching me about Asperger's so that I could understand and support him, and so that I could teach others in his world to do the same.

After a few months of our being in Sydney, the changes associated with our emigration became, relatively speaking, our new normal, and Orlando began to settle into school and life in Sydney, even coming to like his teacher very much. By the end of term two, he was finding schoolwork fun and stimulating and he was largely happy to go off to school in the morning. He started to make friends with a clever, kind and tolerant girl called Winona with whom he liked to read and play chess, and he started to relate more easily to some of the other children too.

As a teen, Orlando still has Asperger's, of course, but it is more muted and presents in low-key and less overwhelming ways than it did in those first torrid months in Sydney. Asperger's manifests differently in different people. For Orlando, it manifests primarily as difficulties with the reciprocity of social relationships and the formation of friendships, even while he wants to be sociable and he gets lonely when he doesn't see his peers for long periods of time. He struggles to empathise and acknowledge the perspectives of those around him, and he is not able to easily read people and non-verbal cues. Because of these struggles, he can be unintentionally insensitive, and even rude interpersonally – for example, when he is not able to notice and take into account the reaction of people listening to him. Sometimes too, he will put someone down when he could easily have avoided mentioning the person's flaws. He is also very easily overloaded by interactions with other people and sensory stimulation and he requires a lot of time on his own.

In 2013, Asperger's syndrome was included in the general diagnosis of autism, where it is a subcategory under the autism spectrum disorder – autism with social communication disorder. This new label is quite an accurate description of Orlando's struggles.

As someone on the spectrum, Orlando has a powerful need for structure, order, predictability and routine, and he has a higher than average resistance to change. He has highly focused interests (like computer building, woodworking, coding, and reading) and he needs to pursue them in order to maintain his psychological equilibrium. He is also easily anxious and depressed and he has a very low tolerance for any physical discomfort caused by, for example, heat and hunger.

However, as with most people with Asperger's, there are very significantly positive aspects to this diagnosis for Orlando: he can always be relied upon to be good, direct and honest (he cannot lie or say what he thinks he should say), he is morally upright and will always choose to do the right thing, he is smart and serious and he is a rational intellectual who is focused on the big picture, able to see the world in intriguing, unusual and interesting ways. He is also an original and independent individual, never tempted to follow the crowd – unless there is a very sound and rational reason for him to do so. For example, he has always had a de-schooling perspective on life, believing that learning in conventional schools is conceptualised in conventional, limited and controlling ways and that school students should have more freedom and choice over what and how and when they learn. Of course, this kind of thinking has been a common philosophical position for teens over time – and the reason why a song like Pink Floyd's 'We don't need no education' is an endlessly popular anthem for youth across generations – but Orlando can argue this de-schooling perspective very persuasively.

There are some people in Angus's extended family who I think may fall somewhere on the Asperger's spectrum. I have always found myself drawn to them because they are innately trustworthy, interesting and clever, good and kind, reliable and dependable, stable and consistent, different and idiosyncratic. People with this Aspie way of being are often people who change the world in big and small ways – not least because they are relatively immune to the impact of their words and actions on those around them. I am also drawn to them because, in so many ways, people on the spectrum are the antithesis of me and my family of origin: most of us in my family are emotional and impulsive, deeply empathic and highly/overly sensitive to social and psychological dynamics, excessive communicators, often focusing on the small picture and the dramas of everyday life and valuing relationships and people above ideas and thinking. People on the spectrum, with their calm and rational approach to life, are a good foil for people like me.

When Joy broke the news to him that he was on the Asperger's spectrum, the diagnosis made sense to him. His cousin and his brother had long called him Sheldon, associating him with the highly Aspie Sheldon Cooper in the TV series *Big Bang Theory*. Still, it became apparent to me in the next few months that the Asperger's diagnosis was very painful for Orlando to bear precisely because it explained his struggles with interaction, communication, friendships and relationships over the years. For him, being on the spectrum seems like a life sentence, because he sees it as signifying to him that he does not have the innate skills to engage with people easily and appropriately despite the fact that he actually craves socialising and relational connections. This is one of the tragic ironies for most people on the Asperger's spectrum.

Orlando also has to live with the sharp differences between him and his twin in these matters: Stirling is the polar opposite of someone on the Asperger's spectrum; he is acutely tuned into personal and interpersonal dynamics, deeply empathic and emotionally connected to people around him and easily able to form close and intimate relationships with people.

After Joy had explained to Orlando about Asperger's, she also told him that he needed to process all of his feelings about his sexuality and his gender slowly and openly in a therapeutic relationship with someone who deeply understood these experiences. She gave us the name and number of a therapist who works with teens with gender and sexuality issues and I had phoned this woman before we were through the doors of Joy's practice and onto the darkening streets of Surry Hills. By the time we were home, I had an appointment for Angus and me to see her the following week, and for Orlando to see her on his own a few days after our parental appointment.

The instant booking of these appointments reflects my unstoppable action taker way of being in the world. This approach is not always the best way of handling problems because sometimes I don't think through all the options before acting, but it is a way of coping that has been largely effective for me in my life. My tendency to quick action is probably also a response to my childhood experience of feeling powerless and unable to act when things at home were spiralling out of control.

On the way home, Orlando and I were talking about this very

significant session with Joy. Well, I was talking a lot, and Orlando was talking as little as possible. I was trying to promote an open and unfixed view of his gender struggles, and he said to me, quite firmly, 'I'm pretty sure, Mum, that I am gender-dysphoric. I've thought a lot about this for a long time.'

I remembered as he spoke that, unlike me, and very like Angus, Orlando is not an impulsive or impetuous person and I thought to myself that, if Orlando was sure that he was gender-dysphoric, then it was highly likely that he was.

When we arrived home, I found an email from Fawn responding to my email to her telling her my tiger dream and about Orlando being transgender. As I knew she would, she totally understood the emotional content of my dream and what my interaction with the tiger signified.

Ah, Lyndsay, my friend, this is huge and I can only imagine the wildly scary space you are in. The visceral sense of fear in your Tiger dream is so apt. I can hear how scared you are – I have never heard you so scared before – scared for Orlando, for yourself, for your family, for your future. How could you not be? Your beautiful boy with whom you have always been so close, always loved so deeply, in whom you have invested so much real love energy, has been struggling in a way that is foreign to you and in a way that you are absolutely unprepared for.

I am so glad he had the good sense to read and YouTube and get hold of as much information as he could about gender identity and sexuality identity – he is so courageous in doing that. He is exceptional for being able to talk to Stirling and with you about this at all. *So* many teens would have just been quiet and terrified about it all. It is a huge relief to me that you can now finally begin to tackle what his depression is really about.

Even though I felt so deeply heard and understood by Fawn, I still felt entirely and absolutely lost. I had never felt so uncertain about life and the future and what to say and do. I felt utterly haunted by the terrifying tiger that, I feared, was going to devour all of us.

2

Coming out as a trans family

In my dream, I was with a group of academic women with whom I had
been friendly at university: Jenny, Debby, Dori, Catherine, and others.
We were taking turns reading aloud extracts from a book of radical
stories about the world. These other women started off reading but then
they couldn't go on because it was too tough to read the stories, which
wouldn't 'stay still' on the page for them. I stood up and offered to read
the most radical story. I felt very scared but I knew that, somehow, I could
do it. I struggled through the story because it was hard to read the text as
the lines were jumping all over the place but I managed, although I didn't
get to the end of it before the bell rang for the lecture to end.

When my alarm woke me up on Day 3, I was very surprised to realise
that I had been sleeping at all. During the night, I had been constantly
conscious of being awake, no matter how often I took Panadol tablets
to take the edge off my heightened sense of anxiety and to encourage
me to sleep. As I brushed my teeth and looked at the foreigner in the
mirror, I felt again the physical presence of the waves of shock that
seemed to wash through me every few hours. My mind began to race
again. Was this really happening in my family? Did Angus and I really
have a child who was a different gender to the one that he was assigned
at birth? It was, actually, impossible to take this idea in whole.

Despite life feeling entirely different, I woke the children at the usual
time, they had their usual breakfasts, and I dropped them at the ferry
wharf at the usual time as they headed off to their usual Friday school day.

The night before, on the way back from cricket training, Stirling had asked me, rather vaguely, 'What's happening with my brother? I mean, what's happening with Orlando?'

'He's going to start taking a different antidepressant and take another kind of medication that will hopefully help him sleep well and feel less anxious. And next week he's going to start to see a psychologist who specialises in gender identity and sexuality struggles.'

I knew that I wasn't really answering Stirling's questions but I didn't have any more satisfactory answers to give him. I was as confused and unknowing as he was.

After dropping off the children (I was already beginning to feel awkward using the collective noun, boys), I went to meet my friend Lindy for a dog walk at Queenscliff Lagoon. Lindy was my first Australian-born friend after we emigrated to Sydney. She and her son, Sam, had lived over the road from us in our very first rental home and our kids had gone to the local public school together. I have always known that there was nothing I could tell Lindy that would shock her or cause her to judge me: she was brought up in the 1970s and 1980s by irreverent, broad-minded, hippie parents and, after leading an adventurous young adult life of her own, she is an open, non-judgemental and free-spirited adult. She is also a very genuine person with the surprisingly rare gift of always talking about what's really going on, and I love that about her. Because our kids were the same age, and at the same developmental stages, she and I often talked about what was happening with them and we had supported each other through our many parenting challenges.

As I saw Lindy, I burst into tears and, while she hugged me, I told her my big news. 'Lindy, Orlando is transgender. He says that he isn't a boy, that he's a girl.'

'Wow, we made a lot of predictions about our kids but we never saw that one coming, did we?'

We walked and talked while our four crazy dogs swam deep into the lagoon and rushed at the beautiful pelican pair that were there every morning. Eventually I got the whole story out and my unshockable friend was as shocked and surprised as me. I felt relieved to unburden myself so completely and so honestly. When we hugged goodbye at the car park, I felt quite noticeably calmer for the first time since Stirling's revelation, probably because I had been able to talk about it face-to-face, to someone I knew so well and trusted so absolutely.

It was a Friday, my day off work. My friend Jacqui also doesn't work on Fridays, so on most Friday mornings I would meet her at the Terrey Hills forest near her house so that we could go cycling in the bush together. On this Friday, Jacqui's friend Simone was also there with us. Simone was a novice cyclist, so we set off slowly on our bikes, cycling hesitantly on the muddy track, our wheels turning to the rhythm of our constant conversation. I filled Simone in on the new developments in my life and she told me that in her work with teens at Headspace (a mental health centre for teens), she had often worked with gender-dysphoric teens. Simone reiterated what I had learnt from Orlando's psychiatrist: that it is common for teens with Asperger's to present with gender dysphoria. We also talked about the high rates of attempted suicide amongst transgender teens: around fifty per cent, said Simone. That was a statistic that utterly terrified me.

Simone and Jacqui, excellent therapists and very special human beings that they are, were supportive and reassuring, giving me a sense that our family would survive and adjust to this crisis.

Usually when I am riding in this forest of many different eucalypt trees, I am struck by how beautiful my surroundings are, even while I am deeply immersed in a connective conversation with Jacqui. After spending time here with Jacqui over the years, I am familiar with the various wild flowers on the side of the track; I know when to anticipate that the track around the corner will be too steep or too bumpy, requiring me to get off my bike and push; I know when there is a fork in the path ahead and which path we will take. Yet, on this day, I got to the end of the ride and I realised that I hadn't noticed anything in the forest at all: I had been entirely and only focused on what Jacqui and Simone had been saying, desperate for them to help me to understand Orlando and gender dysphoria.

I drove home, inspired by my conversations with Jacqui and Simone to finally engage with Google in order to explore gender dysphoria and the experience of being transgender. Until then, I hadn't felt brave enough to explore these electronic terrains but Jacqui, in particular, had encouraged me to find out all that I could. Her husband, Guy, had terminal cancer and she had been remarkable – and very successful – at conducting extensive electronic research in order to understand all the possible treatments for Guy.

So, before I even got into the shower to rid myself of the cycling mud, I sat down at my desk and started the invaluable Googling process, clicking onto links, moving between Google Scholar and Wikipedia and so on, learning in the free-associative way that the internet gifts us. I researched until my head was bursting with trans information, facts, opinions, life stories, the experiences of other trans parents, transitioning stages, links between being transgender and having Asperger's and so on. Indeed, I got so caught up in my research that I lost any sense of time and was surprised when, suddenly, I heard the front door open and I realised that Angus had arrived home from Singapore.

As I went to kiss and hug him hello, someone I had loved for so long, our connection felt odd and different because I felt that I had fundamentally changed since he had left at the beginning of that same week. Angus and I had first met in 1986 in the anti-apartheid student movement at the Durban campus of the University of Natal, where we had been colleagues, comrades and friends, and then eventually fallen in love in 1990. We had been in a committed relationship since then. In the decades since I had met Angus, a great deal had happened that had formed and changed both of us: we had both been elected student leaders, focused solely on the struggle against apartheid; Angus had been awarded a Rhodes Scholarship and he had lived and studied in Oxford for two years; I had lived and worked in London and Oxford for a year; my mother (with whom I had a very complex relationship) had been diagnosed with lung cancer and died a traumatic and early death; Angus and I had co-parented my once troubled half-brother because both his parents (my mother and his father) had died by the time he was thirteen; I had completed six degrees while I considered various career options; I had been actively involved in the political campaign to help the African National Congress (ANC) win the first democratic elections in 1994; we had gone through eight desperate years of infertility troubles and eventually we had had our twins through a surrogacy arrangement with a friend whose pregnancy with our babies had been constantly threatened; I had started and finished the very demanding process of researching and writing a PhD and co-authoring a book on race; Angus's father had died a shocking death (falling from a mountain following a heart attack); and then, in 2011, he and I, and our twins, had emigrated from South Africa to Australia because we felt that we had to find a stable and secure future for our children and that South Africa was not likely to provide sufficient opportunities for them.

Moving countries in our forties had been overwhelmingly difficult professionally, personally, culturally, economically, geographically and politically. Emigration for us had entailed more identity shifts than we could ever have anticipated. It left us often, in those early years in Sydney, with a profound sense of being in a kind of self-imposed exile, feeling that we were unable to live in the country of our birth yet also that we were outsiders and interlopers existing in the margins of life in Australia. It was also very painful when we worked out, not long after arriving to live in Sydney, that Anglo born-Australians were often reluctant to engage with white South Africans, who have a sometimes-deserved reputation in Australia for being arrogant, entitled, rude, racist, overly ambitious, blunt – and more.

So, all things considered, there was *so* much that had profoundly transformed us in the thirty-one years that Angus and I had known each other and yet it felt to me, that day when Angus returned home to our house in Manly after just a few days away, that he and I were not the same people we had been when he had left for Singapore. It seemed to me as though nothing in our lives to date had changed us as profoundly as this news that our child was transgender.

While Angus unpacked his bags, I deluged him with all the trans information and stories I had read on the web that morning. Then I told him again, in detail, everything that had happened from the moment that Stirling had told me about the Would You Rather...? game revelation. I talked and talked, which is my way of processing and coping. Angus was pale and drawn, not saying much at all. He is usually a person of few words but this time he was really, really quiet. After a while, I stopped free associating and regurgitating all that I had read, and Angus spoke, quietly and with very little eye contact.

'I remember when I was thirteen, I believed fervently in God and I even seriously entertained the idea that one day I might be a priest but by the time I'd left school, I was beginning to question the existence of God at all and became an atheist. How do we know that Orlando isn't going through that kind of phase? Teenagers are always trying on new ideas and experimenting with new identities.'

What could I say? I knew Orlando so well, and being transgender did not feel in any way like a phase he was going through. In fact, being gender-dysphoric explained so much about his years of depression and suicidality. I just listened while Angus spoke, and, when he had finished unpacking and had put his dirty washing into the machine, we went for a walk with the dogs along the Manly foreshore, stopping for a late lunch at a local café. During this time, we mostly talked about not-Orlando subjects – like the complexity of the race identities that he had witnessed while working in Singapore – but all of the time I was conscious that what we were really thinking about was Orlando. We just didn't know what to say to each other about our child, about this enormous shift in our world. It was an odd kind of interactional wordlessness that I couldn't remember ever having been a part of our relationship before.

When Orlando came home from school that afternoon, Angus hugged him tightly and told him, 'I know from your mum that you're struggling with big issues and I wanted to say to you that I love you and will support you, no matter what.'

And that was the extent of their conversation about it for what turned into weeks, maybe even months. Neither of them seemed able to do or say any more with each other.

Our unexpected and unusual wordlessness extended to our broader social world. That weekend, we went to a large dinner party at the home of our close friends, Paul and Tracy, and there were lots of people there whom we knew well and with whom we were close. However, although Orlando's identification as gender-dysphoric was absolutely top of mind all the time for Angus and for me, and these were many of our good friends, we didn't mention Orlando's revelation at all. It just felt too impossibly heavy to introduce such a subject. And we didn't yet have the language to do it. I retreated into my glass of Shiraz and Angus was quieter than usual. My friend Jacqui was there and I felt her, deeply empathically, watching me as I stumbled along trying to make small talk about my life, our kids, my work, knowing how troubled and traumatised I was about this secret that I could not articulate.

When we got home, Stirling and Orlando were squabbling with each other – in a typical sibling rivalry way – about who had been less cooperative and responsible about going to bed at the agreed time. I thought about how weird this normality was, as though this massive story about Orlando was not actually going on. I have never been one to avoid talking about what's really going on around me. Indeed, I usually need a fierce openness in my world because it is my way of rejecting all the lies and the dangerous secrets that bubbled under the surface of my family life when I was growing up. Yet, suddenly, in the face of this news about Orlando, I was more silent and wordless than I could ever have imagined myself. I wasn't reluctant to talk about this development in our family; I simply did not know what to say to anyone. It was so unlike me.

Another fundamental struggle for me was the powerful dissonance between how Orlando felt himself to be a girl/woman and the way he continued to dress and act and look like a boy. I knew, from some of the things that he had told Stirling and me, that he yearned to be a beautiful woman, that he wanted to wear make-up, that he hated the hairiness of his body and would like to wax it smooth, that he wanted to wear a leotard and tights to ballet classes (not the boyish shorts and singlet that he currently wore to ballet classes), that he was interested, for the first time, in clothes and how he presented to the world. So there was seemingly a very powerful yearning within him to embody femaleness, and yet, mostly, he continued outwardly as before, dressing just like every other teenage boy on the northern beaches in surf shorts and T-shirts, rolling around on the floor with the dogs, mostly talking and acting as he always had.

I was desperate to engage in a conversation about his experiences and feelings about being trans, and to find ways to help him. At every opportunity, I asked him questions. 'How does it feel to be transgender? When did you first experience yourself as trans? How do you see yourself transitioning? How are you feel about this journey? What would you like from us, from your Dad and your brother and me, to help you right now? Is there anyone you'd like to talk to about this? Are there any changes you'd like to make in what you wear right now? Would you like me to take you shopping for new clothes? Do you want me to help you to shave or wax any of your body hair?'

Orlando, however, evaded, ignored or deflected all of my many questions. His silence about this big subject was disconcerting and unnerving. I had noticed, though that, for brief moments, he was emotionally lighter than he had been in years. On these occasions of lightness, he danced around the house, demonstrating the moves that he was learning in his new ballet classes, simultaneously singing, seemingly exuberantly happy. Stirling was taken aback by this new behaviour, asking me why Orlando was suddenly so flamboyant. I hadn't seen this happy side of my child for so many years and, each time I witnessed it, I felt the heaviness on my heart lift just a bit. Clearly, he felt freed up now that his massive secret was unfurled. At these times, I could actually imagine coping with him being transgender. Maybe, I thought, I might even enjoy the experience of difference inherent in having a (trans) daughter. I celebrated and encouraged these slices of lightness and joy and even started to imagine, with an open heart, what life might look like for Orlando as a girl/woman.

Easily and quickly, though, these moments of lightness would dissipate entirely and Orlando would be deeply troubled again, expressing grave fears about his future as a transgender person. The medication that Joy had given to help him sleep and to mediate his anxiety was making him sleep really heavily and wake up groggy. I knew it was a 'substantial' drug for an adolescent and I didn't want him to take it for long but I also I knew that he needed something to take the edge off his tumultuous emotional state right then.

At that time, bizarrely, ironically, coincidentally and with much synchronicity, my manager at the not-for-profit organisation where I worked sent me to a trans-oriented workshop in Surry Hills run by an organisation called ACON. This workshop was intended to strengthen community workers' understanding of gender-diverse people and the health impact of marginalisation and stigma on such communities. I learnt a great deal at the workshop but I was also forced to confront the brutal facts about life for trans people: incredibly high rates of suicide, alcoholism and drug abuse, and significantly higher levels of unemployment than in the rest of the population. It was extremely scary for a trans parent to be presented with these statistics.

The sharing sessions of this workshop were an outing process for me, and for another participant who also identified as a new trans parent. It was the first time I had spoken publicly about having a transgender daughter. Of course, because we were a group of community workers, it was a supportive and accepting environment, so it was relatively easy to do it but, all the same, it did feel liberating to say out loud, in a public forum, 'My child is transgender. She came out very recently and is transitioning from male to female.' It was difficult but also important for me psychologically that I was able to use the female pronouns about my child in this way in a public space, to say them aloud, testing how it felt, learning to do it.

I am someone who learns a lot from other people's stories and so I contacted another trans mum, Michelle, a friend from my university days who had been to visit me earlier that year in Sydney when she was in Australia for a conference, before we had learnt about Orlando's gender identity crisis. Shortly after Michelle arrived in Sydney, she and I were having lunch at a beachfront café just a short walk from my home.

When I had asked her how her sons Andrew and Damien (who was eighteen) were doing, her answer was startling.

'Well, while I was on the plane, Damien emailed me to tell me that he is, in fact, a girl, that he's transgender and that he's known it for a few years now.'

I remember that moment precisely, staring at her across the café table, everything around us going quiet as I switched off to all but this monumental and, frankly, rather shocking news.

My overwhelming experience at that lunchtime was of Michelle being seemingly unfazed by the content of Damien's email. I, on the other hand, was profoundly taken aback by his revelation and, after a frozen pause, I started asking Michelle endless questions. Did you have any idea that Damien was transgender? What exactly did he say? What does it mean for your family? What health services are there for trans people in South Africa? On and on.

Of course, at that time, Michelle couldn't answer most of these questions as she had only just found out that she had a trans child, but she was calm and relaxed way in a way that I could not comprehend. I knew, at this lunch, that having a trans gender child would have been a much bigger drama for me than it appeared to be for her.

Many months later, thinking back to our lunch together, I was even more astounded at Michelle's laid-back early response to this epic news, especially as my response in the first few days of Orlando's coming out was so intense and so different. Perhaps Michelle's easy-going attitude to Damien's coming out as trans was partly because there had been a few very minor indicators from early in her child's life that he/she might identify as transgender later on in life. Also, my friend Michelle is in the science/engineering world and is generally optimistic and calm, while I am a neurotic and anxious social scientist: perhaps our antithetical academic and emotional contexts partly explained our very different reactions to our children identifying as transgender.

Six months after that lunch, I too had a transgender daughter, so I texted Michelle and we set up a time to talk on WhatsApp about my news. At that appointed time – early on a Sunday morning – I set off with my headphones and, with my phone fully charged, I walked around Manly while Michelle and I chatted for hours.

By then, she and her husband had left South Africa and moved to the UK to live and work because she wanted to build a life for her family in a trans-friendly society where there were free and good medical options for transitioning for her trans daughter. I listened and learned as she talked about her experiences as a trans parent of six months. Her comments to me revealed that Michelle was as relaxed about having a trans daughter then as she had been when she first discovered the reality six months ago:

'Sally, that's the name she's chosen, is absolutely the same person as Damien was: a geeky nerd who still doesn't like to go out much. She just enjoys being home on a Saturday night gaming and connecting with her virtual friends. She still has the same friends as she had when she was Damien: her friends are male and female, straight, gay and bisexual, black and white, and they all accept her transition. Her brother is also cool about her transition and if he has a friend who isn't cool, then he isn't friends with that person any more. The main difference now is that Sally is happier and more relaxed than she was when she was Damien. It's like she's now the best and realest version of herself.'

My life felt very surreal as I wandered along the Manly beachfront chatting on my phone while surrounded by the very domestic Sunday activities of people walking their dogs, parents playing with their kids on the sand and tourists sunning themselves in the weak early morning sun. My conversation with Michelle seemed light years away from the conversations that people seemed likely to be having on the beach. I had so many questions for her.

'Michelle, how does gender reassignment surgery work for males transitioning to females?'

'Only about one-sixth of all transgender woman choose to have surgery and, when they do have it, they have most of their penis surgically removed and then the surgeon fashions a functioning vagina from the remaining penis. Lots of trans girls opt for breast implants because taking oestrogen often doesn't give them sufficient breast tissue.'

Michelle explained that the hardest physical issues for trans girls generally are their deep voices and their physical height and size.

Some of this information was shocking for me to hear at first but I needed to get used to these realities. It had become apparent to me that Orlando knew a great deal about medical transitioning – from YouTube – and I needed to know too.

'Michelle, I'm worried about Orlando's future love prospects and love relationships. Who is Sally attracted to sexually?'

'She sees herself as heterosexual and attracted to men.'

'But what kind of men? Gay men?'

'Nope, just men who are tolerant and open and maybe quite gender-fluid.'

'I'm worried about how our children will meet partners like that. Surely they're relatively rare?'

'Actually, the online dating world is extensive nowadays and offers good relationship prospects to the younger generation in particular. Our children will be fine. They'll find love. The most important thing now is that you must help Orlando to be part of an accepting, tolerant and open community where he can be accepted for who he is. Also, you should allow him to determine the pace of his transgender progress. He must work out when he wants to engage in girl behaviour, dress, activities and so on. And try to find him a therapist experienced in gender dysphoria to guide him through this. Maybe you'd find it helpful to read *Becoming Nicole*, a true story written by an American called Amy Ellis Nutt about a family with identical twin boys, one of whom identified as transgender very young, and how the family dealt with it.'

This conversation made me realise just how much I had to learn about being transgender and about transitioning. When I got home, I made rooibos tea for Orlando and me, and we sat at the kitchen counter together drinking and chatting. Michelle had been very open about Sally's journey and had said that she and Sally were happy for me to talk to Orlando about any of it. As I told him the details of my phone conversation, he seemed open to talking about Sally's transitioning process, even seeming to relish the opportunity. It seemed that it was much easier for him to talk about someone else's transitioning than it was to talk about his own. As he explained gender transitioning processes to me, I was astonished by how much he knew.

'Mum, in stage one you take puberty blockers to inhibit puberty development, then in stage two you take hormones – in my case, oestrogen – so you get breast buds, less body hair, female fat distribution on the body and face, and then, in stage three, you have gender confirmation surgery, and maybe facial feminisation surgery, which includes your head and your chest area, so maybe if my breasts don't grow enough on oestrogen I might want to have breast implants. Along the way of stage two and three you also need to legally change your name on your passport and Medicare card.'

'Are you sure that you are transgender, babe?'

'I'm eighty to ninety per cent sure.' (Months later, he told me that he had not said a hundred per cent because he felt that I couldn't handle this at that time.) 'I really don't like being physically male.'

'Do you want to go through all three stages?'

'I don't want to rush through the stages but I'm sure I'm going to go through them all.'

'How long have you known that you're transgender?'

'For years, I wasn't sure. I just knew I was different. At first, I thought I was gay, then I thought I was trans, then when I was in Year 5 you bought me a trans teen book to read and it was about a trans girl and, when I read that, then I thought I was trans. For years, though, I had a lot of doubts but after I'd read lots more trans novels, then I became more and more sure that I was trans.'

'When were you going to tell us, babe?'

'I'd planned to come out to you when I was sixteen because then I could decide for myself to have stage two treatment.'

'Why didn't you feel able to tell us?'

'I'd read so much about how hard it is for parents to accept that their child is trans and I just couldn't bear to tell you. It's a very hard thing to tell your parents. Also, in the book that you wrote for us about our birth story, you said how happy you were when you found out, before we were born, that we were both male because you didn't feel that you could cope with having daughters after all the girl trouble you had when you were growing up with your mother and your sisters. I really am very relieved now that you do know. I feel very unburdened by telling you.'

'Oh, babe, I'm so sorry about that story. It was easy to tell that at the time because I knew we were having two boys... Do you have a sense yet about whether you're attracted to men or women?'

'I'm not sure. Maybe both.'

Orlando was so self-contained and sure when he was talking to me that morning over rooibos tea. He was only sad and emotional when he spoke of his shock at being told by the psychiatrist that he had Asperger's. I explained to him that we had known the diagnosis since he was six but that the psychologists had advised us not to tell him because he could have become fixed on a binary (either/or) view of himself as an Aspie who could not change (because binary positioning is a feature of people with Asperger's), when actually behaviour change is possible and important for people with the diagnosis.

Despite our very painful discussion about his diagnosis, Orlando was much happier and lighter after we had talked and I was glad to have had Michelle and Sally's situation to act as a conversation starter .

I was so relieved to finally be talking with him about his experiences and feelings about being transgender – or trans, as he preferred to describe himself.

I had ordered the book that Michelle had recommended – *Becoming Nicole* – and, as soon as it arrived in the post, I read it from beginning to end in a few days, putting aside any non-essential activities to devour it. It was incredibly helpful and normalising for me. I found the story particularly interesting and relevant because it was about twins, both born male, one of whom transitioned. In my online research, I had noticed that being a twin was a common feature of trans kids.

I realised that slowly I was starting to feel calmer about Orlando being transgender and I figured that this was probably because I was writing and talking with people with whom it felt safe to express my feelings of shock, anxiety, fear and sadness; and because I was hearing from Orlando about how he was feeling and thinking. I was also learning more and more about gender dysphoria, including first-hand, from someone like Michelle.

I wrote to my friend Fawn about this and she reinforced for me again how important it was to support Orlando and allow him to feel totally supported by us. Fawn wrote me an email which was clearly influenced by her work.

Lyndsay, my experience as a therapist has been that so often parents whose kids tell them that they are gay or bisexual (and transgender too probably) are in absolute denial and quite plainly horrified and completed unprepared to accept it. I have seen how these kinds of parental responses make the children very unhappy and consequently the children shut down and withdraw from the parents. I just want to reinforce how important it is that you hold Orlando at the centre of all this and not everybody else. So, it's OK for now to feel that you are muddling through with him. The most important people are you, Angus, Stirling and Orlando. Orlando is still your child that you know and love and nothing is lost even though at times you might feel afraid of this. You will get through this, my friend. You are getting through this.

After my conversation with Michelle and my email from Fawn, I had a rather graphic dream that woke me in a hot sweat before five a.m. I had been dreaming that I was able to see deep into my right nostril all the way through to the inside of my body, to places I have never seen before. Initially snot and blood and water rushed out in great streams from this nostril, a stream of gunge that seemed endless and threatened to physically overwhelm me, and then slowly it dried up and I could see very clearly deep, deep inside of my nose and it was all clear and fine. There was no sign of the expected infection, sores, cysts or anything else toxic or deathly. It was all normal. Actually, it was even interesting and surprising to see what I hadn't seen before. It seemed to be another dream that highlighted the ambivalent feelings I was having during my waking life, where I felt that the potential trauma of having a transgender child could overwhelm him/her and me and our family *but*, simultaneously, I was aware that this was something we could survive and, as my dream showed me, this might even be an interesting journey for me.

For Angus, though, it was all still rather too raw for him to think about this possibility. He was still not talking very much at all about Orlando's gender dysphoria. I have known Angus for so long that I knew his silence represented an overwhelming and powerful sense of loss on his part. If he did talk about the gender dysphoria with me, it was to express his fears about Orlando's future and the way that parts of society would potentially reject him as a transgender person.

I tried to be as loving and supportive of Angus as I could. 'It's early days for us, darling. We've only known for a week that our son is our daughter. We will adjust.'

One morning, Angus sent me an email from work about a conversation he had had with his good friend Hayley, also a barrister and in the same chambers as Angus.

Sweetie, I spoke with Hayley today about our story. And I cried. I suppose I haven't been able to cry while talking with you because of your pain and anguish. I had to try and hold myself together for you. This is so very painful. I love Orlando so much and I worry so much about the hard path that lies ahead for him.

I was relieved that Angus had been able to share his feelings with Hayley but, despite this sharing of his emotional pain, I knew that he was still deeply troubled, because he was sleeping really badly every night. He is generally a bad sleeper, regularly awake during the night, particularly if he is in the middle of running a court case but it seemed to me that, since Orlando's revelation, Angus was hardly ever asleep any more.

I thought about Orlando all of the time. One morning when I walked into the office and my friend-colleague Nonnie asked me in her gentle and caring way, 'How are you?', tears involuntarily slid down my face. Nonnie was wonderfully empathic and helpful, reminding me again that I would survive and that at least I still had my beautiful Orlando and that this was big-picture stuff for our family. She was a very significant source of support for me, particularly in those early weeks when I was so preoccupied with Orlando's story.

I took solace from every source that I could. My friend Jacqui has an eighteen-year-old son, Thomas, a smart and progressive young man, and Jacqui emailed me Thomas's thoughts on Orlando's revelation that he was gender dysphoric.

Thomas wasn't shocked or surprised about Orlando's revelation. He did say that he was glad that Orlando wasn't rushing to a premature conclusion as this is a complex thing which needs time. He suggested that Orlando may be projecting his feelings of difference onto gender but, in that, he is part of a broader social trend – not that that makes his experience any less real. Gender has become a culturally acceptable place for dysphoria to go. And to question gender has become more possible and more feasible. Many people end up gender-fluid rather than embracing a different gender identity. Thomas asked if Orlando wants to be a woman or if he just doesn't want to be a man? There is much more space today to throw gender out altogether and to simply be a person but if he wants to be a woman that is fine – just a bit complicated. Thomas was clear that he would be sexually/romantically attracted to a transgender person as long as they were the right person.

Thomas's normalising of Orlando's experiences helped me to begin to normalise the situation too. Maybe, I thought hopefully, it was possible that my child would become an adult in a world where there were lots of accepting and open-minded Thomases living in a more gender-fluid, less genderised world. I found myself regularly moving from feeling that being trans was not going to be such a big deal for Orlando when he grew up to feeling totally and utterly fearful about the potential discrimination that he might encounter in the world as a trans teen and adult.

I realised that, having known for a week about Orlando being transgender, it was time to tell our children's three grandparents, all of whom were living in South Africa: my father (Gavin), Angus's mother (Iona) and Alexis, a wonderful friend of mine who had taken on the role of surrogate grandmother when our boys were born (because my mother had died when I was in my twenties, and Angus's mother was a farmer who lived more than an hour's drive away from our home in Durban).

I sent a similar email to each of them.

Buckle up your seatbelts – this is a big email. In my update to you last Sunday, I referred obliquely to Orlando struggling with identity issues. I wanted to tell you more specifically what is happening. Orlando is deeply uncertain about his gender identity. His most dominant experience is that he doesn't feel like he is a boy, that he is gender-dysphoric (his words from all the research he has done on this). He says he has known this for at least a year, maybe more, which makes my heart very sore as, in that time, he has told nobody and sat all alone with his confusion. This all became evident when, off the record, Stirling alerted me to Orlando telling him that he would 'rather be a beautiful woman than a handsome man' and that he 'wished he could wear make-up'. When I put this together with a joke that Orlando made to us about how we 'mustn't assume his gender' and with his interest in reading teen fiction about transgender teens, I asked Orlando if he was struggling with his gender identity and he said yes, that he was gender-dysphoric.

As you can perhaps imagine, it has been, at times, rather traumatic since this emerged last week. Angus and I were pretty blindsided, not having expected this from Orlando at all. We have come a very long way in a week and a half though and are now on this journey with Orlando, side by side, loving him and accepting that his future is going to be radically different to any futures we had imagined for him. I learnt along the way that this is a common struggle for young people with Asperger's.

All three grandparents responded with unconditional love and acceptance. My father responded first and his email made me cry. He had been a very absent father when I was growing up because he had worked such long hours but, by the time his grandchildren were born, he was a devoted, present and playful grandfather whom my children adored.

That is big news, Lynds, but OK with all of us who love, care and appreciate Orlando as I certainly do.

Angus's mother, Iona, also wrote a very supportive email.

I know so little about these things but I have always wondered why some people are prejudiced against those who are not quite the same as they are. It is a blessing that these days there is far more tolerance of people with gender differences.

Alexis, not one for email, phoned to chat and was incredibly loving and accepting. This response was not at all surprising: she had always been a completely loving and accepting grandmother figure for our children, nurturing them and spoiling them in the most grandmotherly of ways, and our twins adored her, not least because she had always spoilt them outrageously with toys, food, and hours and hours of her precious time.

The next thing we had to consider was finding the right context or world for Orlando, and for our trans family. It was apparent to me that we were probably going to have to move to a different part of Sydney.

While Manly is a very beautiful area, it is very nuclear-family-oriented and, despite the liberal live and let live tolerance on the northern beaches, it is not a society likely to be actively encouraging and embracing of transgender people. Certainly, transgender people did not have much of a presence or profile in the area, and so Orlando would not see himself mirrored in that environment.

Angus and I both recognised that it was going to be important for Orlando to live in the most open-minded and socially progressive part of Sydney and that was probably the inner west, where difference, on the whole, was seemingly celebrated and encouraged. In addition, all the trans services that we would need to access regularly are located in the inner west: the Gender Centre in Annandale, 2010 (a gender centre for young people particularly) in Redfern, the transgender counsellor in Newtown, the psychiatrist in Annandale, the clinical psychologist in Marrickville, and so on.

Angus was rather reluctant to move, largely because his uncle, aunt and cousins all lived on the northern beaches, but he recognised that we needed to live in the inner west. He did ask if we could concentrate our home-seeking efforts in Balmain because it is a suburb on the harbour and he was happiest living near water and being able to commute to his work in the city via ferry.

I phoned the Gender Centre in Annandale and spoke to their social worker, Katie, who gave me lots of her time and advice. She seemed familiar with calls from newly shocked and clueless trans parents and she was particularly patient and compassionate in engaging with me. She told me that the most important thing for transgender kids was to have loving and accepting parents and a positive friendship group and social world. In our discussion about a family relocation, she named the various suburbs in the inner west where trans people were most likely to feel at home: Newtown, Marrickville, Glebe, Annandale and Petersham. What about Balmain, I asked? Yes, she said, it's not as trans-friendly as the places that she had already mentioned but still it would be good, particularly as it was close to other more trans-friendly neighbourhoods.

Katie and I chatted about high schools in the inner west, as I had a sense that, in the future, we might have to move Orlando from his traditional Anglican school to a secular, more progressive school. Katie said that we could consider all public high schools in the areas that she had specifically mentioned. She said that the Gender Centre supported a number of trans students in the public high schools in Newtown, Glebe, Marrickville and Balmain.

Orlando is a bright student who loves learning so he had started high school at a private boys' selective school in Sydney and then, when he was desperately unhappy there (before we knew that he was transgender), we had moved him to the Anglican school in the city where Stirling goes. We aren't religious but this school is co-educational and had a reputation for being pastoral with good teaching and learning, so it met most of our criteria for high schools for our twins. However, he wasn't yet out as transgender and so even at this new school, Orlando had struggled. He was deeply depressed and tearful and talked about suicide often. His tears were largely about his fears for his future and his worries that life as a trans person would not be worth living. It was painful and frightening to see him so hopeless and distraught. I spent a lot of time talking with him and comforting him, trying to give him a sense of hope and the possibilities for being able to live a fulfilling and happy life given that his generation was so much more accepting and embracing of difference than previous generations had been.

I told him often how much I loved him. My heart ached when, one day, he told me in reply, 'That's what makes it so hard, Mum. You love me so much that I can't leave you.' Bizarrely, his comment gave me some relief because it meant that there was something holding him back from attempting suicide.

I had taken Orlando to the therapist recommended by his psychiatrist and he had left the rooms of this psychologist in rageful tears because she had reflected back to him how deeply afraid he was feeling about his present and his future. After that first session, he had refused to go back to this psychologist, so his psychiatrist recommended another therapist, Steve, who specialises in people with Asperger's, and this therapeutic relationship went relatively well for some time.

I was doing as much trans networking as I could so that I could learn and support Orlando as much as possible. A work friend put me in touch with a friend of hers, Louise, whose sixteen-year-old transgender daughter attended a high school on the northern beaches. Louise and I met up for coffee one Saturday morning and she taught me about puberty blockers: why they are needed, how to get them, how they work and so on. Louise showed me a phone photo of her daughter before and after being on puberty blockers for two years, and I could see that the teen had feminised significantly in that time, or maybe it was more that she hadn't continued with masculinising as her peers had. Although her friends and the school hierarchy know that she is transgender, Louise's daughter continues to present at school as a boy and only plans to come out fully as a trans girl when she leaves high school. This, I subsequently learnt, is a common choice for trans kids who don't feel that it will be safe to come out as transgender while they are in high school. Some months after that, the friend who had introduced me to Louise told me that Louise's daughter, a good student academically, had dropped out of high school. I felt so sad for them and I wondered if it was just too hard for her daughter to go to school as him.

Following my discussion with Louise, it was apparent that Angus and I needed to seriously consider puberty blockers for Orlando. After doing lots of research, we resolved that we wanted to get him onto them as soon as we could. We knew by then that he could decide at any point to abandon the blockers in order for his puberty process to resume. In the meantime, being on them would interrupt his male puberty process, thus buying him time to make decisions about his future. I talked to Orlando's psychiatrist and we got a referral from her to a paediatric endocrinologist who worked with gender-dysphoric teens and could prescribe puberty blockers. His first available appointment was in early January. It seemed a long way off given that we weren't even in December yet, but we had no other choices, so I took the appointment.

Then there was the question of a new name for Orlando. He had researched girls' names that he might like to adopt and he told us that, for some time, he had been using Millie as his online name. We knew quite a few girls called Millie, so I asked him if we could find a more unusual and unfamiliar name. This naming process felt very significant but also difficult to navigate. When our boys were *in utero*, Angus and I had invested a great deal of time and energy in choosing their names, recognising how names often create and shape an individual's self-identity and how they also often influence the way people respond to each other, especially when they first meet. Names matter – which is why we had deliberated over our children's names for so many months before choosing them. Now Orlando needed a new name and it wasn't clear just how it would be chosen.

Orlando and I discussed a new name one Saturday morning when we had breakfast with my friend Jacqui and her daughter, Bronte (then fifteen). Jacqui initiated the discussion and, after testing out many options, Orlando shortlisted Olivia, Ophelia, Skylar, Amelia and Ella. I was motivating strongly for the new name to begin with an O so that those of us in Orlando's life could easily transition to the new name and were more likely to get it right more often. He said he would think about it further but that his favourites were Olivia and Amelia and, because of the usefulness of its beginning with an O, he was leaning strongly towards Olivia.

This discussion was a pretty confronting moment in the trans parenting journey: in the process of choosing a girl's name for Orlando, it felt that, as parents, we were officially giving up a son and acquiring a daughter. I know that technically we had never really had a son because Orlando had probably always actually been a girl, but we hadn't known that, so, for us, he had been our son.

We needed to settle on a new name because, six weeks after his coming out as trans, we were still using his male name and the male pronouns he/him. The catalyst for the final change happened in the first week of December when Orlando attended his first Transtopia teen trans group at the Gender Centre in Annandale.

Although I had chatted on the phone to Katie, one of the Gender Centre's social workers, neither Orlando nor I had actually been to the centre yet, so on the evening of the Transtopia group, we left Manly early and arrived in Annandale early for the meeting. The centre is on Parramatta Road, one of the busiest arterial roads in Sydney, and it certainly felt incredibly busy as I drove slowly amidst crazy rush-hour traffic looking for the centre. I drove past where it should have been – unsurprisingly there was no giant sign outside – and, of course, being an arterial road, there was no parking close to where the offices were likely to be. Eventually, I found a place to park and Orlando and I walked up to the centre.

I could feel how nervous we both were. The area felt very unfamiliar. We passed by the blinking bright lights of a brothel, and then we were at the advertised address, looking at a rather nondescript and innocuous door. Tentatively, I pushed it open and we walked straight into the meeting area, which was filled with a mismatch of chairs, lots of teen food, and a handful of colourful teens lounging languidly on comfortable couches. Orlando and I stood there for a while, uncertain and unsure.

Cheerfully, the oldest of the teens came over and introduced herself. 'Hello, I'm Juliet, the facilitator. Welcome.'

On closer inspection, it was apparent that Juliet was, in fact, somewhere in her twenties, maybe even thirties. I introduced Orlando, mumbling the pronunciation of his male name, and left, Orlando looking anxious and awkward as I disappeared.

I walked back to an Annandale pub, where I knew (from the Gender Centre website) that some of the trans parents would be meeting for a drink and a chat. Feeling decidedly uncomfortable and out of place, I wandered around the pub, looking for what might be a group of trans parents. Unsuccessful, I eventually went up to the counter and ordered a drink, planning to find a place to sit and read my book until the Transtopia group ended. While I was ordering, a woman came up to the counter to order herself a drink and asked me if I was there for the parents' meeting. I was so relieved. When we had paid for our drinks, I went over with her to the table and she introduced me to the small group of other parents sitting together. I put my book onto the table and soon a few of us were talking about what kind of books we liked to read. Naturally there was lots of trans parent talk too. What school does your child go to? Is it a trans-supportive school? Is your child on hormones? What endocrinologist/psychiatrist/psychologist does he/she see? They were a very friendly and welcoming group and I felt quite comfortable with them, despite having just met them. It seemed to me that many of them did seem rather worn-out when talking about trans matters, but perhaps that was just projection on my part since I felt that way.

And so I started to find my trans tribe.

When the teen support group had finished, and the kids trailed over to the pub to locate their parents, Orlando said that he didn't want to stay for a pub dinner with the group. I could see that he was exhausted from all the interaction. So I said goodbye to the lovely parent group, and we headed back to Manly.

On the hour-long journey home, Orlando told me about the group participants: six trans boys and five trans girls, including him, mostly aged around seventeen to nineteen. At thirteen, he was the youngest person there. He also commented that a lot of the group had colourful hair and many piercings and clearly needed to visually identity as different.

He told me that when Juliet asked them all to introduce themselves, everyone was invited to give their name and their preferred pronouns. He told me that he had asked to be referred to with the female pronouns. I knew then that it was time for our family to move on to using female pronouns, strange as the transition might be for us after thirteen years. Clearly, using the correct pronouns with our child would help with the transitioning process and the identity-formation process. It would also signify to our child – and to us – that we were transitioning too, that we were genuinely accepting of our transgender daughter. The use of the female pronouns necessitated the use of a female name, so Orlando and I again discussed the question of a new name and, by the time we had arrived home in Manly, we had agreed that we would try out Olivia and see if it worked. I liked Olivia and I especially liked Liv, the shortened form.

As we came into the house, Liv went upstairs and I talked with Angus about this big issue. After a brief conversation, we agreed that we would immediately start calling our child Olivia and using the correct pronouns. And, just like that, our child had a new name. It was time to recognise and truly acknowledge that we had a daughter. We could no longer live in a liminal space.

3

The fledgling

I had an extended and repeated dream about a fledgling, a baby bird, flapping around on the ground and struggling to survive because it was too young to be on its own out of the nest. In this dream, I usually caught the fluffy and fragile fledgling in my hands and tried to return it to the nest but, when I woke up, it was never clear if I had succeeded in getting it into the protection of the nest.

A week after Olivia had attended the first Transtopia teen group, I attended my first trans parents support group meeting at the Gender Centre. Despite knowing my way to the centre by then, I still arrived earlier than the scheduled six-thirty p.m. start. The centre entrance is rather confronting for newcomers, as the front door leads directly into the meeting space of couches and chairs. As I entered, I was surprised at how many parents were already there. I felt awkward because I didn't know anyone, so I sat in the first free seat I could find and busied myself settling into my space. Soon, I was warmly greeted by the woman seated next to me. She was dressed, I observed, with unconventional originality and she had dark blue streaks in her hair. I wondered if maybe she was an inner westie, perhaps a citizen of the rather avant-garde nearby neighbourhood of Newtown. She and I chatted easily and comfortably about nothing in particular but our chatter allowed me to relax a bit and feel slightly less uncomfortable, and, yes, she told me, she did, in fact, live locally in the inner west.

There were heaps of temping snacks on the table in the centre of the group but I felt far too self-consciously new to help myself to the delectable-looking melting Brie or chocolate cake. I wriggled into my chair and slowly relaxed enough to look around, as unobtrusively as possible, at the other parents present. I did some wild guesswork about them: some looked young and trendy, others looked older and more conservative, some appeared well-heeled (wealthy), others perhaps were struggling to make ends meet, some might be born-Anglo-Australians, others were perhaps migrants. Mostly, people seemed to be there on their own, like me, but there were clearly a few who seemed connected like couples, mostly heterosexual, some perhaps gay. By the time the facilitator, Lee, began the session, there were about twenty-five or thirty of us squeezed into the space, most relaxed and chatty, others, like me, quite tense and maybe a bit fraught.

Lee introduced herself first, explaining that she had worked at the Gender Centre for twelve years. She had an easy, warm and direct manner that made me feel comfortable and at ease. She explained that, as the senior case worker at the Gender Centre, her primary job was placing young homeless trans adults into the approximately one hundred shared houses that the centre managed. Lee clarified that some of these young people were homeless because their families could not accept that they were transgender and so they had had to leave home, others were homeless because they struggled to find decent paying work because of the transphobia in society, and some of them were homeless because they didn't earn decently because their mental health problems (usually generated by transphobia or gender dys-phoria) meant that they couldn't work much and thus couldn't pay much rent.

As Lee explained this distressing context for these young trans adults, I felt sweaty and light-headed, my anxiety ratcheting up at this distressing reflection of the experiences of transphobia that transgender people had to deal with. I began to free associate to the dangerous tiger that had haunted my dream life. If it was possible, right then I felt even more vulnerable and afraid about Olivia's future than I had in the time since we had known that she was trans.

After her introduction, Lee said we would go around the group, with each of us having a chance to introduce ourselves, to talk about our trans child and where they were in the transitioning journey. We were also invited to ask questions if we wanted to. Some of the parents' stories were encouraging, others were frightening, all of them were deeply moving.

The first to introduce themselves were a young couple whose child was transitioning in kindergarten. They wanted advice on how to cope with the trans teasing that she was having to endure from some of her young peers who had known her as a boy from pre-kindy. Another mother with a child who had transitioned before starting primary school spoke about how positive this experience had been for her child, partly because the other children only knew her child as a boy and had never known the child as a girl (the gender assigned to him at birth).

These contributions generated discussion in the group about 'going stealth', that is, the trans child and family concealing (as far as possible) the information that the child was trans, so, for example, the child would go to a school where they were not previously known and hence seek to pass as their authentic gender rather than the gender that they were assigned at birth. In such situations, very few people, if any, in the child's new world would know that this kid was trans, thus reducing gender dysphoria for the child and potential transphobia from the other kids. Listening to the input from various parents about their experiences of going stealth, it seemed that this choice had both merits and demerits. I knew that, for our family, Olivia going stealth wasn't really an option, given that she could not yet easily pass as a girl.

During this discussion, one of the mothers spoke about how her trans son had moved high schools because he was being so badly bullied at his private Catholic school and that the move had allowed him to go stealth at his new all-boys' public school. While this seemed to be going relatively well, he was constantly worried about being outed and thus did not feel safe enough to engage socially with the other kids much. He experienced the school as quite macho and he was having to work hard at keeping up with the physicality of the other teen boys, not having grown up with the rough and tumble of boys' interaction. She spoke of how he both enjoyed and struggled with having to learn to wrestle in a friendly fashion, to fist pump, play soccer at all the breaks, and engage in other similarly boyish activities.

The other parents of trans boys talked about similar experiences of their trans sons having to learn these kinds of manly interactions, including doing role plays at home with older cousins and siblings to practise their male skills.

As I listened, I thought about how unnecessarily complex and binary our genderised world is, how stark the markers of male and female are, even today. All of this division makes it difficult for our transitioning children who, if they want to fit in with the dominant stereotypical male and female ways of being in the world, have so much to learn, especially because they have missed out on years of unconscious gender social-isation. I knew that, as a powerful individualist, Olivia was likely to resist this kind of conformity and then struggle with the consequences. I had observed that already girls rejected her socially because she would not play the girl game and enact stereotypical ways of being female. This was a conundrum for me too when I was a teenager, because I had felt myself to be an outsider in the girl world, ambivalent about this kind of gender conforming, unable to do what was required of me to fit in, and yet feeling very alone on the margins of the social world.

The next person to speak was the father of a young adult trans woman. He told us that things were going very well with his daughter, who was thriving at university after some very difficult high school experiences and associated depression. Immediately, I felt a surge of hope and optimism and my spirits lifted. I felt relieved to hear a story of a young trans woman living happily. He asked a question about how to get his daughter interested in cycling with the family again, something she had done often with them before she transitioned.

When he had finished, Lee talked about the impact of taking female hormones and how it could affect the levels of energy of young trans girls particularly who, when they no longer had testosterone in their system, felt a notable reduction in their physical strength and physical abilities.

Some months later, I read research that indicated that when trans teens start to take oestrogen/testosterone, it could lead to a change in their interests and in the activities that they had previously been interested in before taking hormones, particularly if the activities were aligned socially with the gender they had left behind. When I read this, I thought back to this father's question to the group that night and wondered whether hormones generated differences in personality or whether, when these trans youngsters began to take hormones and feel more psychologically authentic with their gender, they began to adjust and align their behaviours and activities to their 'new' identity. It seemed to me that there were many unknowns and indistinct causal connections in this intersection of hormone medication and identity formation.

This father also added some very interesting information to the group discussion: his daughter, who was on the Asperger's spectrum, was much less Aspie now that she had been on oestrogen for more than a year, and thus she was finding social relationships easier than she ever had. While, of course, this could be partly about her feeling self-confident because she was living her authentic self, I did think about how statistics show that most Aspies are male at birth, and I wondered whether there was something about introducing oestrogen to trans girls that changed their chemical make-up and that this then mediated their Asperger's traits. This was a fascinating idea to consider: maybe taking oestrogen one day would mediate Olivia's Asperger's and facilitate her being able to engage more easily socially. That would certainly make her life a lot easier.

I wondered about the strange connection between Asperger's and being trans and what the biological basis for it could be. This is something I pondered a lot. Later in my trans parenting journey, I learnt quickly that many trans people and trans activists believe that our responsibility, as trans allies, is simply to support those who identify as transgender and not to ask any causation questions. There are only a few trans activists who believe that an understanding of the biological causation of being trans could potentially lead to support for trans people. I do also recognise that any discussion about the idea that being transgender is a kind of biological variation can be highly problematic because, at the most brutal level, if one can identify a trans gene *in utero*, one could also potentially eliminate it. Also, inherent in the biological causation studies is the premise that being trans is somehow pathological or problematic, a failure biologically. So I have tried to avoid ruminating about causation. Ultimately, none of this theorising makes any difference to Liv, or to our lived experiences with her.

The next speaker was a mother who spoke very lovingly and amusingly about her two teen trans children, one female to male, and one non-binary. The facilitator, Lee, knew automatically that she needed to clarify for the new parents like me that non-binary meant that the individual did not identify as either male or female, or identified as both at various times. This parent spoke about her journey to learn not to misgender her children, but also how hard it was to use the pronouns they/their/them for the non-binary child. I couldn't even imagine how complicated this must be, given the very binary male-female social structure of our world.

Listening to the next mother speak was a heart-rending experience. She spoke of how her eighteen-year-old trans daughter had had to stop taking oestrogen because it had conflicted with the medication that she was taking for her anxiety and her depression. Her daughter was in a love relationship with another trans teen who was also struggling to move her own transitioning journey forward. This mother's heartache as she documented her fraught relationship with her daughter left me feeling intensely sad and scared.

Another mother empathised and told the group about her trans daughter's powerful efforts to separate from her too, including the child refusing to talk to her for many months.

Lee spoke about how, in the early days of transitioning, the relationship between parents and trans children was often unnaturally close given what the child was going through and that this unusual closeness often created tensions between parents and children as the children grew older and yearned for independence. I could see that this was feasible, given that the natural individuation and separation developmental work of teens would be seriously disrupted if they were trans and needed more support from parents than their non-trans peers were likely to need. It was becoming more and more clear to me, as I listened to these parents, that trans parenting was a seriously tough gig, and one that potentially continued in intensity long after the youngster had finished school.

We moved to the other end of the age spectrum with the next speaker, a mother of a child who had transitioned almost from the time that she could walk and talk. This mother spoke of how recently her child had been enormously upset when she saw a baby/toddler picture of herself because, in the picture, she looked like a boy, the gender that she was assigned as birth. This young girl absolutely refused to accept that the child in the picture was her, and her mother did not know how to help her process the idea of herself as trans because she hated it so much: for her, she was just a girl and had never been anything else. That input put paid to my idea that trans parenting was much easier when the child transitioned very young.

Next, a father of a trans son spoke about how his seventeen-year-old son, after years of serious health problems related to binding his breasts too tightly (to conceal them), had recently had top surgery. (Surgical breast removal, explained Lee.) His father spoke about how his son was feeling incredibly liberated by this procedure, overjoyed to be heading to the beach on the weekend with all his mates in their boardies (swimming trunks) – and nothing else. This same father then documented the legal processes they were struggling through as they sought to have their son's gender and his name changed on his birth certificate, passport and Medicare card.

Lee gave him suggestions of trans-friendly people and institutions who could help to simplify this bureaucratic process. I noticed that many of the parents were, like me, writing down the details of these referrals. This happened regularly during the evening when Lee and some of the more experienced trans parents gave out names of endocrinologists, surgeons and psychiatrists who were trans allies and gender specialists. One of the experienced parents explained that, at this time, legally one could change a name on a birth certificate but it was not possible to change the gender on the certificate. It was, however, possible to change both name and gender on passports and other legal documents, like Medicare cards.

During the discussion that evening, it became apparent that some of the parents were keen for their children to be on hormones (oestrogen or testosterone) as soon as possible, while other parents wanted to wait until the child was sixteen or eighteen. Some parents were clearly much more comfortable than others with having a trans kid. Many parents spoke about how their children had not been prepared to be openly trans until they left the confines of school where the potential for bullying was so high.

I found much solace in the stories from parents who had trans kids in their late twenties who were settled and happy, some of whom were living and working overseas, others who were at university or working locally in their chosen careers. Their stories of their trans adult children living ordinary and regular lives were a great source of comfort to me, and presumably others present too. I was particularly grateful to these experienced trans parents for coming along to the group when they probably didn't personally need any support. They seemed to be there because they knew that their stories offered support and encouragement to the new and/or struggling trans parents. Perhaps, I wondered, they also come along because trans parenting is always difficult and meant that trans parents always needed support. I hoped not.

There were also two grandparents present, one of them a grandmother who was there supporting her daughter and grandchild (the mother was present in the group). She spoke about how much she struggled to call her grandchild by the right name and gender. This was a common thread during the evening, particularly with the very new trans parents. Lee was very clear when she spoke about this issue, explaining to us politely but firmly that we had to make a very serious effort to get this right with our child, or grandchild, since it was so fundamental to them and their identity.

The grandmother spoke about how sad she was that she had to take down all the pre-transitional pictures of her grandchild and how hard it had been for her. She was struggling to convince her trans grandchild to provide her with post-transitional pictures to put up around her house, which was covered with pictures of her other grandchildren. Some parents were supportive of her desire for these pictures. Other parents very gently suggested that perhaps she would have to wait some years until her trans grandchild was willing to have pictures up, maybe even pre- and post-transitional pictures, but that for now she should take the lead from the grandchild and let it go. She seemed OK with this idea but I couldn't be absolutely sure. Lee spoke about how research and anecdotal evidence showed that it took about five years post-transition for (most) trans kids to be happy to have pre-transitioning pictures around.

Next a grandfather spoke about his eleven-year-old trans grandson who was living overseas with his parents, one of whom was the man's son. He wanted to talk about how to support his transitioning grandson and asked if there were any parents with trans kids around the age of eleven who might want to meet up with his grandson when he was in Sydney in the next school holidays. Lee told the group about various social engagements available to young trans teens and how to use the private trans parents' website to set meetings up.

A trans uncle introduced himself next. Hen spoke openly and bravely about his own gender identity struggles when he was a teen and how he had nearly completely transitioned, when he changed his mind, and now he identified as non-binary. This transitioning process had put him in a unique position to be supportive with his trans nephew, a generous gift to the young man, given that his own father was resistant to his transitioning.

Then it was my turn. I felt nervous that I would misgender my child and I wondered how I could talk about my love and support for her, while still acknowledging my current struggles. I stumbled through my piece.

'My daughter, Olivia, is thirteen. My husband and I found out a few weeks ago that he, I mean she, was transgender – her twin brother told us that she had told him that she wanted to be a woman. She says that she has known for years that she was different but only in the last year or two, when she was reading trans teen novels, did she realise that her sense of difference was because she's trans. We have an appointment for her to see an endocrinologist in January so that she can hopefully start puberty blockers as soon as possible. We're very supportive of her transitioning but, honestly, what I need help with is my own transitioning, so that I can see her as a girl rather than the boy I've known him as for thirteen years.'

As I explained our story, I realised that I had tears running down my face. Two of the experienced trans parents with adult trans offspring (who had transitioned years before) comforted me empathically, telling me that it would take time, maybe years, to mourn the loss of my son and to move forward but that I would likely find myself welcoming my daughter at the same time. One of these experienced parents spoke about how it had taken her many years to adjust but that now she couldn't imagine her son, a female at birth, as anything but a man. The responses to me from the group participants were extremely non-judgemental and compassionate.

Another brand-new trans parent spoke after me. He told us that his adult child, a professional, aged twenty-four and working in a big corporate law firm in the city, had revealed recently that he was transgender and that he was going to transition to living as a woman. This father seemed to be even more shocked and surprised to discover that he had a trans child than I had been with Olivia. His child didn't yet have the courage to tell his/her siblings so the parents were struggling with a massive level of secrecy within the family.

Another mother told the group how she had known for years that her son was transgender but that the child didn't want to tell anyone else, including her father, the woman's husband. I thought about how it would not be possible for me to live with that kind of secrecy because, after a childhood lived with endless dangerous secrets around me, I could not tolerate secrets. Secrets, to me, felt like lies.

When the other new trans parent spoke about his twenty-four-year-old, he was clearly struggling to talk about his son as his daughter, and someone in the group, very gently and tactfully, asked him if his daughter had chosen a female name. When he told the group the female name, the other parent used the name (and female pronouns) to talk to him about his new daughter. I wasn't sure whether it was intentional or not, but the use of the new name and correct pronouns by others seemed to give the father the opportunity to use his daughter's name and the correct pronouns aloud with us, and perhaps helped him to start the process of transitioning as a parent to having a trans daughter.

Another couple spoke about how their eighteen-year-old child had told them that she was transgender only once she had been on oestrogen for a few months, something she had organised herself. She was also working at two part-time jobs in order to save up enough money to pay for gender confirmation surgery in Thailand.

This input led to a discussion in the group about whether it was better to have gender confirmation surgery in Thailand or in Australia. Apparently, there were two very senior and experienced Thai surgeons, in particular, who were very skilled at doing excellent gender confirmation surgery, but who were verging on retirement. Another set of parents spoke about how they had booked their daughter in for gender confirmation surgery with a doctor in Melbourne and that the process was due to take place in a few months' time. I was shocked to hear that the waiting time for competent and professional gender confirmation surgeons in Thailand and Australia was at least a year.

Another couple spoke about how their trans daughter, aged nineteen, had recently undergone facial feminisation surgery and voice retraining and she was now considering where and when to have gender confirmation surgery. These parents radiated pride and love when they talked about their daughter and how well she was doing, telling us how glad they were that their other daughter, who had originally resisted having a transgender sibling, was now relishing having a sister with whom she could hang out and do girly things.

The last parent who spoke, a mother, told the group that her child's biggest difficulty was not being transgender, but being addicted to the internet and only prepared to engage in virtual reality. Some of the other parents commiserated with this situation, as their teens were similarly overly reliant on virtual relationships and reluctant to venture out into the world. While an addiction to virtual reality, gaming and social media is obviously a very modern phenomenon in the digital revolution through which we are all living, clearly trans teens are more liable to want to retreat to the virtual world because it will seem so much safer for them in various ways. This was something I worried about significantly with Olivia, as she was very deeply engaged in the world of technology.

During the group discussions that night, I learnt a *lot* of new terms and concepts, which Lee was brilliant at explaining: cisgender, M2F, F2M, AMAB, AFAB, T, non-binary, top surgery, bottom surgery, gender fluidity, deadnaming, going stealth, passing, facial feminisation surgery, Gillick competence, and more. I also learnt quite a lot of details about the medical procedures and professionals involved in the various stages of transitioning (social, legal and medical). By the end of the evening, my head spun with many new ideas, new ways of seeing the world and new terminology and jargon.

Never once during that evening did I sense that any of the parents, no matter what their struggles or stories, were being judged by the others. I am not so naive as to categorically assert that nobody was making any silent judgements of anyone else in that group, but certainly my experience was that there was a sense that we were all on this tough journey together and that each of us was there to support the others, and to will each other on to progress and positivity. There was, I felt, a profound honestly and willingness to openly share, a poignant sense of our shared humanity, and a deeply compassionate acknowledgement of each person's struggles and triumphs.

There were so many of us there that night, and so much to talk about, that the meeting, which had been due to finish at eight-thirty, finally finished just before ten. Many of the parents left promptly when the meeting closed but others, like me, stayed around to chat and to ask Lee further questions. She was so warm and helpful, never giving anyone the sense that she wanted to lock the door and go home, despite the late hour.

As I walked into the noisy dark night on Parramatta Road, I felt like I had shifted and changed substantially. I had a strong sense of being one of them, a trans parent. I did not feel sorted and resolved, but I had a clear sense that I was the parent of a trans child and that it was OK.

As I drove home, my head was swimming. I tried to organise my thoughts so that I could tell Angus everything about the evening but my mind was so overstimulated by all I had heard and learnt that my thoughts were jumping around randomly. When I arrived home in Manly, it was late but Olivia was still awake. She had been waiting up for me, as she wanted to know how the meeting had been for me. I knew that she had been concerned that Angus and I, like many of the YouTube trans parents she had watched, might react negatively to having a trans kid. When I told her what a positive experience the evening had been for me and how much I had learnt, she said that she was so pleased that I had gone. Angus told her that he was planning to go to the next parents' support group with me, which seemed to be important to Olivia too.

During the group, one of the parents had explained that she was an administrator of a private online trans parents support group for Australian families and those of us who were first-timers gave our names and email addresses to her so that we could join the group. A few days later, one of the administrators phoned and asked me a few questions – I guess to check out that I was legitimate – and then joined me to the group.

Over time, this group has become an absolutely central source of support for me, an e-space to ask questions, get emotional support and logistical advice, a place to listen to other trans stories and even a place to establish connections and arrange real-life meetings with some of the parents. So often, I have felt that these other trans parents are the only ones who could really understand what I was going through with Olivia. Despite not having met most of them, I have come to feel as though I am friends with Lisa, Susan, Cath, Beck, Claire, Adriadne, Barbara, Karen, Anne and all the many, many others in this supportive group. I have experienced them as being completely non-judgemental towards me and other struggling or new trans parents. I have also been struck by how often a new parent joins the group – at least three every week – and that sense of a growing trans community in Australia gives me comfort and reassurance that being trans is not that unusual. Perhaps, at some point in the future, being trans will be a kind of normal in the way that being gay has become normal – in a place like Sydney, at least.

One of the issues that comes up regularly on the online group is the way that friends and family respond to the news that they have a transgender relative. Angus and I had been talking about this for a while: how our various extended family and friends would respond to the news about Orlando/Olivia. We resolved that it was time to write an email to each of them telling them our news. Angus wrote up a generic email which he then customised and sent off to each person. After explaining about Olivia's transitioning process, his email ended positively.

At the end of the day all one wants for one's children is that they are happy and can live rewarding lives. We are committed to giving Olivia all the support that we can on her difficult journey. One of our key concerns is keeping her safe in a world that is largely transphobic so we are moving suburbs in the hopes that she can go to a school and live in a part of Sydney that is actively encouraging of difference.

The email responses we received were imbued with kindness and love. Here are some of them.

I can't begin to imagine how difficult this must be for Olivia. What a difficult and brave decision to make. It must also be incredibly difficult for the other three of you in the family. You're all strong people and there is enough love to help you to endure.

Olivia, for me nothing has changed: I love you as you are and wish you strength in the decisions you make as you negotiate your way through what must be a difficult time.

Even thought this was a bit of a shock, I want to give you all my complete and whole-hearted support. I am so sad that Olivia had to go through all this turmoil for thirteen years. I am so glad to see your unwavering support for her and the steps you have taken to ensure she feels more at peace. I have friends who are transgender and the constant misgendering is not easy to deal with and can be extremely triggering. If there is anything that we can do to be supportive please let us know.

I explained Olivia's transition to my girls and they went on to educate us through the process, explaining gender fluidity etc. I had a real respect for this new generation. I am so saddened by Olivia's depressive state and at such a young age to be so burdened with so many conflicts in one's mind cannot be easy. I am convinced though that the burden will be lighter as time goes by. Each day is a new beginning where love will always win and if we didn't get it right the day before, the new day presents us with another chance. I always think about catching 'pockets of happiness' on this journey of life and I wish that those pockets of happiness are many in number for all of you.

I just read your email and was discussing it with my girl and we are both wet-eyed that Olivia has been feeling at odds with her body and the world for so long and that we, who love her so much, have had no idea about her struggles and sadness and pain.

I feel so sorry for Olivia/Orlando that she was going through that process for such a long time with so many confusing, painful and desperate moments. It must also be very difficult for Stirling to adapt to the situation, to build a new relationship with his now sister and former brother. I wish for them both all the best reactions from their friends, classmates and their social environment. I wish for all four of you a smooth and enlightening journey where the transition of Olivia becomes more and more integrated and 'normal' in your family interactions and your world – and in between you must look after yourselves, laugh, behave silly and selfish and have fun too.

I have read your email, twice. It obviously takes some digesting. I am full of admiration for how you are handling this. I am very doubtful that I would be at all good in this situation. Summer holidays will, with any luck, let everyone get more used to the new situation before school starts again. That obviously has the potential to be tricky. Much will depend on how competent the school is in handling it. Kids nowadays can surprise with their acceptance. Times have changed since the 70s and 80s. BTW it would not have escaped you, or Olivia, that the 'Orlando' name was perhaps better chosen than anyone could have realised.

Big change is an understatement. Overwhelming stuff but the more I read your email, the more I thought that I am so glad that the kids picked you two as their parents, and you them, and especially that Olivia has a twin that looks out for her in the most important ways. I keep thinking how unprepared most parents must be to start off this journey. It's a steep learning curve of deciding what to do medically, the right school and environment, family adjustments.

Thank you for including me in this big process you are all in. My first thought is that Olivia chose her family so very well and your wholehearted, unequivocal support is going to support her hugely through this passage. Olivia is so brave. I am thinking of you, sending love and courage, not that you need any more of that. I am here to listen for you on this journey.

Please give this message to Olivia: Hi Olivia, thank you for being willing to share your big news with us. I'm really missing you and the rest of the family. When is your next visit? One of the YouTubers that I follow is Stef Sanjati, a transgender woman who talks about her experiences. Not sure if you have heard of her or if you like vlogs?

Now that we had taken the big step of informing all of our close connections, I realised that the next step in supporting my fledgling to grow and develop was to help her start the process of her social and physical transitioning, something she had hinted at for some time. It was school holidays and hence a good time to shop for girl gear. I am not at all interested in clothes, fashion, make-up, jewellery and accessories, so I was no good to Liv as a shopping companion. Like many teens, she doesn't trust her mother's fashion sense anyway! Thankfully, Stirling's friend Danni and her mother, Sarah, both love clothes shopping, so they took Olivia to Chatswood Mall, and she came back with white skinny jeans and girly T-shirts. Then my friend Jacqui and her daughter Bronte (then fourteen) and son, Thomas (then eighteen) took Liv shopping at Westfield Mall in Bondi Junction. I gave Liv money as an early Christmas present and she came home very happy, having acquired lots of new girl gear: skinny dark jeans, tiny denim shorts, silky T-shirts, a necklace, trendy North Star trainers, mascara and so on. Jacqui told me how Liv had swirled and preened in the stores while trying on her new girl clothes, clearly revelling in this expression of her newfound femininity.

I liked how wearing girl clothing quite obviously freed Liv up and made her happy because she was feminising her look. Indeed, it was a lot like watching a baby bird learning to fluff up its wings as it becomes emboldened by the possibilities of beauty and flight. It was, however, tough for me to get excited about this development, because I have never been interested in that girl stuff. Indeed, Angus and I mused about how he and I had met and fallen in love when we were both involved in a political movement that had been committed to breaking down gender stereotyping and yet, ironically, here we were with a trans girl child who seemingly wanted so many of the stereotypical trappings of femininity.

Buying clothes for a trans girl who comes out at thirteen is a bit of a hit-and-miss affair because, of course, her public/outer female identity is nascent. She is still a fledgling in girl terms. In addition, she hasn't had thirteen years to work out what she likes to wear, what clothing styles suit her, how she likes to look and feel in girls' clothes, how she might sit and walk in girls' clothes – all things that girls living as girls from birth learn slowly over time from birth. I am guessing too that mothers of girls from birth are perhaps tuned in to what their daughters like and what suits them – and, course, I had no idea at all what would work for Liv, so I was really no good to her on this front. About half of the clothes that she bought turned out to be unsuitable for her in some way – even if she had tried them on in the department stores to see if they fitted. She often wore clothing items a few times before she worked out that she didn't feel comfortable with them, so we couldn't take them back to the store to exchange them. For example, she just wasn't relaxed in the very tiny denim shorts that she had bought; the white jeans were too tight and hence didn't do any concealing of (male) body parts; and the sleeveless T-shirts gave her a very masculine look.

What worked well for Liv were the short cotton shorts, fitted and V-neck silky T-shirts, slightly baggy long pants, and flowery/colourful fitted jumpers. If something did suit her and she felt comfortable wearing it, then we went back and bought a few of the same item in various shades and patterns. I did buy from relatively inexpensive clothes shops like H and M, Woolworths, Cotton On or K-Mart, so that she could experiment with particular styles and fits and it wouldn't be a financial problem if she rejected various items after a few efforts at wearing them. These large department stores also offered an anonymity that was important for Liv when shopping for clothes, as most of them had gender-neutral changerooms too.

Bras have been more complicated. On the advice of an online trans parent, I made a bra-fitting appointment for Olivia with an underwear consultant at David Jones at the Westfield Mall in Brookvale. When I called to make the appointment, the manager seemed unfazed by my request for an appointment with a fitter with transgender bra-fitting experience, telling me that she had a staff member who did it quite often. It was a more public experience than either Liv or I were comfortable with, because the fitter measured her out in the public space and not in a cubicle, but we did manage to get the first of her bras from this experience (Bonds lightly padded teen bras in size 13A). Over time, we have experimented with a range of Bonds padded bras and worked out which ones are most comfortable and natural-looking under her shirts.

According to the parents on the website, binding and concealing underwear had to be ordered online, either from a local Sydney business or from the Etsy website in the USA where it is handmade and very good quality. I ordered a range of transgender M2F underpants from Etsy and, although they were expensive and took months to arrive, when they did finally arrive, Liv was very pleased with them. They were made of beautiful cotton and they were comfortable and, most importantly, concealing. It is now the only underwear that she will wear in and out of the house.

As part of the feminising project, I showed Liv how to shave under her arms and I took her to have her ears pierced, her legs, arms and face waxed, her eyebrows shaped and tinted and her eyelashes tinted. (I have to say, I was amazed at how these cosmetic changes so notably feminised her.) One evening, Jacqui's daughter, Bronte, and her friend, Millie, made up Liv's face with elaborate make-up, trying to show her how to replicate it, but she has shown little interest in make-up since then. Indeed, after her initial enthusiasm for the outer feminising project, she has generally shown a lacklustre commitment to the various preening activities of femalehood – usually nowadays I have to cajole her to make an effort with her appearance when we are going out of the house.

My focus on her external feminising process was clearly a big issue for Liv: she told me one day when she and I were hanging out the washing together that there are aspects of living as a boy that she missed. For example, she missed a time when I was not regularly pressurising her to work on her appearance. She added that she did wonder sometimes if I was sexist because I didn't used to talk about her appearance when she was a boy but that she does keep reminding herself that I am a feminist, so I can't be sexist!

When I told Angus about Liv's comments to me about pressuring her to look good, he asked me why I do it with her. I guess there are lots of reasons: I wanted her to pass more easily as a girl; I wanted her to cue people that she is a girl – or, at least a trans girl – so that they then respond to her as the right gender and don't unconsciously misgender her; and sadly, I do it with her because I do know that, unfortunately, women are judged far more on their appearance than men are. Given my politics, though, I am deeply ambivalent about putting this pressure on her and I am quite relieved that, as she is further along in her transitioning, she has become less focused on the girly stuff, even if it makes misgendering more likely.

By the time the summer holidays were in full swing, Liv was presenting as a girl full-time and, a few weeks later, she made it clear to us that in six weeks' time, when Year 8 began, she was going to go to school as herself, as a girl, as Olivia. Based on her experience with the trans youth groups and what I have read, some trans kids are able to tolerate being in the closet until they have finished high school. In many ways, this is useful because then they can avoid struggling through the tortures of adolescence while dealing with trans bullying. Perhaps too it is easier to turn eighteen and come out as trans because, at that age, trans youngsters are able to make their own decisions about transitioning. However, some trans teens, like Liv, cannot tolerate this dissonance between their inner and outer selves and need to go to school as their authentic selves, even if it is likely to bring them transphobic troubles somewhere along the way in high school.

I was very happy for Liv to go to school as her girl self too: for me it was vital that she was able to live authentically and didn't have to cope with all the deception that goes with being trans and being in the closet. She was worried, however, that going to school as a girl in the girls' uniform, expecting to use the girls' facilities and to be called Olivia (with appropriate pronouns, she/her) wouldn't go down well at the Anglican school where she and Stirling were students. Stirling was also worried about it. Indeed, he was often very upset when talking to Angus and to me about Liv going back to school in January because he was so worried that she would get bullied by the macho boys in their cohort.

It turns out that Liv had a sense of this impending rejection too because, just before Christmas, she told us that she didn't think she would be accepted as Olivia at her school. She talked about how, during the marriage equality postal plebiscite a few months before, some of the teachers and students at her school had been vocal about their rejection of marriage equality. She concluded, probably rightly, that those who were against marriage equality were very likely to be transphobic. She said she was even more afraid of being shunned by many of the other kids at her school who didn't understand trans kids and would feel freaked out by her.

I emailed the school and told them that we needed to talk about how they would adjust to having Liv returning in Year 8 as a girl. Within a few days, the acting principal phoned me to talk about it. He told me that the school's council had discussed the matter. While he spoke, it was apparent that the council did not feel comfortable with having a trans student at their school. He explained to us that the council had said that they had never had a transgender kid at their school and hence did not have the facilities and resources to accommodate our child. For example, they didn't have unisex toilets or change rooms. In addition, they felt that, if they had a trans kid at the school, it would be appropriate for the council to send out a letter to every parent in the school notifying them that there was a transgender student enrolled in the school. The board was concerned that with all the children in the school knowing that our daughter was transgender, it might lead to bullying of her or her brother within the school. The acting principal also informed me that he had liaised with the school counsellor, who had advised him that it would be particularly difficult for my son to have a transgender sister at the school as he could be bullied about it. He highlighted the leadership skills that my son had demonstrated during the previous year and commented that this situation with his sister could compromise his future leadership opportunities. Then he made clear it that if our daughter left the school immediately, they would waive the notice period fee (one term's fees).

I ended the call and told Angus all the details, and he, like me, was devastated, not least because it was a reflection of the transphobia that Liv could well have to deal with in the world in the future. We debated having a legal fight about it with the school but concluded that there was no point because we didn't want Liv to be at a school where she was not welcome. In addition, we were dealing with so much at this time in our lives that we didn't have the energy to take the school on. We also knew that it wasn't wise to fight the school right then as we had to leave Stirling there because he and we couldn't cope with more change. So we just accepted their implicit rejection and withdrew Liv, even though there were only three weeks to go before Year 8 was due to begin, and we had no obvious schooling options for her. Naturally, this became a massive dilemma for us.

Simultaneously, we were worried about Stirling and trying to find ways to support him. He was really struggling emotionally and psychologically. One night when I went to kiss him goodnight in bed, he asked me to lie with him and talk. As I lay with him in the dark, he talked and talked. It had been apparent to me that, while he was often very empathic towards Olivia and that he sometimes liked the rebellious idea of having a trans sister, on the whole, he felt a great loss about this monumental change. He talked about how hard it was to think about his memories of growing up with his twin brother, wondering about how valid his memories were now in light of the news that Orlando had never really existed but was, in fact, Olivia. He was struggling significantly with the discontinuous sense of self presented to him by this change and he was, understandably, angry about all the turmoil in our lives, like our plans to move across Sydney, and the consequences of potentially returning to school with a transitioning sibling. Liv's Asperger's also seemed more pronounced at that time – perhaps because change is so hard for Aspies and she was amidst so many changes. It made her quite difficult to live with and impacted significantly on Stirling.

I listened and listened and empathised with Stirling and tried to get him to see things from Liv's perspective too. It was so hard. I asked Stirling again if he would consider seeing a therapist but he refused to go back to therapy, telling me that it was boring. Given that I trained as a psychologist and we have had quite a few upheavals in our lives, my children have been in therapy from time to time in their young lives and perhaps, as a consequence of having those regular early experiences, they have become quite resistant to therapy.

One of the most important people in Stirling's life is his cricket coach, Ash. Ash has had a tough upbringing and is a remarkable human being with good judgement and very insightful perspectives on life. For years he has effectively functioned as Stirling's mentor, a man other than Angus on whom Stirling can depend for support and guidance in the difficult journey of adolescence. I emailed Ash to tell him about Olivia's transition and our attendant move to Balmain. I knew that I needed to tell him, because our change of location might affect where Stirling might train with Ash and, also, because I hoped that Ash could support Stirling through his struggles. Ash wrote a wonderfully caring and supportive email in reply.

The support that you have shown to your child is something we could all learn from. I don't know, nor can I imagine, what you guys have gone through but this is an amazing commitment to make for your child. I know that Stirling will support Olivia no matter what and that he will be happy as long as she is. Olivia will have a head start in life now. Obviously, there will be hurdles, but a year down the track everything will be so much easier for everyone. I will be there 100% to support all of you and especially Stirling.

The next week when Stirling had training, Ash was really gentle and kind in the way that he talked with Stirling and with me about Liv. He reassured us – a few times – that the hard times would come and go, and that life would be good for all of us in the end. Every week when I take Stirling to training, Ash asks after Liv in a deeply caring way and this role modelling of love and acceptance has been very influential for Stirling.

In our trans journey, support has sometimes come to us in unexpected ways, from unexpected people.

4

Semigrating to Balmain

I dreamt that there had been a very unexpected weather change for Sydney: there was snow and sleet expected in December. In our home, we were all hugely excited about this and we opened up all the doors and windows and slowly the snow and sleet and ice drifted in. It was blue, silver and white and quite, quite beautiful and misty. Our dogs became encased in solid ice, frozen and still. It was absolutely freezing cold and suddenly we realised that we didn't know how to get rid of all the snow and ice from inside the house and warm everything up again. Everything was beautiful but also so very cold.

We had three weeks to find a new school for Liv and we were totally fraught about it. I networked widely and was advised about a public high school in the inner west which could be a good school for Liv because there were other kids transitioning there. As a public school, it was bound by legislation to adopt practices and procedures for making a school a positive place for LGBTIQA+ students. Coincidentally, at a Boxing Day party at the Surry Hills home of one of Angus's colleagues, Angus and I had chatted to one of the 2017 school leaders and she had been full of praise for it. Liv and I also had tea with one of the girls who had just graduated from the school and she, and her mother, were largely positive about it.

Given that it was the holidays and schools were closed, we couldn't meet with the principal or any other school authorities to ask questions and find out more about the school. We resolved that we would just have to go on good faith and put in an application for Liv to attend the school. Liv and I spent ages working on the application and then posted it off in the second week of January. I knew that the school was only scheduled to open to the public in the last week of January but I hoped that senior leadership would be back before then. It was all pretty nerve-racking but we decided we would move to the inner west and hopefully enrol Liv in the school when it opened.

When we emigrated, we had settled on the northern beaches because it was where Angus's family lived: his aunt and uncle, cousins and more cousins, and his cousin's young families. In time, my sister and her partner and child also moved there. We lived on the Manly Flats, a kilometre or so from Manly village and our neighbourhood was quiet and beautiful. Our small and modern house was just a few hundred metres from North Steyne beach, where Angus and Stirling loved to swim, surf and ski in the ocean. I rode my bike along the beachfront to get to my job in a local community centre, and we all loved to walk the dogs at Queenscliff Lagoon. There was no doubt that being so close and connected with the ocean and the beach was very positive part of daily life for all of us. Commuting was relatively easy too: Angus and the teens caught the ferry to and from work and school in the city. We also liked how we were able to see family and friends on the northern beaches easily and often.

Despite all these positive lifestyle factors, however, I had never felt at home in Manly. For many people, the slogan adopted by Manly tourism that Manly is 'Seven miles from Sydney and one thousand miles from care' is central to the charm of the place. For me, the slogan reflected the often parochial and exclusive feeling of Manly. I understood clearly why the northern beaches was referred to by people who lived elsewhere in Sydney as the insular peninsula. Since moving there, I had yearned to live in a place that was more diverse, more progressive, more vibrant, more inclusive and more connected with the city.

At first, Angus and Stirling were not particularly keen to leave the northern beaches. They expressed their concerns about moving away from family and the ocean. What was also difficult for them was the feeling of semigrating: emigrating from Durban to Sydney had been so incredibly hard for us that ripping up our fragile roots in Manly and moving to plant them across the city felt a bit like a semigration.

Moving from Manly to Balmain was easiest for Liv: she wanted to live in a place that she hoped would be accepting (and hopefully reflecting) of her transness.

I knew that Balmain was probably the least edgy and the most gentrified of the inner west suburbs but I was prepared to make the compromise because I knew it would make Angus happy to live close to the water and beautiful harbour walks of Balmain – and he and Stirling could still get the ferry to school and work. Having a calm start and finish to the day was important to Angus's state of mind, especially given his highly stressful work as a barrister. Over time, Angus, who is always good at seeing the big picture, became increasingly clear that this move was the best decision for our family, and so Olivia identifying as transgender became the catalyst for our move.

There was some difficulty with our extended family, some of whom initially did not support our move, phoning and emailing us with questions and comments.

Is it really so critical for you to move, especially in such a rush? Does Olivia have to go to that particular school? Would she not be better off being home schooled for a while? Stirling is already struggling to adapt to losing a brother, does he also need to move when he doesn't want to? Having a transgender child is stressful but now you are adding more stress on top of that. A bit of time at home for Olivia while she gets used to the whole transition would surely be better for her too. I can't see how you four can deal with so much in such a short time without something breaking?

Angus and I were really upset about these questions. Our life felt so difficult at that time and we had struggled and thought through this move to Balmain. We both felt that, hard as it was for Angus and

Stirling to semi-grate, it was the right decision for our family. Angus wrote to those in his family members who had been raising these questions/comments.

You should feel assured that I have thrown every alternative and permutation around and it seems to me that it is best that we leave Manly, at least for now, and that we do this in time for the new school year. Moving house to a suburb a short journey across the city is not such a big deal. I have a lot on my plate right now so I can't explain everything – I can do that in due course – but I would just like to say a few things.

We have been thinking for a while of selling our Manly house as it is too small for us. We have also been thinking of moving closer to the kids' school and my work – long before the transgender issue arose. There are good reasons for this: Stirling is a very social animal and he needs his friends around and they live largely in the Inner West. Olivia is much less relaxed in social contexts so it is important that it is as easy as possible for her to be with friends. The area we are considering is also better for universities and opportunities in and around the city. As much as the Beaches are great, they are isolated. Work opportunities are better for Lyndsay that side of Sydney. Most of my colleagues live that side and I could do with more social contact with likely friends and connections.

Olivia is transgender. We, and the professionals we are consulting, have no doubt about that. But even if she isn't then we can move again if we want to do that. But if she is transgender, it is critical to her well-being (which is under threat in various ways) that she is able to come out and come to terms with herself in society as soon as possible. Moreover, there is a ticking time bomb here which is puberty. The further she goes along that road before taking puberty blockers (which, as you know, are reversible) the more difficult it will be for the rest of her life – a life that is already bound to be difficult. So we can't just sit around and take time to see what happens and what works out or not.

And then there is the question of schools. As I have explained school starts at the end of the month. That is a critical date. So which school will she go to? A few members of the family have suggested that she should stay at home and be home schooled. We do not see that as a viable option. Olivia is a socially anxious person. What she needs is interaction with the world. To isolate her at home would be very bad for her and could even lead to her refusing to go to school again. Olivia gets enormous benefit from being in the school learning environment and it would be terrible to take that away from her. All we are doing is trying to find the right school environment.

Questions have been raised about Stirling. Although he has found the idea of the move difficult, he is happy to go to Balmain and tonight even said that he is looking forward to it. That is where his friends are. Of course, he will miss being in Manly and he will miss Jamie and Robbie and the young cousins especially, but we will not be that far away. But, in any event, frankly this decision is too important to be made on the basis of the preference of a thirteen-year-old. He will adjust and he will be fine. On the other hand, if we don't move and we don't do it soon, Olivia may not be fine.

It is hard to describe how liberated Olivia is by coming out. She sings and dances around the house. She loves her new look (make-up, girl's haircut, shaved legs, girl's clothes) and she wants to go to school as Olivia. Of course, that will be a tough thing to do but it is also a freeing thing to do and this is the psychologically healthier choice as far as we and the psychiatrists and psychologists see it. It is an enormous relief for us to witness the lifting of her depression and suicidality. Of course, it is not going to be easy for her going to a new school and making new friends and so on but we believe that this is the right thing to do in this context.

So, yes of course, moving is hard but it is also exciting and promises new opportunities and we look forward to what those might be.

Angus concluded his email with a piece by Olivia about her trans journey. Afterwards, there was thankfully wider family support for our move to Balmain. Unfortunately, however, moving to Balmain wasn't logistically simple: we struggled to find a four-bedroom house to rent because most homeowners weren't keen to rent to people with dogs and we have two much-loved Beagliers, Archimedes and Serena. This problem was odd given that urban legend has it that Balmain has the highest person-to-dog ratio of any suburb in Australia. It certainly seemed to me, when walking around Balmain, that everyone had a dog. Ultimately, we managed to rent a rather ramshackle old stone house when we offered to pay more than the weekly rental price in order to compensate for the presence of the dogs in our new rental. We then had a week and a half to pack up our Manly lives and get ready to move to Balmain.

First, though, on 11 January, we had the long-awaited appointment with the paediatric endocrinologist. The doctor's rooms were across town and our appointment was at eight a.m., so we had to be up early and out of the house by seven. We got there in time to seek out a coffee and while we sat in the early morning silence of the hospital café, Liv and Stirling were tetchy and troubling each other endlessly over nothing and everything. I guess we all felt the tension and significance of this visit. I certainly had no idea what to expect but I was hopeful that we would at least come away with a script for puberty blockers.

After our coffee, we found the endocrinologist's rooms and sat waiting in the vast open waiting room. I looked around as surreptitiously as I could at the other families sitting in this space, wondering if they too were there with trans children. When the doctor came out to call us, all four of us trooped into his rooms. He had to find a chair for Stirling, which indicated to me that perhaps it wasn't the norm for the entire family to be there. He sat behind his desk, reserved and professional, but also relatively warm, asking us for a brief summary of the journey that had brought us here. We looked at each other and Angus suggested that I tell our tale, which I then did, with some additions from Angus and Liv.

Within a short while, Stirling looked as though he was having a TMI (too much information) moment and he asked if he could wait outside. The doctor assented and Stirling very quickly disappeared to the comfort of his Instagram feed in the waiting room. The doctor then asked Liv lots of questions, explained the stages of transitioning to us, answered lots of our questions and got her to complete a long survey about her experience of being gender-dysphoric. Then he took her behind a modesty curtain and did a full physical examination in order to establish how far advanced she was in her physical puberty journey as a boy.

He told us that he had received a report from Liv's psychiatrist saying that Liv was gender-dysphoric and he felt that this accorded with his assessment of her. Consequently, he said, he was prepared to prescribe puberty blockers. He explained that Zoladex, the one that he would be prescribing, had very limited side effects, but that there were no long-term studies about the effects of the drug, so he could not guarantee that there would be no long-term effects.

He also explained that, before she could start the puberty blockers, she needed to decide whether she wanted to store sperm in it for *in-vitro* fertilisation (IVF) if she wanted to try to have her own genetic offspring in the future. This had to be done before taking the puberty blockers, as they inhibited sperm production.

There was a rather tense moment when Liv asked him if he would give her testosterone blockers instead of general puberty blockers, and he refused, telling her, 'I can't give you testosterone blockers because that would effectively be giving you a very low form of oestrogen, given that all male bodies have a low dose of oestrogen. At this clinic we don't support giving teens cross-sex hormones until they have been living as their chosen gender for at least a year, preferably longer, and have been through intensive work with a psychiatrist and psychologist for a significant period of time. We're not prepared to dispense such hormones until a teen is Gillick competent and sixteen years of age, approximately. That's because there's some research evidence that some teens change their mind and decide that they are, in fact, not gender-dysphoric. So, at this stage, we can give you a puberty blocker that effectively puts you in a holding pattern while you seek help and support and socially transition.'

Liv was silent after this, her head down as she avoided any eye contact with the doctor. Soon after this, the doctor began to wrap things up with us. Before we left his rooms, though, he said to Angus and me that Liv undoubtedly seemed gender-dysphoric to him and that, over the next few days, we should discuss as a family if we were sure that Liv should have puberty blockers and also whether she wanted to store sperm. He advised us to talk to the Gender Centre for support and to look online for breast padding, binding underwear and other feminising gear for trans girls. Olivia had done very little to dress up as a girl for this appointment; indeed, she looked just as she might if she had presented as her old (male) self. I mentally kicked myself. In retrospect, it could have impacted on his assessment that Olivia was not presenting and living as female.

While Angus and Stirling fetched the car, Liv and I walked over the road to a pathology lab, where she had extensive blood tests, including a testosterone level test, and then we headed home. The mood amongst us was heavy. I had not realised that Liv had gone to the appointment actually hoping to be given testosterone blockers. As Angus drove us home, she explained to us what we hadn't understood all that well during the appointment with the doctor: that she had wanted him to give her testosterone blockers because they allow for the latent female hormones in her body that every born male has to flourish and have a (limited) feminising effect. In contrast, the puberty blockers that he had prescribed for her stopped *all* hormones being produced in the body, so there could be no feminising effect from taking them, just a halting of the process of male secondary sexual characteristic development. I had had no idea about this distinction before the appointment. Even though it had been apparent that he wouldn't have been flexible about what medication to give Liv, I did wish I had done more research and been better prepared.

During the rest of that journey home, none of us said anything. When I turned to look at Liv, I saw that she had silent tears running down her cheeks and my heart ached for her. When we got home, we all went to our separate spaces in the house to try to process the experience with the endocrinologist. Within a few days, he emailed me the results of Liv's blood tests: she was already three-quarters of the way through puberty. He said that he thought it was still worth her having puberty blockers in order to inhibit the final stages of (male) puberty, including importantly the development of facial hair and an Adam's apple.

So, on 30 January, Liv and I set off to the endocrinologist's rooms for her to have her first puberty blocker injection. He gave us a script for Zoladex and we went to collect the capsule from the local pharmacy. While we waited at dispensary, the pharmacist explained to me that because it was a drug used to suppress sex hormones, it was primarily used to treat breast and prostate cancer. The shock of this news ricocheted through me as I figured that it must be a fairly serious drug. I paid the $1,100 for this single dose and, as we walked towards the endocrinologist's rooms clutching the precious package, I tried not to think about the medication's usual use.

When we got to the doctor's rooms, he first wiped down the upper outer quartile of Liv's right butt cheek with an anaesthetic cream and then told us that we had to wait for an hour before the area was numb. We sat in the waiting room, waiting for the cream to work, both looking distractedly at our phones and willing time to pass. I thought about all the tough years of hope and despair that I had spent waiting in IVF waiting rooms for hormone injections in the upper outer quartile of my butt cheek when I was trying to get pregnant through IVF.

Finally, the doctor called us and we went through for Liv to have the injection. I was very conscious about not looking at the needle because he had warned us that the one he had to use for inserting the capsule was significantly larger than usual needles. I am often hopeless in medical situations like these because medical procedures, particularly where there is blood, make me feel faint and dizzy. Angus copes much better than me with blood and gore but he was at work that day so I simply had to cope – especially as Liv insisted that I was right there at her side, holding her hand. As the needle went in and Liv flinched, I felt the referred pain and I wanted to sit down with my head between my knees to avoid fainting.

But I didn't. I held her hand and took the referred pain, a bit like an electric shock. This experience seemed to me to be an apt metaphor for this gender-dysphoric journey: Liv feels the direct pain and I feel it indirectly through my powerful connection to her.

And that was it. Liv's hormonal transitioning had begun. She was very pale as we hobbled towards the hospital car park, telling me that her butt hurt like hell. I thought about how we were going to have to do these injections every ten weeks. At least in the future we didn't have to drive across town to the endocrinologist for Liv to have the injection because we could buy the Zoladex at our local pharmacy and take it to one of our lovely GPs, Simone, to do the injecting. Simone had told us previously that she had other transgender patients and hence was familiar with administering these seriously invasive injections.

Despite the physical pain of the injection, Liv was very glad to have had it. She recognised that she had begun the medical transitioning process. As we drove home from Westmead Hospital, I felt her mood lift significantly and the lightness between us grow.

Liv's transitioning process continued a few weeks later when we semigrated to the inner west where, hopefully, she would be able to feel more at home, more accepted and reflected. We packed up our Manly house over two days and then, the night before we were due to move into the new place in Balmain, we stayed in an Airbnb rental home close to our new place. It was a scorching hot January night. We wandered around our new neighbourhood and ate delicious Vietnamese food at a local café before heading 'home' to try to sleep. It felt so much hotter than Manly and we were all quite restless. The dogs were as disconcerted as we were, padding agitatedly around the house after we had switched off the lights, clearly unable to settle in this unfamiliar space. Eventually, I put them into bed with me and the three of us were able to sleep. Angus didn't sleep much at all.

Early the next morning, Angus and I went for an acclimatising walk around the neighbourhood. I felt so excited about being in Balmain – despite not being able to locate myself and not knowing where the best coffee was to be found at that time of day. I loved the harbour water everywhere, the slightly grungy feel of the place, the old terraces, the stone homes, the density of very urban living. I could feel Angus's disorientation and dislocation, though, and I knew that this experience was much less positive for him than it was for me.

After breakfast, I dropped Stirling at Balmoral oval for a cricket camp. Yes, it was moving day and he should have been helping us to move into our new rental home but he was so rattled by the move that it was easier to have him away for the day and for us to move into the house without him.

By the time I got back to Balmain from Balmoral, Angus and Liv were helping the movers bring in the furniture at our new rental. It was chaos, of course. Angus didn't like the rental house much and was finding various faults with it: the sofas didn't fit in, the garden was a mess, there was no covered outdoor social space to sit, the air conditioning wasn't working well. While some of these issues were objectively real, I also knew that the fault-finding was part of his struggle to cope with the change. I avoided focusing too heavily on the positives of the house and our new neighbourhood because I knew that it would make him feel that I wasn't hearing his inner struggles with this move. I was very aware that, even though he had come around to the idea that we needed to move, it was still very difficult for him.

Liv was really cheerful and worked incredibly hard – without a single complaint – at packing and unpacking. What was also out of character for her teen self is that she chose to have the smaller bedroom so that Stirling could have the large en suite one.

She told me, 'My brother had to leave Manly so I could go to school on this side of the city so he should have the bigger room.' It was quite insightful of her, because it did make a big difference to Stirling's state of mind when I brought him home from cricket later that day and he found that he had such a lovely bedroom.

After a quick approval of his new bedroom, Stirling was gone, heading off to visit his mate Fin, who lived just a few blocks away.

Within a few days, Stirling was enjoying living in Balmain. He has so many school friends in the area that he was almost never home: in the first few days, he was off swimming for hours at the Dawn Fraser local harbour pool with Vanessa, Alice and Darcy, then he was off walking the dogs with Fin and his dog, and hanging out at Fin's place a few streets away, before heading off to spend much of the day at Max's house in the adjacent neighbourhood of Annandale. When school started, he loved walking five minutes down to the wharf with Angus in the morning and getting a ferry to Circular Quay and a train to school, or heading off to Fin's house so that they could get the bus together. He talked often though about how much he missed Manly Beach and our northern beaches family, most especially his cousins, Jamie and Murray, and his uncle Robbie. He still loves to hop on the ferry to Manly to visit them and when he comes home from these visits, he tells us that he is homesick for his Manly family.

I was happy and at home pretty much immediately in Balmain. Indeed, I have felt much more myself since we moved to Balmain than I ever felt on the northern beaches. While I know that it's unlikely that I will ever feel Australian, I do certainly feel like a Sydneysider since we moved to live in the inner west. I love the feeling of being part of the city. Our rental house was a hundred and fifty metres from Mort Bay park and, as we arrived at the park for a walk, we had a phenomenal, panoramic view of the Harbour Bridge.

Sadly, Angus wasn't finding it nearly as wonderful to be living in Balmain. He missed the peaceful Manly beach lifestyle and his family. He doesn't adjust to change as easily as I do. Well, truthfully, one of the ways that I manage change is just to split off from the past situation and completely immerse myself in the new one, working hard not to think about the past. This is how I survived emigration in my forties: I tried not to think about South Africa at all once we moved to Sydney, seeking to immerse myself entirely in Sydney life.

After we moved into our rental home, we had a few days to get Liv ready for school. Firstly, this entailed finding someone who was prepared to attach professional hair extensions onto her very short hair to help create a more feminine look. We finally found someone in Rose Bay who said he would do it but that it would take a whole day and part of a night (and a lot of money) to do a good job. Nobody else was prepared to do it because her hair was so short so I dropped her off at ten a.m. in Rose Bay and the job was finally finished at midnight. It was not cheap and it was not comfortable for Liv to endure the process but when I arrived to fetch her, I was quite taken aback at how different she looked with long hair. She clearly felt very different too and was preening and swinging her hair around with great pride – and relief too perhaps. It clearly made a very significant difference to her sense of how she presented in the world as a girl, and so it was worth the financial investment.

To prepare further for Liv presenting at school as a girl for the first time, she and I had a meeting with Lee, the senior case worker at the Gender Centre. We talked about what school bathrooms and change rooms she should use (the girls' ones and not any unisex toilets she was offered), what name the school would have to use on their legal documents (both names because the state legally still had Olivia on record as Orlando but we should insist that Olivia be the name used by all teachers in their interactions with her and reporting on her) and what to do if Olivia was misgendered or bullied (take it up immediately with the staff she comes to like and/or trust). We spent hours with Lee as I was really anxious about Liv starting school – more anxious than Liv seemingly. Lee was endlessly patient with me. We also talked about the process of legal transitioning, of changing Liv's legal documents to reflect her new name and real gender identity. I was very much deterred by the apparent bureaucracy of the process but, later in the year, Liv got onto it and worked to make it happen.

The school was only able to offer us an interview with the Year 8 coordinator a few days into the start of the new term. This meant that Liv couldn't start the year with all the other Year 8 students. This was hugely stressful but I had worked as a teacher for four years in a public high school in Australia and I knew that the start of the school year was chaotically challenging, particularly as public schools have to enrol every child living in the school's catchment zone who wants to come to that school.

So, on Friday of the first official week of school, Liv and I met with the Year 8 coordinator. She was reassuring and open, suggesting that Liv consistently assert herself as a girl so that the other students around her would take her lead. She made it very clear that the school insisted on and embraced diversity and inclusivity. After the interview we met the head of well-being and the principal and I was relieved that they seemed both welcoming and encouraging. They agreed that Liv could start on Monday.

As Liv definitely had a place in the school, we went off to buy her school uniform, including a school skirt. This was the first time that she had worn a skirt and she looked good in it, albeit unfamiliar to me. While we were at the uniform shop, I asked her if she wanted to buy the boys' school shorts as well as the skirt but she said no. When Monday morning arrived, however, and Liv got up to go to school, she told me that she was wearing the boys' shorts to school. Obviously, it just felt really hard to wear a skirt for the first time to a new school. I reminded her that when we had been in the uniform shop she had said that she didn't want any boys' shorts and so she went off to her bedroom and put on the skirt with the unisex polo shirt.

Before heading off to school for day one, Liv and I walked Archimedes and Serena around the harbour at Mort Bay park. It was quite a moment for me too to see her out in public in a skirt. I thought she looked lovely. She told me that she felt comfortable and free wearing a skirt rather than shorts. I had had the skirt shortened so that it was a miniskirt, which is a requirement for a girl to fit in in a Sydney high school, particularly a public high school.

After a lap of the park with the dogs, it was time for me to drop Liv at school. I could tell that she was really nervous when she walked off into the labyrinthine school building with the Year 8 coordinator. As she disappeared, I felt incredibly nervous too, wondering and worrying about how her first school day as a girl would proceed for her. I desperately hoped it would go well.

While Liv and I had been walking the dogs in the park, I had taken phone photos of her in her new uniform. I emailed them to Angus when I got home, giving him all the details of the morning. Angus then forwarded them in an email to tell his friend Edwin, a judge and a human rights activist in South Africa, about Olivia's transitioning. Edwin emailed Angus back later that day.

> Thank you for sharing this beautiful and unsettling news with me as part of your close circle. What a day today must have been for Liv – and for all of you – with Liv starting school as a girl. Perhaps later you will be able to feel the excitement of Liv's courage – and the admiration I feel for you and for Lyndsay, that Liv felt safe within your home to find herself, and to start this perilous journey in a perilous world.

Edwin's email was deeply poignant, a reminder that as a gay man now in his sixties, he had encountered a lot of prejudice and discrimination in his life. It turns out that his sense that Liv was about to begin a perilous journey in a perilous world was painfully, dreadfully accurate.

5

A perilous journey in a perilous world

I dreamt that I was going on an expedition where I would be climbing the highest mountain in the world and we would be climbing in the snow. When the people I was going with arrived to fetch me to take me on the trip, I was totally unprepared: I had not packed or even thought about packing. I rushed around throwing things randomly into my suitcase. I didn't appear to have the packing guidelines for the trip so I didn't know what to take and I couldn't seem to find what I thought I needed to take with me. In the meantime, my two children were squabbling around me, commenting on how incompetent I was being. I realised that I hadn't even bought the required hiking shoes for snow hiking and that I was totally underprepared for the Arctic conditions, so I was going to be absolutely freezing. I wondered if I would survive, given how unprepared I was for this massive expedition.

When I fetched Liv from school on day one at her new school, one of the first things she said to me was that she had already been challenged about her gender:

'One of the wild boys in my class asked me, "Are you a girl or a boy? You look a bit like a girl but you're interested in boys' things like gaming, computers and coding."'

'How did you respond, Liv?'

'I told him I'm a girl and girls can be interested in those things too and it's a stereotype to think that we aren't.'

Other than this incident, Year 8 had started off well for Liv. Thank goodness. I was overwhelmingly relieved.

The next day, when I fetched her from school, Liv told me that she had connected with a group of girls and they had invited her to sit with them at recess and lunch. She described them as energetic, raucous, amusing and full of quick banter. She was in the extension class and reported that the lessons were generally stimulating, and that most of the teachers were warm and friendly. Being scholarly and loving to learn, she was surprised to discover that it wasn't cool even in the extension cohort to be studious in class. Fortunately, she has never been a slave to the crowds, so she didn't care about this culture and she took it as a compliment when one of her classmates called her the Girl Who Knew Everything.

She was open with her classmates about being trans because she doesn't believe in living in stealth, in hiding the fact that she is trans. During the holidays, she had shown me a video that she had found on YouTube where a high school trans girl living in stealth in a school in the USA was anxious all the time about being caught out as transgender. The video shows how, when she was at a sleepover and was finally forced to tell her friends that she was transgender, they responded very badly, telling her that she had lied to them. Then the father of the girl who lived at the sleepover house phoned the trans girl's parents and asked them to fetch their daughter because of what had happened. It was a pretty traumatic enactment of something that was probably quite feasible for trans kids living in stealth.

In the first week, Liv told her lunchtime girls' group that she was transgender, and, she said to me, there seemed to be no issue with it. However, after a while, she found that one of the girls was repeatedly hostile towards her presence in the group and, even though it wasn't clear if there was an issue with Liv being trans or not, Liv started to hang out in the library at lunchtime, where, she said, all the outsiders were made to feel welcome. The librarian seemed to work hard to make Liv, and the other LGBTI students in particular, feel at home in the library.

Liv did, however, believe that she passed as a girl much more than she actually did at this early stage of her social and medical transitioning. This disjuncture between her appearance and reality became apparent when an autistic boy in her school kept telling her that she must be a boy and when she was misgendered by the school receptionist a number of times (even though she told the reception team that her name was Olivia). She was also misgendered a few times by her teachers, despite their being briefed about her being a trans girl. A few weeks into the term, I went to raise my concerns with the well-being coordinator and, fortunately, the misgendering seemed to subside.

However, even though Liv did seem to be managing at school and was doing well academically, she was often highly emotional, tearful and vulnerable at night, expressing her fears about her life and her future. She and I had to do a lot of processing, sometimes for hours, before the heaviness and tears abated and she felt settled enough to sleep.

Although Liv and I have always had an overly enmeshed relationship, our connection had intensified significantly since I knew she was transgender. I worried about her all the time. Indeed, I was so stressed with all that was going on with Liv that, one day while I was facilitating a well-being group at a primary school, I had weird and unusual heart palpitations and my left arm was tingling – potentially the signs of a heart attack. It was a pretty scary moment when it happened to me, as it was lunchtime and the classroom where I was working that day was far away from the other facilitators, so I couldn't call anyone for help. I told myself that I was just stressed and that I should just breathe slowly and deeply and I would be fine. I was aware that coughing vigorously could potentially prevent a brewing heart attack so I alternated between coughing hard and breathing deeply and, after a while, my heart settled down to normal, the bell rang, the students rushed into the class and the second session of the day began.

That evening, on the way home, I went to see one of our GPs, Simone, about this strange experience. She sent me for blood tests and an ECG and gave me a referral to a cardiologist for a major heart check. I did think that it was a weird kind of irony and synchronicity that my heart, which so often felt (metaphorically) deeply troubled by Liv's struggles, might be having a little cardiac crisis.

Fortunately, the results from the tests were good and it seemed likely that I had been having a mild panic attack during the school lunch break (even though I hadn't had panic attacks for some years). However, subsequently, I have tried to remind myself every day to remember that, as a pessimist, I tend to focus more intensely when Liv tells me the sad and difficult stories about her day, and less when she shares positive stories. For example, at that time, when she was having trouble adjusting to being in a new school, she had also regained her love for computer coding and was making significant breakthroughs in her coding projects. And she really enjoyed her dance classes at her school and at a local dance school. She also liked her teachers and classmates and was enjoying most of her school classes. As part of my rather pessimistic world view, I was prone to ignore or not hear the positive experiences that she was reporting to me, focusing instead on only the troubling stories.

One of the ways that I have sought to be positive and optimistic about the transitioning of our family has been to engage in communal trans activities. The Mardi Gras in March was a perfect opportunity: I bought tickets for Liv, Stirling and their friends and I to see a trans teen film at the Mardi Gras film festival, I planned for Liv and I to go to the Mardi Gras fair, I organised for her and I to be on a Trans Pride float, and I bought tickets for the Mardi Gras Ideas Festival for our family to go along and to listen to transgender celebrities/personalities speaking about being trans.

I was very excited about all this and so I was pretty taken aback one day when Liv complained to me that she felt that I focused too much on her transness,

'Not everything in life is about being trans, Mom. I don't want to be more trans than anything else. I'm just me. Please stop making everything about me being trans. I don't want to do *everything* at the Mardi Gras.'

That was a tough moment for me. I felt that if we were able to participate in these events, we would be part of making the transphobic world more accepting of trans kids like Liv. In addition, for me, as an unstoppable action taker, participating in these events gave me a sense that we were doing something to be part of Liv's transitioning journey. I also relished any opportunity to learn about the nuances and specifics of transgenderism and to immerse myself in a transgender world and hence normalise our experience of Liv being transgender. *And* I believed that Liv would feel validated at these events and then she would be happier and less gender-dysphoric. It seemed to me that there were so many positives that arose from us being involved in the Mardi Gras festival.

But I had to accept that, for Liv, she experienced me and all my Mardi Gras bookings as me being, in her words, pushy about the trans stuff. When I posted about this dilemma on the trans parent group website, I got lots of parents responding with stories of similar experiences where they had been told by their trans kids to 'Stay in your lane, Mum' and not to push their kids to engage with trans activities.

Despite Liv's resistance, I did manage to get her and her trans friend Mia, and Stirling and his friend Danni, to see the trans teen movie *Just Charlie* at the Mardi Gras film festival and they all seemed to enjoy that.

But instead of taking Liv to the Mardi Gras Ideas Festival, Angus and I went with our friends, Jacqui and Guy and their son Thomas to listen to the ten or so trans (and trans ally) adults aged between twenty and eighty talk about their trans experiences. It was deeply moving to hear these brave individuals telling their personal stories. What was particularly interesting was how they linked their transitional processes to social change about gender identity and being transgender. The show was brilliantly produced and deeply poignant. I was often in tears of sorrow while I listened to how incredibly difficult it had been to be transgender historically but, often too, I was in tears of gladness because these speakers were living very ordinary lives as trans people, with lovers and partners, friends and family, and working in rewarding jobs while living contented lives.

Angus and I felt so much more hopeful and positive about Liv's future after the evening and I wished that Liv had been there to appreciate the remarkable journeys of these inspirational people.

Then, when the Mardi Gras parade was a week or so away, Liv told me that she had changed her mind and that she would, in fact, like to be with me on the Trans Pride float with the other fifty or so trans-activists and allies. At that late stage, she couldn't be part of the dance as, for weeks, we had been practising our dance moves on Sunday afternoons and Liv had stopped attending after the first dance workshop. However, when I spoke to the brilliant choreographer, Lisa Freshwater about the possibility of Liv being involved, she conferred with her co-organisers, Peta Friend and AJ Brown, who said that there was still space for Liv to come along and hold one of the giant colourful letters in the front of the float.

Unfortunately, Liv's enthusiasm for being part of the parade had waned by parade day: from the time she woke up on Saturday 3 March, she was grumpy and unsettled about going to march. By the time we were dressed in our parade uniform (camouflage pants and a pink T-shirt declaring 'This is me'), she was reluctant to leave the house. I reminded myself that she has always found big social events difficult and that she generally tries to avoid crowds and loud noise. She also finds it difficult to go into unfamiliar and unpredictable situations. Whatever her concerns were, she wouldn't say and so we set off for the bus stop with her walking two or three steps behind me, tearful and with her arms wrapped closely around her body. We sat together on the bus. with Liv glowering at her phone and pretending I wasn't there, and me feeling sad because she wasn't excited about what I had thought would be a momentous occasion for her.

We were early, so we stopped off and had tea and cake at a hotel in the city. Still Liv didn't cheer up; she just scrolled through her phone feed, mostly ignoring me. We finished our tea in a sombre silence and headed for St Marys Cathedral, where we were due to meet up with the others who were going to be on the Trans Pride float. The irony of trans people and trans activists organising to meet up for the Mardi Gras parade at this iconic Catholic place of worship was not lost on me.

As we walked up towards them, some of our group, dressed identically to us, greeted us excitedly, and suddenly Liv blossomed, joining in the conversations with these relative strangers, posing for the many pictures we all took, seemingly as thrilled as all the others to be there. I was overwhelmingly relieved.

Once the Trans Pride mob was all present, and we had our identifying arm tags on, we walked through the security gates that had been erected at Hyde Park, and into the holding area allocated to the marchers. When we were through and assembled together near the Oxford Street starting point for our group, we waited for a few hours – with twelve thousand others – for our moment to march. By this stage, Liv was transformed, chatting and engaging, closely observing all the interesting scenes around her, not once impatient or bored.

When, finally, we were asked to line up on the street, we still had an hour or so before our designated time to march. Then the real party began. Our very inspiring song 'This is me', a Keala Settle song and the theme song for the movie *The Greatest Showman*, was playing over and over from the jeep that was due to lead us through the streets of Sydney. So, instead of just standing about waiting, we performed our choreographed dance long before we had even started marching down the streets.

As people walked by in the direction of their float, many were drawn to the elated excitement in our group, stopping to join in with our contagious and euphoric singing and dancing for a few moments. It was an intense and heady, wild and noisy experience. Liv joined in for some of the time but, being Liv, she also needed to sit on the side wall for a while, taking time out from the high energy of the moment.

Eventually, it was time to set off on the march. I was in the dancing team and Liv was in front of me holding up a giant letter S, part of the signage which combined to read 'This is me'. It was the first Mardi Gras I had been to and I could not believe the extent of the crowds along Oxford Street: they were ten deep at places. And, with my heart bursting with happiness, I thought about how every one of those thousands and thousands of people supported my trans daughter. We moved along past them, dancing over and over to our song. Every single time the song started up, I got goose bumps at the painful poignancy of its lyrics for those on our float, most of whom were transgender.

I watched Liv often during the hour or two that we were marching and dancing, and she was clearly exhilarated and deeply validated. There is a phone photo taken by someone in our group of her while marching, and she is throwing back her head and laughing, looking as though she felt, at that moment, an unfettered, sheer joy at being alive and being celebrated for who she is. I know that she loved the experience because, when we got to the end of the march, she told me that she really wanted to do it again next year.

Most of the people on our float were adults, so when we finished marching, they headed off to the parade after-party at Moore Park. As a youngster, Liv obviously couldn't go to the party, so she and I set off to walk from Moore Park to find public transport to get home. We were walking through the roadworks in Surry Hills, a bit lost and very tired, when a Silver Service taxi with its light on came past us, and so we hailed it and jumped in. Within a few minutes, I regretted this choice because the taxi driver was clearly not a Mardi Gras supporter: he was complaining endlessly and aggressively about all the silly, noisy people dressed up crazy tonight. I didn't feel safe with him because Liv was trans and he seemed conservative and angry. I was very happy when we got home and could get out of his car.

It was just as well that Liv had had this affirming experience of marching at Mardi Gras, because things at school were not going well. I had noticed that she had been unusually sad and flat for some time but she wouldn't talk about it, except to comment often on how much she hated her body and how much she wished she could have oestrogen now. I have learnt that when she is clearly processing something difficult, I just have to be present with her and wait until she feels able to talk about whatever is worrying her.

Eventually, one night when I was driving her home from the Transtopia teen support group, she opened up to me. She told me that the previous week, a boy at her school, whom she didn't know but who she thought was in Year 9, had passed her in the corridor at school and asked her, 'Do you have a dick? Are you a trap?' (A trap, Liv told me, is a term for a gay boy/man who allegedly tries to look like a girl in order to trap a boy/man into engaging with him sexually.) Liv had just ignored the boy and walked away, with him shouting down the corridor after her, 'Hey you, dick, answer me.'

That wasn't all, though. She told me that, when she had been walking home from school one afternoon, another boy in the uniform of her school, also not known to her, was riding past her on his bike, and he slowed down and said to her, 'Holy crap. You don't have a c—, so you must be a boy.'

Liv was devastated by these incidents. It seemed to me that, in addition to her sense of being under attack, what she was seriously upset about was that the incidents revealed to her that a relative stranger could clock her as transgender, highlighting that she did not sufficiently look like a girl. Her powerful rejection of her body at that time then made sense to me. I knew that, from the day she had had her hair extensions attached, she had believed she passed as a girl. I just hadn't known how to gently suggest to her that people might still be able to clock her. She had been *so* excited about feeling that there was significant alignment between her internal and external self that I just hadn't been able to pierce her bubble.

She also told me that her trans friend at school, Mia, was getting into serious conflict with another student who had clocked her as trans; how some of the girls in her year would come up close to her in the change room and stare at her body with some inexplicable level of hostility; and how some of the kids were mean to her for no apparent reason, leaving her wondering if it was because she was trans. I found myself wishing that she could pass more easily as a girl so that she didn't draw the attention of strangers, that her transness was invisible, as Lee at the Gender Centre always says.

Despite my fears and anxieties, and while I was primarily empathic, I was taking the advice of some of my friends and trying to help her toughen up so she could become more resilient because I knew that as a trans teen she was going to have to deal with these kinds of transphobic incidents again. It was hard for me not to just empathise with Liv and seek ways to have these boys punished for their cruelty but instead I said to her, 'Liv, you behaved with great dignity in the face of such narrow-mindedness, showing that you are the bigger person. You showed them that you're bravely committed to being your authentic self, something that they probably know nothing about. I am so proud of you. You are incredibly brave.'

She heard me out and then told me, 'I'm not brave, Mum. I just have to choose between a rock and a hard place when I choose to be in or out of the trans closet and the choice to be out is working better for me.'

After some hours of our chatting like this about what had been happening at school, Liv was calmer and able to move onto some positive stories about school. She told me about the rainbow garden that the LGBTI teacher was building with the LGBTI students, and about the lovely librarian and dance teacher who created a fun and safe space for kids like her to code and game and chat at recess and lunch every day.

She was, however, constantly being challenged to be brave. For example, one evening when she and Stirling were walking the dogs in Mort Bay Park, Liv was horrendously harassed by a group of teens and adults living in the dilapidated apartment block near the park, one of whom was the Year 9 boy who was giving her trouble at school. As she and Stirling walked, they shouted out at her, 'Have you got a dick?' 'You're a disgrace.' 'What's wrong with you?'

Stirling reported to me that Liv had ignored them, while he had shouted rude comments back at them. On the way home, Olivia had reportedly told him not to tell me about the incident because I would make a fuss and worry too much. Stirling did tell me – I guess partly because it had upset him so much – but it was interesting that Liv didn't want me to know about it. I wondered if perhaps she was tougher and more resilient than I was about her being trans.

Liv's bravery was also stretched when two of her primary school friends, probably the two boys she had been closest too since Year 3, texted her and asked if they could come and visit her. I had told their mother that Olivia had transitioned and so these boys knew about it and were texting 'Olivia'. It was a strange experience to see them trying so hard to relate to her as her new, girl self. Ultimately, the experience of their visit was too hard for Liv to replicate and she has not seen them again. Perhaps one day she will be able to manage this.

As part of the process for being able to have hormone therapy one day, Liv had to see a child psychiatrist who works with teens with gender dysphoria. Actually, Angus and I had to be there too and we had a very long session – two and a half hours in all – first, all three of us chatting with her, then Liv chatting with the woman on her own, and then Angus and me answering questions. The psychiatrist's conclusion, after all of this discussion, was that Liv was undoubtedly gender dysphoric but that she felt that she needed to get to know her better before she could make any recommendations about cross-sex hormone therapy. At one point, I told her that I thought it was cruel and controlling that the medics wouldn't give my teen oestrogen when everyone was in complete agreement that Liv was clearly gender-dysphoric and it was evident that she was bravely living as a girl in a transphobic world.

Unsurprisingly, this didn't go down well with the psychiatrist, who was quite hostile with me after that, but I just didn't care. I felt that if I wasn't speaking up for my child and her right to choose to have oestrogen now, then nobody else would. Australian musician and journalist Eddie Ayres, who transitioned in the second half of his life, writes in his book

Danger Music about taking testosterone for the first time at the age of fifty, 'Finally I had in my body what most people would never have to think about – a chemical expression of their true selves.' I knew that this is really what Liv wanted: a chemical expression of her true self.

Of course, part of me did wonder if, once she had oestrogen, Liv would then become unhappy because she wanted gender confirmation surgery as soon as possible, and then perhaps, in her desire to remove all traces of her male self, she might urgently want feminising facial surgery (which includes breast enlargements, nasal reshaping, voice box shaving and so on). That is the nature of gender dysphoria, though. The experience that Liv has with herself and with others because of the dissonance between her physical/assigned gender and the gender with which she identifies is so debilitating for her that we have to help her to align the inside and outside of her as soon as we can, and as best as we can.

Soon after seeing the psychiatrist, Liv was due for the next dose of Zoladex. Before it could be administered, she had to have a blood test to assess the levels of testosterone in her system after ten weeks on the puberty blocker. In January, before she had the first injection, her testosterone level was 6.6 and ten weeks later, a blood test showed that the level was 0.3. We were so relieved that the blocker was clearly working to inhibit her testosterone.

When I went to a local Balmain pharmacy to buy the Zoladex, I had to explain to the pharmacist what I needed it for, and she had that by then quite familiar response to learning that my child was transgender. 'Oh, wow, that's so hard for all of you. How are you doing? How is her twin?'

This kind of response is an ambivalent experience for me. I know this pharmacist as a generous and considerate person and I realise that her intention was to be caring and supportive, and indeed it *is* hard for all of us that Liv is gender-dysphoric. However, I look forward to the day when someone says to us, 'Wow, isn't it exciting that your child is able to live her authentic self. That must be fantastic for all of you.' There are some people who respond positively in this way, but not very many.

I paid the pharmacist the $1,100 for the precious Zoladex and Liv and I went off to our wonderful GP, Simone. One of the aspects of Simone that I really appreciate is that, when she relates to Liv, she takes it for granted that being transgender is normal, and that any gender dysphoria that Liv is experiencing is a fault of the transphobic world in which she lives and not a flaw within her.

The Zoladex injection hurt like crazy again. Once more, I had to experience the referred pain as Liv flinched and gripped my hand when Simone used the syringe to insert the giant Zoladex capsule under the skin of the upper outer quartile of her butt cheek. Liv bowed her head as we walked out, her hair extensions covering the tears on her cheeks, but she didn't complain much, even when the giant purplish-blue bruise appeared in the next few days.

What was really scary for me was that the transphobic bullying at school was becoming much worse: systematic, repeated, group-based and physically threatening. I sent off an email to the well-being coordinator, trying both to be a strong advocate for my child and to keep the school staff on our side.

Things have not been going well for Liv at school. She is having quite a number of experiences of being bullied. For example, yesterday at recess she was sitting eating on her own while she waited to go into the library (an important safe space for her) and a boy (maybe in Year 7) came up to her and said, 'My friends dared me to come and ask you if you are a boy or a girl,' and when Liv swore at him and told him to go away, he ran back to his group and they all had a good laugh while looking at her. Then at sport in the afternoon, a boy who has bullied her before (she thinks he is in Year 9) shouted across the field to her, 'You've got a penis,' and all the kids around them looked at her and laughed. Then the boy, also in Year 9, who lives near us and who has also bullied her before, was making threatening faces at her at sport and getting up close to her and saying, 'You're a boy,' a few times over, while his friends watched on.

Liv was in a state by the time she got home. She told me that she spends a lot of time hypervigilantly looking out for this Year 9 boy in particular, and that she goes far out of her way to avoid him if she sees him anywhere in the school. She's feeling quite scared at school now. I should add that she has never spoken to any of these kids, she doesn't know them at all, and that she's not the type of kid who is nasty to anyone and who might have provoked this kind of bullying.

When I spoke to the senior staff at the school, they told me that they could only deal with these problems if Liv identified the perpetrators. I talked to Liv about the importance of her identifying the bullies because then they might not bully her further, and also they might not bully other kids. For a range of reasons, however, she was not prepared to do it.

'Mom, you know I'm not good at recognising people's faces. Also, I told you how Mia has been bullied worse since she dobbed on the kids in Year 7 who have been bullying her for being trans. That boy who bullies me – the worst one – lives really close to us and he walks past our house to get to and from school every day and, if he knows that it's me that has dobbed on him, then none of us will be safe here at home. I work really hard to avoid him all the time and I make sure he doesn't know where I live. I can't risk him finding out and targeting me even more than he already does. I can't do it.'

With all of this going on, I was becoming increasingly worried about Liv's psychological and physical safety. I would not let her walk or get the bus to or from school, so my life was organised around dropping her and fetching her at the exact times that school started and finished so that she didn't have to hang around at school. I also spent many hours in the afternoons and evenings chatting with her and trying to help her to process her fears and sadness.

If I was working and could not fetch her from school, I asked her to walk home on the main roads rather than through the quiet neighbourhood streets where she was more vulnerable to the bully boys. I knew, as I asked this of her, that I was contributing further to her feeling of being unsafe in the world, because I was drawing attention to the potential that she could be targeted by the bullies. She started saying she didn't want to go outside at all. It was an untenable situation all round. Often, she would send me a litany of texts from school. For example, one morning I received these:

'I am unhappy'

'I feel hopeless, lonely and sad'

'I hate everything'

'Sad'

She had so much trauma to deal with every single day. And even talking about it, allowing it all to surface and be raked over in therapy or in conversation with me, was clearly sometimes re-traumatising for her. It was totally destabilising for me too and would leave me feeling extremely tightly wound up, desperately worried about her and what was happening to her mental (and possibly physical) health at school.

Stirling worried extensively about Liv too. He said to me one evening when he and I were walking the dogs, 'Something bad is going to happen to Liv sometime, Mum. We have to take her out of that school.'

When I talked with my therapist at that time about how tormented I was by the prospect of what might happen to Liv, explaining that I had begun to have daytime flashbacks to the image of the bully whom I had seen walking past our house, she told me that I shouldn't be overly protective towards Liv. It was a very low time for me and, as I sat there in my therapy chair, I felt silenced by her and silently dialogued with her. 'If you don't have a trans kid, you cannot possibly ever understand the always, ever-present, impending fear of violence towards your child just for being who they are. *So* many people, you included, like to tell me that the world has really changed for trans people, that society is so much more accepting now than it was, but Liv's experiences, the experiences of the parents of other trans kids, the hostile glances from people in the street clocking Liv, tells me that she is *not safe*. Do you, and the other people who have told me not to worry so much, know how many trans kids are attacked physically on a regular basis? Do you know how extraordinarily high the suicide rates amongst bullied trans kids is? No. So this is *my* fear and it is based on the hard realities of life in a transphobic world and I will do everything that I can to protect Liv. I *will* try and shield her from potentially harmful interactions in the world as much as I possibly can. I *will* drop her and fetch her from school every single day even if that compromises my own working life. I have *no choice*. Yes, I am totally exhausted and I don't sleep well because I am always worrying about Liv's safety but that is just "my lot". It's much, much worse for Liv.'

I never said this aloud to my therapist because I knew she would say that I was overreacting, but I felt this fear very deeply. Indeed, at that time fear was the dominant experience for me of having a transgender child. For example, I didn't let Liv walk on her own any more, or even with only Stirling for company. One night after dinner, Liv, Stirling and I set off to walk the dogs and we got to a spot where a pack of boys was sitting smoking at the bus shelter, vaguely hidden in the dim light. All three of us immediately and instinctively turned round, cutting our walk short. I could feel our collective fear of these boys, what they might do and say to Liv. We all knew that, in order to be sure to be safe, we had to avoid them.

We didn't feel safe in our house either because the worst bully lived so close by. Angus and I resumed our search for a house to buy and I discovered that my criteria had changed: what I wanted and needed was a place where Liv could be safe. Previously I had wanted to buy a house in the heart of the 'vibey' Balmain village (near to our rental house) but after the bullying, I was very happy to go with Angus's preference to live in a quieter area of Balmain because I knew it was likely to be safer. We eventually found a beautiful house in a quiet area about a kilometre and a half from the village centre, but we had to stay in the rental house for a few more months while we renovated the house we had bought.

It was one thing to try to control the world outside of school so that it was safe for Liv, but we could not leave Liv feeling unsafe and scared at school. After much discussion with Angus, he and I resolved to investigate other school options. When I mentioned the possibility of moving schools to Liv, she just looked weary, too weary for a fourteen-year-old, and her response to me was devastating. 'What's the point, Mum? I'll be bullied wherever I go to school.'

It was evident to me that she had a form of resignation syndrome, a strong reaction to ongoing trauma, a kind of mental and physical shutdown because she had lost hope. I told Liv that she was not going to a school where, every single day, she felt anxious and hypervigilant during the school day. It was just not conducive to her learning or to her mental health.

When I suggested to friends and acquaintances that we would be moving Liv to a new school again, some people suggested that she should stay at Balmain and develop the necessary skills to cope with trans-bullying. I would not and could not accept that.

One afternoon, when I was driving with Stirling from cricket training, I spoke with him about the possibility of moving Liv to a different school. His views surprised and shocked me,

'For Liv, a private school would probably be better than a public school because in private schools, the mean kids are too scared to bully because you can be expelled, but it's really hard to expel kids from public schools. Also, the parents at private schools are more likely to be university-educated and therefore more likely to be open-minded, so it's less likely that their kids will bully trans kids.'

I felt sad that the usually open-minded and tolerant Stirling should have this view of the world, even though it was probably true.

And then he added, 'If you move Liv to another school, you must move me too so that I can help her make friends and settle in. She should learn to manage the bullies like I have, by challenging or putting them down, or even physically fighting with them, in order to get them to leave her alone and go off to bully other kids, but the problem is that Liv is just not like that: she avoids conflicts and can't put others down.'

Again, it was apparent to me that Stirling so often feels responsible for Liv – probably a good reason to have them at different schools.

I did some networking amongst the trans parent community and discovered that the International Grammar School (IGS) in Ultimo, a private, secular, co-educational school that educated students from pre-kindy to Year 12, was regarded as inclusive and embracing of all kinds of difference. So, I emailed the principal, Shauna Colnan, told her a little about Liv's story, and asked her if Liv and I could meet her that week. It wasn't ideal timing, as Angus was in court all week so he wouldn't be able to come along with us, but we needed to move quickly to find a new school as term 1 was soon coming to an end. Shauna replied immediately and suggested we meet with her two days later.

When we arrived at IGS in Ultimo early on that Thursday morning, Liv was very pleased that the school was over the road from a coding academy that she had often attended for holiday workshops. I was taken with the very urban beauty of the purple/pink school building and the giant mosaic on the outside wall. I also noticed, with much interest, that the students looked rather free and even relatively unique in the eclectic-looking uniform that they were customising to wear to school.

When we met Shauna Colnan, her greeting was warm, genuine and welcoming. We sat down in her office and she chatted about the school and answered Liv's many questions.

'What's the approach to technology use in the school? Do you have streamed classes and, if so, which ones? What subjects do students do in Year 8? Do you offer dance as a school subject? Do you have compulsory Saturday sport? Do Year 8 students write exams at half year and at the end of the year? What extracurricular activities does the school offer? What is the library like?'

On and on she fired questions at Shauna – and Shauna's thoughtful answers suggested that she was engaging, enthusiastic, progressive and smart.

Shauna also had lots of questions of her own for Liv. My heart ached just watching how hard Liv was trying with her questions and answers. Situations of this kind are not easy for her. Most important for me was the way that Shauna addressed Liv: she was leaning towards her and radiating an interest that suggested that she actually wanted Liv to come to the school. I felt hope rise inside of me, hope that perhaps this woman's school could turn things around for Liv.

When she spoke about IGS, Shauna spoke with such passion, foregrounding inclusivity and commitment to diversity and difference in learning and pastoral care. She mentioned many other attractive features of the school, including modern teaching methods, great academic results, a tutor group system across the high school to encourage cross-year engagement and support, the integration of students from kindergarten to Year 12, and good public transport options to and from the school.

I was also very interested in the school's uniform policy: they have a non-gendered approach to uniforms – that is, students can wear whatever clothing is listed on the extensive uniform list (skirts, tunics, long shorts, short shorts, tartan pants, grey pants and a range of shirt options). This seemed to me to be a good sign about the school's general attitude of tolerance, acceptance and diversity.

The other question that was very important to me was, 'How do you deal with bullying?'

Shauna's detailed answer about their clear anti-bullying strategies was deeply reassuring for the mother of a bullied child.

Shauna organised for us to be taken on a tour of the school by one of her staff and then we met the head of high school and the head of academic learning to talk about what subjects Liv could do if she came to IGS. Both of them were really engaging and welcoming.

As we left, Liv and I both commented on how much we liked Shauna and the school. I wanted to enrol her immediately but I knew we had to talk with Angus that evening before we could make a decision. Angus is much more cautious and slower in decision making than me. When he and I spoke after dinner, he said that he felt very strongly that we should talk to parents who had children at the school to find out just how positive a place it was so that we were very sure about it as a school for Liv. We knew we couldn't move her to another school which didn't work out well for her.

So I networked with friends, and friends of friends, and managed to talk to the parents of students in Years 3, 5, 6, 8, and 12 at IGS, a teacher who had worked at the school, and a student in Year 12. There were no lukewarm responses: all of them loved the school, albeit for different reasons. I asked all of them whether they were aware of any bullying in the school. One parent had a child who had been mildly bullied the previous year in the primary school, but the staff had dealt with it immediately and thoroughly, and he hadn't been bullied again.

A few day later, Shauna Colnan emailed us and told us that a place had come up in Year 8, and so we signed Liv up to start at IGS in term 2. It was to be her fourth high school in eighteen months, a pretty tough gig for an Aspie kid who loves school and hates change. She was sad about leaving her previous school because she was really starting to feel at home in the extension class, making friends and enjoying her classes. I felt such wretchedness that this school had not been a safe place for her.

On the last day of term, her last day at the school, Liv didn't want to go to school. She was still facing pressure from the school authorities to identify the bully boys and she still didn't want to do so because she was afraid of being targeted by them in our home area. Also, she didn't want to say goodbye because, she said, 'Saying goodbye feels awkward and hard.' I thought she should go to school because then she could say goodbye to the students and staff that she liked, establish some kind of closure and not feel that she was left with unfinished business. Eventually, she and I agreed that she would go and I would cancel my work meetings for the day so that I could be at home – five minutes' drive away – and she could text me to fetch her within minutes if she needed to.

At eleven a.m. she texted me to ask if I could please fetch her at eleven-thirty, as she would have said goodbye to everybody and given her favourite teacher (the librarian and dance teacher) a card and a chocolate, and she would be ready to leave. I went off to fetch her, completely at her beck and call, which is not something I had ever imagined for myself.

In a different world where I didn't have a marginalised child, I would have thought it entirely inappropriate that I was so available to my teen in this way. So many of the parenting rules and parenting values that Angus and I have agreed on over the years are challenged and changed by us having a transgender child. Before this experience, I would have insisted that she go to school all day on her last day at a particular school – even if she didn't want to – because in the process of doing so, she would be building resilience and forbearance, the ability to sustain herself through hard times, and the ability to delay gratification. In facilitating her learning those lessons, I would have seen myself as a responsible parent doing my job to prepare her for tough times as an adult.

However, for a trans kid who is being badly bullied, it is not so simple. Just being trans in this context meant that she was learning resilience and forbearance every single day. Many of the usual rules of parenting just do not apply for the parenting of trans kids. It was cruel and wrong to send her into a situation where she felt fundamentally unsafe and to tell her that she had to stay there until the end of the day.

Thankfully, Angus and I could afford to move her back to a private school and we could afford too to move to a home relatively far away from the bully. I would have been desperate if we couldn't make these protective choices. I am very often aware of how much harder the trans journey must be for families without access to resources, to enough money to buy good medical care and psychological support. And I am also incredibly grateful to Angus that he has worked so hard as a barrister, taking on extra cases here and elsewhere in the world, so that he can earn the money that has allowed us to afford all the health care and resources that we have needed for Liv's transitioning. I know that the financial demands of the transitioning process have been sub-stantial, and that the burden has been heavy on Angus.

And so ended Liv's one term at this school. Despite the good teaching and learning, the very inclusive extension class and a few real trans allies, it had been a very painful experience for Liv.

When I fetched her from school that very last day, I took Liv to my favourite Darling Street café for lunch, hoping perhaps that I could pretend for a while that we were normal, not outsiders to the mainstream, not a mother who had just had to fetch her daughter early from school because the daughter is trans and afraid of trans bullies.

As soon as we entered the world of the café, I was immediately aware of how we were different, this trans mother and her trans child because people, frankly, *stare* at Liv, not just once but repeatedly, their eyes moving backwards and forwards, eyes on her, eyes off her, eyes on her, eyes off her. I guess perhaps they are trying to figure out if she is a girl or a boy; I know that people generally do not feel comfortable with ambiguity. Sometimes when people do this, I smile at them to disarm them and hopefully embarrass them into keeping their eyes to themselves. I do it to suggest to them that all is good and normal – we are just a mother and daughter eating smashed avocado and baby tomatoes on charcoal and quinoa bread while drinking pots of English Breakfast tea with cow's milk. In these moments when I adopt (feign?) this kind of deliberate innocence, I am trying to convey to the hardcore onlookers that there is nothing interesting to look at here.

At other times, I convey the attitude that there is nothing to look at by simply ignoring people, switching off (or appearing to switch off) in the hope that my behaviour consciously and unconsciously models to Liv, and those staring idiots, that *we* don't notice that she is any different from them. I also hope it models to others that I am OK with my daughter being trans and that they should work on adopting a trans-friendly attitude too.

Sometimes, however, being the object of the Repetitive Gaze makes me murderously rageful. One afternoon when Liv and I were eating at a sushi train in Balmain, a man, also there with his daughter, was repeatedly glancing over at us. I started glaring at him, holding his gaze with a radiant hostility, hoping that he was getting the message that if he didn't stop staring, if he looked at Liv just one more time, then I was going to walk over to him and shout at him, 'What is it to you, mate? Why the hell are you staring at my child? Why are you othering her in such an invasive way? Am I staring at your child? *No.* What is wrong with *you?*'

I wanted to attack him as a representative of *all* the people who stare at Liv everywhere. Of course, I didn't do this because –

1. Liv would be mortified because she is self-conscious, conflict-avoidant and non-activist.

2. I am afraid of direct conflict myself given all the conflict in my family when I was growing up.

3. This staring man is part of the mainstream and we are the outliers, and I wasn't certain that everyone around us would have our backs in a conflict.

4. I lived in hope that Liv was not noticing the public surveillance and, if I was to make a massive scene, that would undoubtedly change her potentially blissful ignorance.

I know that Liv does notice the eyes on her, though. I know this because she comments on the absence of them. When she and I went to the Mardi Gras festival in Victoria Park near Sydney University, Liv commented, very soon after we had walked through the security checkpoint that it was good to be in a place where she was surrounded by acceptance, where nobody was looking at her because she was different. I know that I too felt relaxed there that morning; despite the oppressive and overwhelming heat. I felt like I could breathe, liberated from my anxious hypervigilance, able to forget that Liv was transgender, able to interact with my daughter as 'just Liv' and not as my trans daughter.

While we were at the festival, surrounded by rainbow couples, individuals and families, I thought for the first time that I could understand the political philosophy of separatism: I could understand entirely why black people and gay people, and other marginalised groups, so often choose to be exclusive socially, maybe even choosing to live and work separately from non-black and non-gay people because it is *so* tiring consciously and unconsciously to be 'other', different, an outlier, the object of the gaze of most/many, the minority to an often-hostile majority. I could see why lesbian mothers wished to have a street in Newtown for lesbian parents so that their children could grow up seeing themselves as 'normal' and not be 'othered' all the time. I understood why, at the trans parents' group, when the parents of young trans adults talk about how their kids are doing, they often report that their young adult offspring choose to hang out primarily with trans friends and to choose trans lovers. More than many people perhaps, transpeople are confronted with internal rejection (gender dysphoria) and external rejection (transphobia) and so the place to get their validation and acceptance most easily is with others who are like them in this fundamental way. It's also safer, I reckon, for people who are different to live in communities like Newtown where they can be effectively 'invisible' because there is so much difference around them.

Months later, when Liv returned from the Gender Centre's trans camp, she told me about how she had felt so relaxed and accepted among the twenty-eight trans kids on the camp that she wished that one day she could live in an area just for trans people. I told her that in Sydney Newtown was probably the closest she would get to that and she agreed that it could be a good place to live. Newtown is and isn't a good place for Liv to consider living one day (assuming it stays as it is now – an open and accepting place for difference). Unfortunately for her, Liv is not naturally drawn to diversity and difference. She would much rather *not* be a trans person. She is not an activist who wants to challenge and change society, she just wants to get on and live her own life, do her own thing. Even though she loved being part of the Mardi Gras parade, ultimately trans activism is too political for her and she would rather not feel the need to go along. I can't actually see her being comfortable living in Newtown.

Liv and I are different in this way. During Mardi Gras, I told Liv that, in some ways, her being trans is a gift to me because, for whatever complex set of psychological reasons, I like to be different, I want to challenge the status quo and to live in the margins. With Liv being transgender, I now have a legitimate place on the edges; I am officially an outsider to the mainstream, challenging the inside. For me, even being married feels like a compromise and a conventional life choice. I inherently choose to champion the causes of the marginalised. My therapist suggested to me some time ago that perhaps I reject the mainstream and identify with the oppressed because I grew up oppressed by being in a dysfunctional family where my needs weren't often considered. I guess there is probably some truth in that.

And I know that there is a serious need to challenge transphobia because it really is a transphobic world that we live in, even in Sydney, even if only benignly in some places. For example, Angus and I often talk with each other about how, when we engage with acquaintances who ask us 'How are your twin boys?' and/or 'Why did you leave Manly for Balmain?' and we tell them about our transgender daughter, then we can judge by their clearly shocked responses just how much the world hasn't changed for trans people.

For example, the other day a really kind, relatively distant, family friend, about forty years old or so, a man who has travelled the world, came to our house to fetch something and asked me why we moved to Balmain. What is there to do but tell the truth – even if one doesn't feel like having that Big Conversation? So I told him, 'Because our child Olivia identified as transgender last year and we needed to be closer to trans services and actively trans-friendly schools.' As I said this, I witnessed him actually physically reeling backwards a little, just a noticeable little bit. And then he had so many questions to ask about this transformation in our lives.

I am now used to this reaction. Most people are shocked when I reveal this information to them. And then they say something like 'Wow, that's big' or 'That's tough.' Or more often they don't even know what to say and they are silent and wordless for a while, their shock writ large on their faces or in their body language. One man, a tough 'rugby guy' in his late fifties, started crying when I told him. Sometimes I get the sense that people are thinking – perhaps unconsciously – 'Thank goodness that isn't me or my child.' They may say, for example, 'Wow, you are amazing,' but sometimes their admiration feels tinged with a deep pity for me and our family, and a relief about their own 'normal' family. Someone we know relatively well, a highly educated professional man-of-the-world, aged about forty-five, said to us, quite frankly, that he unquestionably would not be able to deal with it if one of his children identified as transgender.

When I observe people's shock at finding out for the first time that our child is transgender, then I know that absolutely the world has not really changed significantly for transgender people and my child is not lucky to be transgender at this time in history.

Anyway, back to our smashed avocado on charcoal toast lunch… While we were eating, Liv was telling me that her teacher had returned their Japanese assessment tasks that day and she received 100%, the top mark in her extension class (one other girl also got 100%). She told me how her teacher had said that she was very impressed at how thorough Liv's Anime project had been and how complex her classroom presentation was. And, in that moment, as Liv proudly shared this story, I felt a bittersweet crack in my heart: amidst all that trans bullying she had had to endure at school, after all the name-calling and shaming, Liv had found it within herself to put enough effort into her Japanese project so that it was worth 100%. I was overwhelmed by her ability to have found the psychological space to have been so thoroughly engaged with the assignment.

And then Liv described the project of the other girl in her class who got 100%, telling me how brilliantly this girl had integrated the visuals and text of her project onto a kimono, using kimono material as the pages to cover interesting stories for the reader paging through the project. And again, my heart contracted, this time because I recognised the extraordinary humanity of Liv's generous description of this other girl's creativity. I thought about how, despite her experiences of the darker and uglier sides of humanity in the school bullies, despite everything that had happened to her, she was able to acknowledge and celebrate the talents of another human being.

Angus and I often talk to each about how every single day we are humbled by how brave Liv is, going out into the world as a trans girl. She doesn't yet pass all that well: she is nearly six foot tall, she has a long way to go before she can go unnoticed, and she makes very little effort to conceal her difference – yet she went to school in term 1 wearing a school skirt every single day, despite the reaction of those mean kids.

Her courage really stood out to me one morning when I went to get a coffee at a local café, and I walked past a bloke sitting at one of the tables and noticed that he was barefoot, with his toenails painted bright, shiny red. On the way out, I observed that he had a smart, short, grey haircut and was wearing rather blokey shorts and a rather daggy, boyish, grey T-shirt. I wondered if perhaps he was transgender and whether being outdoors with his shiny red toenails was his daily moment of being out in the world as trans. In the past, I might have judged him for lacking the courage to live fully and authentically as a woman all of the time but, after all the trans bullying and transphobia that Liv had experienced, I completely understood why he might not be out and proud. I also appreciated, though, after seeing him/her, just how brave Liv really is when she goes out every day as a girl into the transphobic world.

So many trans teens are still in the closet, out only to very close family and friends, or perhaps on puberty blockers but continuing to live as the gender that they were assigned at birth, often waiting until they are finished school to come out to the world as trans, and I totally understand why they would do so. Still I am relieved that Liv – tough as it is – is keen to live and present to the world as her authentic girl self. It feels to me like a much healthier choice for her. Also, it is so much less complicated for us not trying to live differently at home from how we live in the world.

Over and over since we have known that Liv is transgender, I have committed myself to not-othering, to not consciously observing the difference in the world around me, no matter how hard and counter-intuitive it feels. For example, when I see, out of the corner of my eye, a man wearing lots of make-up in the Thai café near our home, I strenuously resist every single urge I feel to look twice, thrice and so on. When I see a black woman crossing at the zebra crossing in this rather white part of the world, I do *not* look at her any longer than I might look at someone else. She doesn't know that I am looking in joy, intensely happy to have someone who is black in otherwise rather white Balmain. She may experience my looking at her as an 'othering experience' – which I guess it is, albeit benevolently. When I see a woman in a burqa/hijab collecting her son from Liv's school, I smile warmly at her and look away instantly, willing myself not to be curious and look again. When I see the two women who are clearly in a love relationship walking their collie dog down to our park, I don't make more of an effort to greet them simply because I am so happy to have a gay couple in my street. When I see a much older woman in a love relationship with a much younger man, I steel myself not to look again. If a disabled person is in queue in front of me in the super-market, I am not nicer to them than I am to someone who is ably bodied. If I see a couple in a 'mixed-race' relationship at my coffee shop, I strenuously avoid giving them any attention. When I see a middle-aged woman in the gym who looks trans, I smile at her and studiously avoid any surreptitious glances to clock her.

I do all of this because I recognise that it is not my right to 'other' those who are different, to notice and observe and fixate on their difference. *But* it is their right to be seen as equal, ordinary, normal and commonplace. So, to this end, I am deeply, morally committed to teaching myself to avoid fixating on difference. I do this because I hope that it has a knock-on effect and maybe people will stare less at Liv and notice her difference less. I realise it is likely that, as human beings, we are, in some primitive way, programmed to notice difference because of the potential threat that the difference could pose to our survival centuries ago, and so I choose to engage in a kind of evolutionary reprogramming. I believe that as humans we have evolved so significantly over the centuries that our biology has been eclipsed by our sociology in countless successful ways and that our programming to observe difference needs to change as well. Perhaps it is even the case that survival of the human species, in a very Darwinian way, is now dependent on the observation of commonalities and similarities rather than differences.

I am particularly committed to this reprogramming of myself since I have noticed just how much Liv's bravery has been dented by those bullies who have so closely drawn (negative) attention to her difference. I noticed this dent when she and I went to buy her new school uniform for IGS and Liv asked if we could buy her one skirt and two pairs of the tartan pants, because she was probably mostly going to wear the pants to school. I felt sad as I realised that, in one term, she had lost much of her confidence to wear a skirt to school. Although the entire IGS uniform is officially non-gendered – that is, boys and girls can wear any aspect of the uniform that they like, and the tartan pants are quite feminine and traditionally the pants worn by the girls, which means that Liv is still wearing a girl's uniform when she wears them – still she does not want to wear a skirt to school any more. Maybe she just feels safer in the pants. She did not want to explain to me her preference.

The pants in size 16 (she is seriously tall!) had to be custom-made and were only due to arrive midway through term 2, so Liv had to wear the skirt to school when she started at IGS. She did, in fact, wear it on day one but hasn't worn it since then. From day 2, she wore the PE uniform and when the tartan pants arrived, she alternated between wearing the short shorts and the pants. It will feel like a significant and magnificent day if, and when, she ever feels able to wear a skirt to school again.

6

The storm of gender dysphoria

I dreamt that I was trying to guide Liv along in a synchronised swimming water competition but I kept going underwater because people on the surface of the water would inadvertently push me down with their feet. I was floundering, nearly drowning, struggling to come up for air to breathe, and this meant that I couldn't help Liv with her swimming.

Just because Liv had been impressed by IGS, it didn't mean that she was ready to make the transition to another new school. Indeed, the April holidays were a serious challenge for her and, hence, for me. It didn't help that Angus and Stirling were in India on a cricket tour over the holidays. Liv is very attached to Stirling and finds it very hard when he is not around. For Stirling and Angus, frankly, I think that it was a relief for them to be away from the drama and trauma of our home at that time.

One morning, Liv was so troubled that I was really thankful that she had an appointment with her therapist, Steven, that day – even though she said that she didn't want to go and talk with him. I used the carrot to get her there when I reminded her that her endocrinologist was not going to give her cross-sex hormones (or oestrogen as she preferred to call it) until she had engaged in a lot of therapy. So, very reluctantly, she agreed to go. She walked into his room, her face reminiscent of a very dark thundercloud. I felt sorry for the therapist. After fifty minutes, she came through to me where I was reading at reception and, with some hostility, told me that he wanted to talk to me.

He and I talked about how hard things were for Liv at that time. He said that she had cried with him about feeling afraid at having to move schools again. She had also cried about our impending holiday in South West Rocks the following week with family friends because she didn't feel that she would fit in with any of the teens: not the macho young teenage boy crowd or the girly young teen crowd (because she is not a feminine girl). Then she had cried because she was missing her dad and her brother. She had told Steven that she had never been separated from Stirling for sixteen days like this and that he was so loving and accepting of her and he was the most important person in the world to her.

Steven and I talked about how I could support Liv as she transitioned to IGS. We talked about how I needed to catch the bus to and from school with her for the first two days, trying to help her to recognise familiar faces even by the second day so that she felt safe because she had some kind of community support when she was at the bus stop and on the bus. We talked about how to help her work out where to sit in the bus to feel the safest (near the front, near the driver, not on the top if it was a double-decker bus). What a bizarre conversation it was: talking about how to protect my daughter from people who might be mean to her while she was quietly going about the business of being herself.

One of the things I have had to get used to about having a transgender child is the feeling of my child not being safe in the world, a feeling that had more or less disappeared when my children turned eight or nine years old and became relatively sensible and rational beings no longer needing me to watch for their safety. Trans teens, though – because the world is so often actively intolerant of them – need a parent in that same protective way that they did as toddlers. So the normal developmental trajectory of adolescence is not available to them in the same way as it is to their non-trans peers: Liv can't individuate and separate from me in the way that her twin can because she needs me in a similar way to how she did when she was a toddler.

When I had been talking with Liv about what she would do during the holidays on those days when I was at work and she was at home, she said she would do her own thing and that it was probably good for us to have a break from each other. I was surprised to hear her say this as she seemed to want me around all the time. If felt as though, in wanting her space a little, she was recognising the complexity of the natural developmental individuation process for a trans teen. On the one hand, she needs me to be a part of the logistical processes of her journey, for unconditional love and acceptance and for protection from the transphobic world, but, on the other hand, she needed to establish her independence from me and her Dad, building core alliances with her peer group which should be the dominant part of her social world at this age. No wonder so many of the parents of older trans kids in the trans parents group talk about their kids pushing them away as soon as they can live independently. Sometimes I can actually feel Liv's deep ambivalence about her dependence on me (and her dad) and I wonder how it is going to play out in our future.

Despite Liv's concerns about going on holiday to South West Rocks, we agreed that we would do it. On the way there, we stopped over for the night in the Newcastle Novotel to break up the six-hour drive from Sydney. When I had been looking for a place for us to stay overnight en route, I didn't even consider booking into a small hotel or a bed and breakfast; I knew that we had to stay in a large hotel to guarantee our anonymity, a space where we didn't have to have face-to-face contact with anyone other than the concierge if we didn't want it.

I remembered how, in South Africa, long before my children were born and I was working for a non-profit organisation that required me to travel around the country extensively with a group of young black people, that these young people would refuse to stay in small, personal places like bed and breakfasts, always seeking out the larger hotels for accommodation. Even grotty Holiday Inns were preferable to them over quaint and well-appointed, personal boutique hotels where there was the potential to have a close-up encounter with a racist white owner or manager.

I have come to realise that for our family now it is the same issue: the bigger the place, the more likely we are to feel safe and anonymous and 'protected' from explicit or implicit transphobia. In some ways, sometimes, it's quite a humbling experience for me that I have come to know, just a little, what it feels like to be part of a significantly marginalised social group. I had always thought that being a woman in a dominantly male world had taught me that feeling but I have realised it hadn't really done that; I realise now that, on the discrimination scale, being a woman is generally far away from the experience of being transgender.

When booking our room at the hotel, I had asked the concierge for a recommendation for dinner and, based on his advice, I had booked, in advance, for us to eat at a Mediterranean restaurant called Rustica, which was adjacent to the hotel. We arrived at the hotel at around dinner time, so soon after we had settled into our fourth-floor room, we headed off to Rustica for dinner.

In a very European way, the tables at Rustica are seated quite close to each other in order to maximise space. At the table on the one side of us was a middle-aged blonde woman sitting with her long dress pulled right up her thighs and repeatedly clocking Liv. I pretended not to notice, hard as that was, because I didn't want Liv to notice her and feel self-conscious. I worked hard at keeping my eyes focused on Liv and at pretending that I didn't notice Blondie's not-very-surreptitious spying. Also, Liv was so animated with her techno-monologue, and so beautiful and brave, that I didn't want to interrupt her flow.

At that moment, I thought to myself that the best response to the ever-present eyes on us would be to work hard at just ignoring them, to the point where I really didn't even notice. This is a serious challenge for me, as I am inherently highly extroverted and tuned into the people around me. Asking me not to notice the glances of those around us is like asking me to change a fundamental part of myself and to be someone else. I knew it was worth it, though, because it would likely reduce the pressure that I felt from my hypervigilant approach. Still, it was months before it became even possible for me.

Having a trans child has challenged me on many different levels. One of the many unexpected issues I have dealt with in this journey has been being overly grateful to people who are embracing of Liv's transness. For example, at our dinner at Rustica, our lovely waiter made my night when she came up to our table and said, 'What can I get you ladies to drink?' I don't know if she had been cued by my explicit online booking for my daughter and me or whether she was cued by how Liv looked, but I was so grateful to her for recognising that we were both women that I was absolutely charming to her.

Later on, when she asked, 'What are you ladies ordering to eat?' I talked to her about what my daughter liked to eat and I felt so happy. I gave her a huge tip at the end of the evening and said, 'Thank you' to her in a way that was heavily loaded with meaning. I hoped she would be as welcoming, inclusive and accepting of other trans (or otherwise different) people who come to the restaurant, or into her life.

We had a similar experience in the hotel lift: a middle-aged rather conservative-looking man in a semi-suit got into the lift when Liv and I were returning from the hotel gym in the morning. I tensed up just a little bit, on the defensive before anything transphobic had even been said or done, but anticipating it nonetheless. When he said to us, very cheerfully, 'Morning, ladies,' I felt such overwhelming gratitude to him for not misgendering Liv that I was *really* nice to him, greeting him warmly in return. It is a bit ridiculous that I am sometimes so grateful to strangers in this way. This kind of obsequiousness feels rather out of character for the person that I used to be before I was a trans parent.

A similar situation arose in our home neighbourhood one night when Liv and I were out walking the dogs. It was dark and I tensed as we walked past the Dry Dock pub, anticipating perhaps that some of the men smoking outside might harass Liv – and they did, not for being trans but for being female. One of them grunted and called out lecherously, 'Good evening, ladies.' I was so pleased that he had identified Liv as a girl that I nearly greeted him back. If I had been on my own and he had done that to me, I might well have told him where to get off. Sometimes I am shocked at how being a trans parent has changed me in so many unexpected ways.

More and more, I have come to wish that Liv could easily be 'invisible' in the public sphere so that she doesn't have to deal with so much othering from strangers. The toilet issue would be so much easier and less fraught too if this was the case: since she has been living as a girl she has, obviously, been using the female bathroom in public spaces. This has been quite an adjustment for me as I am not used to her coming to the bathroom with me. Every time we go into a public bathroom together, I tense up just a little, hoping it will go smoothly, and that nobody will clock Liv and be, in any way, transphobic towards her. Liv reports the same feeling: a deep anxiety that someone in the girls' bathrooms might clock her and confront her for being there. She says she feels this every time she goes to the bathroom. She told me that one day at school someone knocked on the door of the toilet stall that she was in, and she immediately froze and feared the worst – and she was enormously relieved when it turned out that the person knocking just wanted to know if the stall she was in was occupied or not.

It's not just strangers who can be transphobic: sometimes close family and friends have been unwittingly and unconsciously transphobic, even those who I know support Liv and her transitioning. If they, people who are kind and close to us and aware of the journey we have been on with Liv, can be so unconsciously transphobic, then that leaves me wondering, what about the rest of society?

My anxiety about us living in a transphobic world impacted on my feelings about our impending beach holiday because I was worried whether Liv might have to deal with any unconscious transphobia from our extended party of about forty kids and adults. The holiday was also fraught – even before we left home – because Liv was *so* anxious about wearing swimmers and about swimming. Clearly right then, the swimmers issue was a part of Liv's identity transformation as she shifted her physical presentation of self from male to female. I had been backwards and forwards to surf shops to get her potential swimmers to try on but very few of them had been acceptable/bearable to her and I didn't know if the few items that she had chosen would even work well for her once we got there. When, months before, she had first raised the issue about not feeling comfortable to go swimming on our beach holiday, I had ordered trans swimmers online from the USA but, unfortunately, they hadn't arrived by the time we left for the holiday.

As we drove to South West Rocks, I noticed that, often, in our many hours in the car, she would be literally staring at herself in the mirror, commenting on her looks to me, making faces, moving her head this way and that as she looked at herself. This was unfamiliar behaviour for her and it seemed to me that she was, literally recognising, identifying and even constructing her femaleness. I know that she feels like a girl inside but this process of constructing a female external identity, shifting from the physicality of male to female, is enormous, mostly uncharted and so damned hard. I am often aware that she has missed the pervasive, usually covert, female socialisation processes that other girls had been subject to in their first thirteen years of life and I am guessing that this means that her version of femininity may be very different as a consequence. This is something I feel very ambivalent about: I am glad she has escaped that kind of controlling femininity socialisation and that she is free to be her own version of a girl, but I also sometimes wish for her that it was easier to adopt the socialised mannerisms and preening that girls learn from very, very young. It would make her presentation of herself so much simpler.

The question of what it means for Liv to be a girl vexed my friends too: during the few days that we were in South West Rocks, my very good friends Jacqui and Karen asked me, on separate occasions, 'What it is that Liv likes about being a girl/woman?' This is an obvious question, given that Liv doesn't adopt the traditional femininity, habits, interests, grooming, clothes and so on of being a woman. All I could say to them was that Liv 'feels herself to be a girl inside herself'. We were staying in a house with Jacqui's daughter Bronte and her friend Millie, both rather classically girly teens, interested in fashion, make-up, preening, wandering around all day in their bikinis, changing their clothes a number of times a day, following the lives of celebrities on Instagram and TV shows, and so on. Liv isn't interested in any of that. She likes gaming, technology, coding, reading, thinking about ideas and not people.

I know many people, me included, would find Liv's transness so much easier to integrate into our mental picture of her if she worked harder at looking like a girl, but that's just not her thing. In one of her sessions with her psychologist, Steven, he suggested that it might be helpful if, at this stage of transitioning, she put out more physical signs of being a woman – wearing make-up and so on – and she told him that she would try. There has been very little evidence of that, however. Bronte and Millie spent ages doing Liv's make-up when all the teens were planning to go out to the movies in South West Rocks and Liv was a very reluctant participant in the process, even though in the end she looked really pretty. She is not naturally inclined to the aesthetic fussing that goes along with traditional girlhood.

She and I talked about this issue at South West Rocks. We were sharing a room in the rather packed holiday home and, one morning, when we were both awake early and reading in bed, I asked her, 'What do you like about being a woman?'

And she turned the question back to me and asked me, 'Well, what do you like about being a woman?'

I couldn't think of anything to say in response.

'Exactly,' she said, 'It's not a question that you can answer. I like being a woman because I like being myself. I may not always act or look like a stereotypical woman or girl, but I feel like a girl inside.'

Indeed.

One night, when everybody in the holiday house was off at the nearby campsite for drinks, Liv and I went into the little town of South West Rocks to find some dinner. The Cantonese restaurant was one of the few places open, so we went there. I knew that, as a small country town, South West Rocks was likely to be a conservative community, so immediately I was hypervigilant about how people would respond to Liv. The tables were placed very close to each other. I made sure I was facing the man in the middle-aged male/female couple next to us because I am aware that men are far more likely to be a threat to Liv than women: men do more staring at her generally and they are more dangerous because they can more easily physically hurt her. It felt as though people in the restaurant did take extra notice of us, but it was one of those rare nights where I didn't care too much. Hypervigilance gets pretty exhausting after a while.

Liv being clocked relatively easily makes her being trans a big part of our lives. One day at home when she and I went off for a dog walk and we were chatting away happily about nothing in particular, I inadvertently made eye contact with a man and woman who were pushing their twin babies around the park. The man held my eye for a few seconds too long and after we passed them, I felt their gaze on us still so I turned back to look in their direction and he was *still* looking at us. I met his gaze with my semi-hostile gaze as if to say, 'Stop staring at us, mate.' But he was undeterred and kept on glancing at us. By then I wanted to approach him and say to him, 'In what way is my child an affront to your masculinity? In what way does my child threaten your world? In what way does she challenge your limited view of humanity? *Stop staring at her.*'

Eventually, we just moved on. I felt sad-cross because I had forgotten about Liv being trans when we set out for our walk: she was just my teen-child with whom I was having a good chat and I felt annoyed and depressed about how, suddenly, I had been made aware of her being trans.

I inherited the anxious gene from both of my parents and my dysfunctional childhood enhanced this anxiety and fostered my sense of the world being unsafe. My historical experiences also created in me a powerful sense that I needed to challenge and confront people wherever necessary (partly inherited from my often-angry mother). I know that this is not useful and productive so I have worked hard all my life to change this about myself, to settle into a calmer, less anxious and less angry way of being in the world. Now with a trans daughter I have often found myself sliding back into being anxious, afraid and angry in the world because my child is so vulnerable and so likely to be bullied and/or attacked for nothing other than who she is.

Some people like to say that our children are sent to teach us particular lessons in life and, while I am generally not someone who espouses that kind of magical/fantastical thinking, it does seem to me sometimes as though I am being presented with endless opportunities with Liv to work on my own developmental journey to be calmer and more at peace with the world.

And, of course, society has changed to some extent. The cover of the April 2018 edition of *Vogue Australia* magazine had four young internationally famous Australian models featured: a black woman, an Asian woman, a rather quirky-looking dark-haired woman and a trans-gender woman, Andreja Palic. Below their group photos is the caption, 'The new Australian supermodels'. There is a long focus on these four women in the pages of the magazine, with more gorgeous photos of them. Then in the September issue of *Vogue*, there was an extended feature on a non-binary teen called Audrey who lives with her parents in Melbourne. So the transgender marginalised are becoming more mainstream, at least in some places. I guess that that is change.

Anyway, back to South West Rocks. When we had been there only a day or two, Liv insisted that she wanted us to make an early return to Sydney. We were staying in a house with lots of people and she doesn't find it easy to spend protracted periods of time with anyone other than her immediate family. After some resistance, I eventually agreed and we told the group that we were leaving, three days earlier than every-one else.

Bronte, Jacqui's daughter, who is as forthright and frank as me, suggested that perhaps I was a pushover for agreeing to leave early because Liv wanted to leave whereas I wanted to stay. I thought about it and figured that, in many ways, Bronte was correct: I had been a pushover. One aspect of being a trans parent for me that goes against my grain is the reality that I am a bit of a pushover with Liv, easily convinced to do what she wants to do – even if it is not what I want. I feel as though Liv's life is *so* hard that I will do whatever I can to make it better and that often means I am overly accommodating of her needs.

I do worry about the negative impact of this parenting limitation on Liv's character development but I don't know how else to parent her, because my primary objective as a trans parent is to find ways to keep her happy and alive. She is so much happier these days but I often remember my first ever trans parents group, where the facilitator told us that the rate of suicide attempts amongst trans teens was 50% and I burst into tears at this shocking statistic, remembering how suicidal Liv had been in the two years leading up to her coming out as trans. I clearly remember thinking during that meeting that I would do anything and everything I could to keep her alive.

The long drives between Sydney and South West Rocks were good for Liv and me, as we had a lot of time to chat. She told me that she was going to get involved in absolutely everything at her new school because, she said, she knows that teachers like students who are 'participants' and, if they like her, then she will be safer. There is so much that is hard about this decision, including the way it reflects how she feels that she has to consciously design strategies to create a safe environment for herself and that she has to be so strategic, so benignly manipulative, in her way of being and living, which is just not in her innate character.

I also used this car journey to finally tell Liv that it was Stirling who had alerted us to the fact that she might be trans. Liv not knowing that he had told us just seemed like too much of a secret to be keeping within our family. She said she was glad that he had told us but that she was also glad that she didn't know at the time, as she would have felt upset that he had broken her trust. I explained that I was very grateful that he had told us because it meant that we could start her on puberty blockers before it was too late, and because it meant that she could be freed from the confines of such a huge secret (and the associated depression and suicidality), and begin to live her authentic self.

When I see how coming out has brought an end to Liv's terrible, dark depression and suicidality and I witness her sense of personal liberation, then I am 100% convinced that she is a girl. When the medical specialists tell me that they don't rush to give teens cross-sex hormones because some teens change their mind and decide, ultimately, that they are not trans, then I think to myself that Liv is absolutely not one of those who will change her mind.

As soon as we arrived home in Sydney, Liv asked me the date and time of her appointment with the psychiatrist that was scheduled to take place during these school holidays. I knew that she had been ruminating about this meeting for weeks, given the power of the psychiatrist over her life: she could decide if and when to recommend to the endocrinologist that he give Liv cross-sex hormones. Liv believes strongly that non-trans people should not have the right to decide whether and when trans people get hormones, because they cannot possibly understand how important these hormones are for trans people. She has often told me that having hormones for a trans person is more important than having gender confirmation surgery. And so, over the next few days, I felt within her a powerful tension building up to the impending appointment.

I was personally struggling to understand why the psychiatrist and endocrinologist wouldn't agree to give Liv oestrogen at this stage of her life, especially as they, and Liv's therapist and gender counsellor, had been very clear that Liv was 100% gender-dysphoric. Indeed, of the many medics we had seen, not one had disputed the diagnosis, and all of them had confirmed it. In my view, it was cruel not to give her oestrogen, but we knew that this psychiatrist wouldn't recommend to the endocrinologist (yet) that he should give her oestrogen. This was partly because Liv is not yet sixteen, the unofficial minimum age that many doctors seem to fix on in order to prescribe oestrogen to trans girls, but also because Liv only came out as transgender a few months before and hence hasn't been living as a girl for very long, and because she hadn't been in therapy or with a psychiatrist talking about her gender identity for long.

The strain was also evident in our house because Liv was feeling so anxious about starting another new high school in term 2. It's awful for a kid on the Asperger's spectrum to have to deal with so much change, given how seriously averse Aspies are to change. But the transphobia of our world necessitated all this change as we sought to find her a happy and safe place where she could learn without being bullied and where, hopefully, she could perhaps forget about being trans much of the time, and just be herself.

While the April school holiday period was tough because of Liv's tearful anticipation of a new school, there were, however, some highlights for her, most especially the discovery of Vanessa, a ballet teacher who had agreed to do one-on-one ballet classes with her. When I had had an initial chat on the phone to Vanessa, I told her upfront that Liv was transgender, which is my usual way of smoothing the path ahead of Liv and preparing people so that they could avoid being inadvertently transphobic when they met her. When I outed Liv, Vanessa immediately told me that she is gay. I guess she was giving me this particular personal information because she knew that it would likely reassure me that Liv wouldn't have to worry about her being in any way transphobic – and she is right, I did feel reassured. That Vanessa is gay is significant to Liv too – I am guessing it allows her to feel more accepted.

Quite apart from gender and sexual identity issues, the ballet lessons seem to take Liv's mind off her troubles: when she gets into the car after the lessons, she is covered in sweat and looks so different: elated, relaxed, at peace with herself, not anxious or fraught in any way. She tells me that it is only during the ballet classes that she is able to forget entirely about her troubles because she is totally immersed in the moment, working as hard as possible to do the exercises perfectly.

Vanessa has been so supportive of Liv: later on, when there were days that we had to cancel ballet classes with her at the last minute because Liv was feeling too sick, Vanessa would text supportive and compassionate messages, telling us that she was looking forward to seeing Liv the following week. She became an unexpected and significant trans ally for Liv in her journey.

As it was the holidays, Liv went off for the time-sapping process of having her hair extensions neatened up by the bloke who had put them in a few months before. I tried to convince my own hairdresser to take on the task but she couldn't because she didn't use the same process and chemicals as he did. So I took Liv off to see him and all the time she was there I worried about possible transphobic behaviour, given that he was an evangelical Christian who had told me previously that his church could heal Olivia and make her non-trans. I texted her often during the seven-hour stint she had with him and she didn't reply – she told me later that she had forgotten to switch her phone ringer on – and I felt incredibly anxious about her. I went to the salon about half-way through the appointment – ostensibly to bring her lunch, but really I was checking that there hadn't been any trouble with him offering to pray for her not to be trans, or anything similar. When he finally finished, Liv came out looking gorgeous, flicking her long, straight, shiny golden locks in the girliest way.

When we were walking the dogs later that day, she was processing the day's experience with me. 'Do you know, Mum, the pain of sitting there in chair doing nothing for all that time today while the guy reattached my extensions was worth it for the end result. It's like taking the puberty blockers – they make me feel nauseous and they give me a headache but even if the symptoms were ten times worse, I would still have the injections to avoid developing an Adam's apple or a male facial shape or male facial hair. My biggest terror, even though I know it's not rational, is that the puberty blocker isn't working.'

While Liv was processing her transitioning relatively well, the impact on Stirling was raw at this stage. One evening, while he and

Angus were still in India, Angus texted me to tell me that Stirling had been in tears and had been really down. When he started to talk with Angus about his sadness, he said that one of the things that was upsetting him was that there was trouble at home with Liv being so unhappy.

We hadn't factored in just how difficult the transition would be for Stirling. He had been hostile towards Liv transitioning at first, irrationally telling me that it wasn't possible that she was a girl. The impetus for his shift towards a more empathic connection with Liv came after he had seen *Just Charlie* at the Mardi Gras film festival, a film about a teen called Charlie who comes out to her family as trans. Charlie's father is harsh to her as he can't accept that his 'son' is actually his daughter, while Charlie's mother and sister are caring, accepting and supportive of her. A few days after we had watched the movie, Stirling came to me and said that he had changed his mind about therapy and he would now like to see a therapist to talk about Liv because he wanted to be more like Charlie's mum and sister in accepting the transness of his sister and less like Charlie's mean father.

My friend Jacqui recommended that we take Stirling to see Andrew, a therapist she knew who practises in Balmain. Andrew is the most gentle and beautiful human being, and after a few sessions with Andrew, so much seemed to change for Stirling. Slowly he came to accept Liv as his sister, even being protective over her and telling her occasionally that he loved her. Over time, he has become her greatest ally, loving and supporting her, and insisting that others do the same.

While I am really moved by how close Stirling and Liv have become, I do really worry about the impact of this monumental change on him. Every part of his identity until now has been about being a boy twin with a twin brother. One evening, a Facebook memory came up on my computer screen of a photograph of the two of them, at age three or four, sitting close together and laughing, right at the apex of Van Heyningen's Pass in Injisuthi in the Drakensberg mountains in South Africa. It has always been one of my favourite photos, reminding me of the way that Angus and I had cajoled our precious twins up this monumental mountain, hour after hour, distracting them with dung beetle activity, feeding them treats and inducing them to climb further and higher. It was a momentous moment when they finally got to the top and could see out over the beautiful valleys. It was a walk we did many times as they were growing older.

Stirling was sad when he saw the photo, asking, 'Mum, is that Orlando or Olivia in that photo?' I didn't know what to say because that is a struggle that I have too. Of course, it is the same person in some core ways, but it is also not. I know that, for Olivia, photo memories of the past are a painful reminder of her living in secret, living the wrong gender. So, for Stirling, especially as a twin with shared memories, it must seem sometimes as though, with Liv's transitioning, many of his memories are erased, and hence parts of his sense of self are eradicated.

The photo issue comes up relatively often. One morning, Liv and I were in my study looking at something on my computer and my Facebook memories came up with pictures of our family on a cycling trip in Victoria two years ago. we had a glorious time during a week of cycling from village to village and staying overnight and eating at gourmet restaurants. Liv and I looked at the photos, many of them of her as a boy with shaved short hair, and I saw and felt a dark cloud pass over her as she became utterly silent. So I just scrolled down the Facebook page and away from those memories.

When we moved from Manly to Balmain and we packed up the more than twenty-five photo albums that I had made of the children from the time that they were in utero, to their birth and their growing years, I realised, with some yearning and sadness, that they were not memories that we could really enjoy unfettered any more. The photos are now tainted for me because I wonder if he was conscious of being she when each photo was taken, and how terrible it might have been to be forcing down that massive secret, afraid to tell us in case we rejected him/her. I hope that, at some point in the future, we are able to find a way to merge our past and present so that we can have a more continuous sense of our individual selves and our collective family identity.

When we moved into our new home, we decided to create a photo wall of framed and old black and white family photos that we had hung in a group on a wall in our house in Durban. Included in this collection is a photo of me with Orlando at about age two, him sitting on my shoulders and smiling happily. I asked Olivia what she thought about putting the picture up and she said she feels fine about baby pictures being up, as babies don't look like girls or boys at all. So, the picture is up and she is OK about it.

Lee, who has worked at the Gender Centre in Annandale for more than twelve years, says that usually it takes at least five years of a trans kid living authentically before she/he can feel safe and settled enough in the new identity to be able to tolerate seeing photos of her/his old self. This is definitely something to work towards but, in the meantime, I do totally understand why Olivia doesn't want to be confronted with the photos of her old, inauthentic self. This journey of transformation is so hard for her that it is just as well to find ways to make it easier for her. She tells me often how she hates to look in the mirror because the person she sees there is not how she feels herself to be, that the image doesn't feel like it is her at all. At times like that, I think about what Lee says to us at the parent support group meetings about how our gender identity is located in our brain and not in the body.

Lee also talks about how facial feminisation surgery for trans girls is often not so much about making the girls look more feminine or pretty but is mostly about eradicating the traces of the male self that has looked back at the trans woman from the mirror over so many years; that it's impossible for the transitioning woman not to see herself as the man she once was when she looks in the mirror. That makes a lot of sense to me.

And actually, maybe it is helpful for us too not to have the old photos around while we all work at internalising and integrating the new Olivia into our heart and soul and brain. I worry a lot about how deeply Olivia is embedded into my unconscious. Sometimes I still dream about her as a young boy. In the first few months of her transitioning journey, I had to expend quite a bit of energy being very careful not to misgender her or call her by her old name. A few times, in the early months, I said to Stirling and Olivia, 'Right, boys, please would you…' and, as the word boys left my mouth, I would see Liv looking downcast and crestfallen, her very being fundamentally denied by me in that moment. I always apologised profusely and she was loving and forgiving but I saw in her body language that I added to her substantial trans wounds and scars. This is getting easier as I internalise Liv as my daughter but misgendering her is still a significant fear for me.

And I have to confess that, even nearly a year after Liv's transitioning, the photo memories that pop up on Facebook that are of Liv before she transitioned still occasionally and unexpectedly reduce me to tears of sadness and loss. I have been shocked and surprised when, at some of those moments, I found myself missing that boy.

One day when Liv and I were driving and chatting, she spoke about how she couldn't understand why trans parents so often yearned for the child that was. I told her that, happy as I was to have her now as my daughter, sometimes I missed the boy I had thought she was, the boy I had been so happy to have when he was born and who was part of my life for thirteen years or so. I was aware of the heaviness of this conversation, so I repeated again how much I loved having a daughter and how much I loved her and also that I knew that she was still the same person that she had always been. But it was too late: she had begun to cry, telling me through her tears, 'I'm so sorry, Mum. I wish that I could be normal.' Then I started to cry and I wondered if, perhaps, I should not have told her about my occasional tears for the boy that was – and wasn't.

According to Lee's research and experience at the Gender Centre and beyond, there is a 'rough formula' for working out how long it will take for parents to truly internalise their child's new gender: for every two years the parent has known the child as the wrong/old gender, it takes six months for in-depth processing of the new gender into the parent's being so that it is instinctive/natural and internalised. So, given that we had learnt that Olivia was transgender when she was thirteen, it will be three to four years from that time before we don't have to remind ourselves all the time that we now have a daughter. That means at age sixteen or seventeen we will instinctively see her and know her as a girl.

Lee also spoke at the parent support group about the term that trans teens use for misgendering: deadnaming – that is, when someone uses the trans person's old name, then they are deadnaming the trans person because they are using the name of a person that is dead to the teen who is now living their real/authentic self. The new parents in the group are shocked by the term, finding it very painful because their old child is not dead to them. Once I got over the shock of it, though, I totally understood, because I realised that the word/concept dead-naming does illustrate, albeit in a rather extreme way, just how much the trans child resents and resists the old identity which is so closely tied up with their name. Parenting is so much about self-sacrifice generally and it seems to me that trans parents have to dig even deeper than non trans parents in order to sublimate their needs and emotions so that they can let their child flourish as their true, authentic selves.

Despite my willingness to embrace Liv's transitioning, our visit to the psychiatrist made it clear that we were really going to have to struggle to get the medics on our side. Our visit did not go well. That morning Liv had woken up in a total state and come straight to me needing me to hug her because, she said, she had had a terrifying dream where she was being forced to be a boy again. Poor kid. When we got to the psychiatrist's rooms, Liv was silent and withdrawn. She went in first, and then it was my turn. The psychiatrist asked me how Liv was doing, and, during our conversation, she was misgendering Liv, referring to her as he. The first time, I gave her the benefit of the doubt and ignored it; the second time I corrected her. WTF? She was supposed to be a specialist in gender-dysphoric teens. Of course, we went home without any recommendation from her for the endocrinologist to prescribe her oestrogen, and both Liv and I felt that she had not heard or understood us.

Later in the day, Liv and I were out walking the dogs along the harbour and she told me that the psychiatrist had asked her if Stirling was gay. Liv said to me, in a very humorous way, 'Does she think we're a family of LQBTIQA+ wannabes: you with your short dyke haircut must be interested in woman and my brother's gay and I'm trans!'

She and I laughed and laughed, exhilarated that we could laugh together about these matters. Suddenly, in that moment of lightness, I became deeply conscious of the beauty in the world around us: the perfect angles of the harbour bridge, the iridescent light in the sky, the silky dark depths of the water, the joy in the curve of our dogs' tails. I felt such an intense and heightened happiness to be laughing with my precious child amidst all the sombre, harshness of so much of our life at that time.

As we walked, Liv's tone continued to be light and she talked about how she wanted to take hormones so that she could grow breast buds in the first few months, and then breasts in the years after that. She joked about how she wished we could all be starfish, creatures that have all genders contained within one body. Having so much lightness and laughter about such previously heavy matters was truly liberating. And it felt like a kind of progress. I laughed so much, at least in part, because I was so happy to be joking and laughing, and not crying and worrying, about trans matters.

Liv also talked about how, just like her therapist, the psychiatrist had talked with her about her perhaps wearing false breasts and more make-up, and she said to me that she could not understand why people are so fixated on her *looking* female and presenting as female, when really that isn't the issue for her, because what she wants is to really *feel* physically female and *be* physically female (with breasts, and so on). I guess what she means is that she wants the outer physical form of her body to be genuinely congruent with her gender identity in her head – without her having to use the trappings of femininity like make-up and false breasts in order to artificially achieve that. Such a complex issue.

These light moments were few and far between, however. Liv was so anxious about starting at a new school that she was in tears a lot, often moody, difficult and unhappy. I found myself losing patience with her, which I knew wasn't kind or fair but sometimes it was hard to know what more I could say to do or help other than telling her, 'I know it's hard, babe. I acknowledge that to have to start a fourth high school in less than a year and a half is challenging.' She told me that she could think of little else but the pain of starting a new school *again*. So naturally it was the same for me. With the two of us, it feels sometimes as though we are joined by a rope that doesn't stretch, always attached by a metaphorical and short umbilical cord. Liv hugs me many times a day and tells me often that she loves me and I can feel her connection with me as both tangled and tangible.

One day during this time, I went off to have a coffee and a debrief with Jacqui, and by the time I got back home a few hours later, Liv was anxious, clingy, restless, tearful, lost and irritable. When I asked her what was worrying her, she said, 'Starting at a new school on Monday.' When I asked her what precisely it was about starting a new school that was hard, she told me, 'It's just so hard to start all over again.' I suggested that she find something to distract herself and eventually she went to her room and started to read one of the new books she and I bought her, and slowly I started to feel her sad-nervous energy dissipate, just a bit.

Instead of reading, her choice in that situation would have been be to lose herself in the virtual world but I am wary of that, given that a close family member – a young adult who is also transitioning male to female – has been an internet addict, reluctant to engage with the world as a trans girl, preferring the safety of virtual connections via the net. It seems likely that, even more than for non-trans kids, an addiction to a virtual world is a serious problem with trans kids. So many parents in the parent support group and on the trans parents website talk/post about how reclusive their trans kids are, how their socially anxious kids avoid the (transphobic) real world and just engage online/virtually, which is so much easier for them. I am trying hard to avoid this happening to Liv, a tough gig given that technology is front and centre of her identity (she builds computers for a hobby) and in her potential career plans (she is considering being a software games developer, robotics engineer or the like).

Liv's deep engagement with me during these toughest times deepened the parenting divide between Angus and me. While the four of us have been accustomed to me doing much of the overt emotional parenting work in our family, given my interests, training and personality, Angus had previously always been closely involved with the parenting of both children and deeply bonded with both of them. Since Liv's transitioning, though, at first she only really connected with me and she and I became more deeply enmeshed, creating a kind of dyad divide with Stirling and Angus on one side, and Liv and I on the other. What comes to mind is that sometimes, in the early days, I was inside Liv's story and Angus was on the outside, looking in helplessly, unsure how to engage with her and how to share this parenting load with me.

Liv did try to convey to Angus that she wanted more time with him but it was difficult for the two of them to find something that they could do together and it was difficult for them to connect. One night after a therapy session with her gender counsellor, Anthony, we got an email from Anthony in which he wrote to us about this absence in her life.

> Olivia asked me to communicate to you her desire for a closer relationship and more time with her father. It goes without saying, but just as sons need their fathers, daughters very much do as well. I described to Olivia last night how parenting is a relationship and, like all relationships, they need nurturance and tending to. I use the idea of a garden which needs time and tending as a metaphor

for a relationship. Olivia was really clear that her garden needs more tending to from Dad.

Angus and I talked in circles about this and how to shift the dynamics in our family. It was a few months before we found a child and family psychologist, Belinda, who was able to do parenting therapy with us and help us through this impasse. Our Saturday morning sessions with her became a key time for Angus and me to sit together and reflect on our parenting practices and what we could do differently/better. But that was a way off. First, we had had to endure the intensive storm of gender dysphoria that Liv was to go through, repeatedly and very, very painfully for a few months, testing our parenting skills in ways that we could never have imagined.

7

The tsunami

I dreamt about the dog I had had when I was at university, my adored
Maltese poodle, Lucy. In my dream. Lucy and I were walking on very
dangerous rocks on the beach, walking where the waves could wash us
into the sea at any time. Lucy was struggling and acting dead because
she didn't want to walk in this scary situation. Eventually. I got her around
the rocks and onto the beach sand, even though it was illegal to have
dogs on the beach. She was limp with fear and trauma. I felt the same.

Within a few moments of waking up on the first day of term 2, Liv was
anxious, tearful, silent and grumpy. She put on the lovely navy and bottle
green International Grammar School skirt and polo shirt and roughly
combed her hair. I managed to get her to put on the bare minimum of
make-up, her hand pushing my hand away with great irritation when I tried
to erase the stripes of foundation that she had wiped down her neck. I made
her favourite breakfast: salmon and avocado on toast, and she ate it with great
reluctance, snapping at me and at Stirling for anything and nothing. Finally,
Angus and I got into the car with her and drove slowly over the Anzac bridge,
mired in morning traffic. We had the radio on loudly to drown out the heavy
silence in the car. In the back seat, Liv just scrolled through her phone, no
doubt trying to find a way to screen out the impending reality she so feared:
the first day of another new school, the fourth in eighteen months.

Despite the rush hour traffic, we were ridiculously early, because
driving to IGS from our house is so easy: we were at the school in Kelly

Street in Ultimo at least forty-five minutes before we were due to meet the head of Year 8, Thomas Marchbank. We parked and headed off to a local café where the barista has a smile that makes everything feel good – even if just for one moment. Angus and I sat close together with our piccolos, talking distractedly to each other about the newspaper news of the day, and Liv, reluctantly, had a cappuccino, reading Quora feeds on her phone, still not saying much to us.

I had absorbed a lot of her nervous energy so I was quite strung out by the time Angus and I got Liv to the school reception at the appointed time of eight-twenty. The receptionist phoned Thomas and he was shortly at reception, a youngish man sporting a fuzzy beard and a kind smile, greeting us with a radiant, warm friendliness. This kindness was verified when he handed Liv a small foil packet of Greek biscuits, telling her that his wife had baked them over the weekend, and that they were delicious, so he had decided to bring Liv a few of them to welcome her to IGS.

Within a few minutes, our small talk was over, and Angus and I left Liv with Thomas. I commented to Angus that she had given Thomas a flicker of a smile but that he had his work cut out for him if he was going to win her over. Angus was silent and looked troubled as he headed off to get the bus to work. I wasn't working that day, so I drove back home over the Anzac bridge and spent the whole day wondering and worrying about how Liv was doing in her new school environment.

When the school bell rang to denote the end of the school day, I was waiting outside the school entrance. Suddenly Liv walked past me, presumably having been in a different building and now returning to her home base. She was chatting animatedly to another girl, the two of them walking close together and completely absorbed in their conversation. When I called out, 'Hi, Liv,' to let her know that I was there, she did the teen flick of the head to vaguely acknowledge me and then went off to get her school bag. I took her cool distance as a good sign and perhaps the suggestion that she felt, at least a bit, at home already!

In the car on the way home, she regaled me with stories. 'Mr

Marchbank is just great and he gave me a tour of the school and he is my English teacher and everyone says he's the best. When you saw me, I was chatting to one of the girls in my class called Adi and she's really nice. During tutor group, which we have at the start of every day, one of the students in a senior year came up to me and gave me her or his mobile number and said I must call any time I need to. I think that they may be transgender and not actually hitting on me. The school seemed really diverse, and it felt so good to blend in rather than stick out.'

On and on she talked. I was relieved that it had gone so well. It certainly looked as though the school was diverse when I had been standing and waiting for Liv: the approach to the uniform and student presentation appeared to be very casual, with students wearing a wide range of clothing items and customising their uniforms and their appearance. It seemed such a simple and symbolically inclusive approach.

Later that afternoon, Thomas Marchbank called me on my mobile to ask me how the day had been for Liv. I told him about her interaction with the kid in her tutor group and he said that the school had specifically put Liv into that particular group because the older students were so supportive, and also because the group of older teens included a transgender kid, out and proud and very together and generous-spirited. I was so pleased that they had thought to do this because positive trans role modelling is essential for Liv.

So, day 1 at IGS went well. Liv woke up on day 2 much more cheerful than she had been at the start of day 1. She didn't put on the skirt, though, choosing instead to wear the girly and rather brief PE shorts with the polo shirt. She and I had agreed that I was going to catch the bus to IGS with her that day as it was her first time travelling to the school on the bus. As we walked up our street onto Darling Street, I could see the bus stop diagonally across the road. Immediately I noticed, in the bright early morning sunshine, that there were two students in IGS uniform standing there: one a girl with a definite greenish tinge to her wild and uncombed hair, and the other a boy, looking altogether male, except for the fact that he seemed to be wearing lipstick and mascara. We got our coffees at the bus stop coffee shop and waited for the bus.

While we waited, I wanted to chat to the other IGS students hanging around waiting for the bus, but Liv warned me not to embarrass her by doing so. When the bus arrived, there were a number of IGS kids on the bus already, and at the many bus stops where we stopped on the thirty-five-minute trip between Balmain and Broadway, an IGS student or two got on.

The younger students looked neat and conventional but many of the older students looked different; for example, many of them had unusual streaks of colour in their hair and/ or customised uniforms. Some of the senior girls had very short, even shaved, hair, which is generally quite unusual among schoolgirls in Sydney. Liv was surreptitiously glancing at each one of the IGS students who got onto the bus, while pretending she was only interested on the Quora news feeds on her phone.

Along the way, a boy called Tom got onto the bus and shouted out, 'Hello, Olivia.' Tom is one the students at the dance classes that Liv had attended on Saturday mornings in Rozelle. By the time we got to the bus stop at Broadway shopping centre, Tom had come up close to us on the bus and was chatting away to Liv. When we got off the bus, the two of them went off in the direction of school, Liv calling out goodbye to me, and so I walked around the corner to Glebe Point Road and got the bus home.

We repeated the exercise in the afternoon: I caught the bus to Broadway and met Liv outside her school and the two of us caught the bus from Glebe Point Road back to Balmain. Being a self-conscious teen, she wouldn't chat with me on the bus, preferring to catch up on her newsfeed, but when we got home, she was spilling over with great stories about her teachers and classmates. That night when she went to shower, I heard her singing, which was the first time in what seemed like years. When she was eating dinner, she told us that she was quite looking forward to school the next day.

I felt such a weight off my shoulders when I recognised that she had had two happy days at school. It seemed to me that, to some extent, she was liberated from being 'all about trans' at IGS, that there could be other identities for her in her new school, that perhaps she would be able to study undistracted to a large extent and live the life of a teen and not live her live only/mostly/largely as a trans teen.

Of course, life at IGS wasn't perfect for her. A few days into the first week, a girl in her class accidentally misgendered her and Liv said that she wanted to cry right there in class. Then her French teacher, whom she really likes, misgendered her a few weeks into the term – twice in one week.

'What does it take? What does it take?' she asked me over and over, tears running down her face. Being misgendered is so painful for her. 'I wish,' she said, 'that I was normal and all I had to worry about was my next assessment.'

It is difficult to separate out Liv's Aspie struggles with her trans struggles given the overlap between them. For example, as an Aspie, Liv struggles with connecting and making friends and she is increasingly aware of how people take a while to warm to her. Also, she has had to move schools so many times to find a trans-friendly environment yet for an Aspie this extensive, constant, repeated change is difficult. She liked IGS a lot yet she often had a meltdown about going to school. One morning, she stormed out of the house to get the bus to school, shouting at me that she was broken. My heart cracked at the idea of my fourteen-year-old feeling broken.

So, despite enjoying her new school most of the time, Liv was still having extensive gender-dysphoric moments and meltdowns, sometimes for days on end. Her emotional outbursts were exhausting, involving a full-body experience: weeping and throwing herself prostrate onto the couch with her head buried in the cushions, crying hysterically in the bathroom while showering, refusing to cooperate, shouting at the rest of us in the house and being very hard to live with. Regularly, she would text me from school, keeping me connected with her and her trauma. One day, just after she got onto the bus to travel to school, she started texting me and this was our exchange over the next few hours.

O: Why, Mum?

L: Because of love, connection, challenge, change, innovation, Stirling, Archimedes, Serena.

O: I just want home.

L: It's not much fun at home as the cleaners are here today and the bloke is here repairing the tiles and I'm working. And you get bored at home.

O: Better than school.

L: (lots of heart emojis)

O: I hate school.

O: And I hate my stupid self.

O: Mom?

L: Liv, please try to focus on class and not on texting me. I love you and I'm here for you. I'll be there at four to fetch you. I'm trying to get an appointment for you for therapy with Anthony.

O: I can't.

O: I can't do it no.

O: I want to die.

L: Olivia, you can do this, my babe. You absolutely can do this. Please cope, babe. Shall I call the school and ask them to take you to the school counsellor? I can call Tom Marchbank and ask him to come and see you. Think about how you feel at dance with Vanessa and use that to distract you. Please, babe, you know how much Stirling, Dad and I need you.

O: Don't talk to the school please.

L: Babe, if you're not safe, then I must.

O: No. Don't talk to the school.

L: OK I won't if you tell me that you're safe.

O: I am safe, I guess.

L: (heart emoji)

O: I can't bear staying.

L: Babe, it's the law that you have to go to school. I go to jail if you don't go to school. Please make an effort to cope. I've ordered you good recess and lunch. Can you focus on that? You can bear it. I know you can.

O: OK. I'll suffer for you.

O: Please cancel all my banana bread orders. The banana bread is disgusting now for some reason.

O: I love you.

L: I love you too, my darling girl.

O: Love you, Mom. I want to hug you so bad.

L: Ah, my precious girl, me too.

During one of these texting sessions, I was with my own therapist and my phone kept vibrating as Liv's messages poured in. I was telling my therapist, in torrents of tears, about how worried I was about Liv's self-hatred and possible suicidal ideation and I read her some of Liv's texts to illustrate my concerns. She told me that Liv was actually managing fine in the big picture and I should just text her right away and tell her that I was not able to reply as I was in therapy and so she should stop texting me. This was a difficult experience in my therapy process and, ultimately, one of the reasons that I moved on to a different therapist. What I had really wanted was for her to hear how terrified I was that Liv would harm herself in some significant way. Right then I did not feel able to text Liv and tell her to stop texting me.

One of the many dreams that I had at that time illustrated to me the endless struggles I was having to support Liv. I dreamt of an endless flight of very steep stairs: I was walking and walking up flight after flight and just as I thought I was coming to the end of a flight, then suddenly more steep stairs would morph into existence and I would have to keep on walking up and up and up one flight of stairs after another. It seemed that I would never ever get to the top. It seemed that way with Liv's struggles too – like we would never get to the end of them.

One of the hardest things to manage at that time was the fragility of Liv's happiness and how quickly she moved from a settled state of being into emotional trauma. For example, one Sunday afternoon, she was fine and then I took her to buy her a new ballet leotard (as her old one was too short for her) and we discovered that in the ballet shops there were no leotards in her size because she is so tall. We entered the last shop, the Bloch dance shop which she loves, with Liv in a neutral mood and we left with her in a dark, wretched fugue of gender dysphoria and unhappiness. She came home and threw herself onto her bed weeping a tsunami of rageful tears about getting taller and taller.

I struggled to endlessly empathise and, one night, after a therapy session with Liv, her gender counsellor emailed me.

Olivia has been taken out of an environment (her previous school) which had her in a pretty constant state of fight/flight due to the ongoing threat of bullying and everything that comes with trauma from a physical and emotional impact. Now that she feels safe, she is describing herself as burnt out and depressed which is exactly what it feels like when the body and mind come out of that state after being in it for a prolonged period of time.

She needs consistent patience because from the outside it may seem as though she has more reasons to be happy at the change of environment – unfortunately our bodies and minds aren't black and white like that and it's going to take her a little while to start feeling better. She describes feeling on edge at times at the new school and this is an indicator of what is happening – it's a consequence of her recent traumatic experiences – her body is sometimes reacting as though still in that previous environment.

I heard what he had to say and I knew that I had to dig deeper and find more resources to emotionally support Liv. I was quite traumatised by her crisis, however. As were Angus and Stirling. One night when Liv was howling and raging in the shower and the raw sounds of her trauma were reverberating through our house, Angus went to sit with Stirling in his bed to comfort him (and himself, I think). He asked, 'Stirlo, do you get upset when Liv is this distressed?' and Stirling's reply was 'Yes, but I can't let myself get upset because Liv needs two parents to look after her.'

Poor boy, Liv's trauma was so hard on him in so many ways. At that time, he also had to deal with transphobic kids at school who teased him about having a trans sister. When a fake and cruel Instagram account came out amongst his Year 8 cohort at school purporting to reveal the intimate secrets of various students, mostly about their alleged sexual activities, Stirling was exposed for having a transgender sister. He responded with a post saying, 'This is not a secret. Everybody knows that my sister is trans and that's cool with me.'

But he wasn't feeling as robust as he liked to present to the world. One evening when he came out of the therapy room, it was clear that he had been in tears. When the therapist, Andrew, called me in to talk to the two of them, Stirling told me that he was only ever happy when he was playing cricket or the video game *Fortnite* with his sister. He asked if he could have half an hour of the online game every day of the week (instead of only an hour on a Saturday and an hour on a Sunday). I said I would talk to Angus about it. Normally the answer would have been no, but we don't have a 'normally' any more. So, despite our misgivings, Angus and I agreed that Stirling and Liv could play *Fortnite* for thirty minutes every day. Bizarrely, there was a very positive secondary benefit to this concession: Stirling and Liv really bonded over the game, playing together online every day for forty-five minutes (it was never actually thirty minutes!) while seated at their adjacent computers. And when they weren't playing, talking endlessly about the game also proved to be a great, neutral subject for discussion between the two of them.

People often say to Stirling (or about him) that it must be very hard for him to lose his twin brother and acquire a twin sister but actually I think that he is one of the few people who really does feel as though Olivia is the same person as Orlando. For him, the bigger challenges of Liv's transition are moving away from the northern beaches and dealing with Liv's traumas. One evening when Liv was in the midst one of her gender-dysphoric traumas, he said to Angus and me, 'I wish I had a normal sister.' Despite his pain at that moment, I recognised that the beautiful thing about his comment was that it reflected that, for Stirling, the difficulty was Liv's moods, not her being transgender.

Around this time, I was talking to Angus about how totally over-whelmed I felt by our children's emotional struggles and he said to me, 'I feel overwhelmed, and you deal with 95% of all that's going on with them. I can't even imagine how overwhelmed you must feel.' Indeed. That night, when I couldn't sleep, I was thinking about the motherload and the image that came to mind was of me being almost unable to walk because of the load on my shoulders.

I know that it has also been hard for Angus to cope with how obsessed I was with the children and how little attention our relation-ship – his and mine – has had since we knew that Liv was trans. I was often reminded of the time when our twins were in-utero in our surro-gate, Brigitte, and I was totally fixated on taking care of her while she incubated our twins. At that time, Brigitte's pregnancy with our twins was quite tenuous, with weekly crises and visits to the hospital and serious threats to the existence of our babies and Brigitte's health. This meant that I spent most of my time taking care of Brigitte, and vicari-ously, of course, of our babies. When Brigitte got retrenched from her job because she couldn't work well any more given all the physical compli-cations of our pregnancy, I spent most of my time in her home and took care of her needs, as well as those of her two-year-old twins and her partner, Jackie. I bought all the food – endless fruit and vegetables for Brigitte, and ciders for Jackie to ease the strain– and I cooked for them often, while also tending to Brigitte, who was couch/bed-bound because of our pregnancy.

During these tough times in the surrogacy I would get home at night at eight or nine, absolutely exhausted, unable to find the emotional energy to engage with Angus. I could only go straight to sleep until it was time to wake up and to head off to Brigitte's house to take care of her and her family again. One evening, I was home earlier than usual and sitting on our veranda having a glass of wine with Angus. I was absolutely starving hungry but I knew that there was no food in the house, as I hadn't been shopping for us for a while. I was staring out at our beautiful city view when Angus said, very earnestly and for the first time ever, that he was seriously worried about our relationship because I seemed so distant from him all the time. I was shocked, feeling that he was being selfish, given that our babies' lives, the babies we had dreamed of for eight long years, were potentially on the line.

But I was also worried about my relationship with Angus and so I talked to my friend Fawn. She persuaded me that Angus and I needed to go to couple therapy to get through this impasse and I realised she was right. So he and I went to see a wise and compassionate therapist, Jenny, and, under her guidance, Angus spoke about how he felt that he had lost me to the babies even before they were born, and I spoke about how he didn't seem to care enough about the babies. We talked and talked. Eventually, after a few weeks of this couple therapy, Jenny was able to get us to really hear each other and to learn to take care of each other and Brigitte and the babies. By the time they were born (they arrived early, at thirty-two weeks, because Brigitte had pre-eclampsia), we were able to bring them home at ten days of age, hearty and healthy, and we were able to, jointly, take care of them, loving them and each other wholeheartedly.

The time of our life since we had known that Liv is trans had a similar quality to those difficult times because, again, all my emotional energy had been going into our kids and there had often been literally nothing left for Angus. He became quite silent, seemingly struggling to cope with Liv's anxiety, Stirling's sad and confused depression, and my obsessional engagement with them both. I did feel his loneliness and disconnection, his feeling of not being cared for, the lack of the familiar closeness between him and I, but I felt utterly unable to change it because I didn't have any energy reserves left.

Of course, while life felt very hard for Angus, Stirling and for me, life was most difficult for Liv, who had to deal with her overwhelming gender dysphoria and related trauma and depression. I am guessing she felt quite alone with this, given how difficult it is to communicate the feeling of gender dysphoria, what it must it be like to hate parts of your body and to experience the dissonance between your apparent and your real gender. Even if Liv was travelling well for a few days, gender-dysphoric depression could suddenly overwhelm her and leave her lying flat on the couch, dark and heavy, or desperately tearful, silent and deeply sad. And when I asked her what she was feeling, she just said 'sad' and when I asked her why she felt sad right then, she could only say, 'It just comes over me, Mum.' And yet, for days, she might have been happy and purposeful. Gender dysphoria is such an unpredictable and difficult experience – it seems to creep up anytime, anyplace, sometimes with a stimulus, sometimes not.

One Sunday night, after a very troubled weekend with Liv's trauma, I lay in the dark in her bed with her back to me and, a bit like psychoanalytic therapy, she just opened up and talked and talked at me in a monologue. 'Mum, my life is just not worth living with the hand I've been dealt: being trans and Aspie. I'm seriously worried about how depressed I am. Nothing I do gives me any pleasure, even the things that I used to love like reading and gaming and coding. Nothing matters to me any more.'

My heart literally ached listening to her and I was absolutely silent with despair. Later on, when she was finally asleep, Angus asked me what she had been saying to me, and I said I didn't think he could handle her emotional pain right then. When he said that, as her other parent, he had to share the burden, I told him what she had said, and I could see it made him desperately sad too. We couldn't do anything but hug each other and go to sleep and hope that the next day would be better.

When I woke up early the next morning and lay there ruminating about my late-night conversation with Liv, I thought again about what a conundrum it is for those who are both trans and on the Asperger's spectrum: for Aspies, change is an absolute anathema to them, so they will do everything that they can to avoid change and to maintain the status quo, yet, for a trans teen, everything is about engaging in fundamental change as they seek to change chemically/hormonally, physically, socially, vocally and so on. No wonder Liv was fraught about the hand she had been dealt.

She woke up soon after me, just as depressed, refusing for ages to get out of bed to go and shower, very reluctant to go to school. It felt like I was literally forcing her to do every single thing that would get her on the way to school but I knew that she was managing emotionally better at school than at home, probably because of the structure and distractions and the need to 'hold it together' in the context of her peers. She was also making friends and they seemed to make it possible for her to come out of herself. Indeed, even though she often didn't want to go to school, being there often broke her dark mood. So I helped her get ready to go to school and I walked with her to the bus, her striding ahead of me, radiating a sad-anger. She got on the bus without even saying goodbye to me. Then she started texting me from the bus, and it carried on until noon.

Liv: I wanna go home.

Me: (heart emoji)

Liv: I'm done.

Me: Olivia, I'm going to contact the school counsellor to come and see you.

Liv: No.

Me: It's too scary for me to get messages like this and do nothing.

Liv: No, I can't speak to anyone I don't know.

Me: OK, babe, I won't call them but if you're not feeling safe, then you have to talk to someone.

Liv: (emoji of a broken heart) Do what you want to do. I don't care any more.

Me: Babe, I love you. I'm off to take Stirling to his assessment and I'll be in meetings there.

Liv: Why

Liv: Why

Liv: Why

Liv: Why

Liv: Why?

Liv: Maybe you should call the school.

Me: OK, I'll call Thomas Marchbank and ask him to get the counsellor to see you. Is that what you want me to do?

Liv: No.

Liv: I want home and Mom and dogs and Dad and brother.

Me: I hear you, darling girl. I'm in Bondi Junction with Stirling and can't text now. I'll bring you a wrap from Nalini's when I fetch you at four.

Liv: Yes, please, a paneer wrap.

Me: (emoji thumbs up and heart)

However, when I fetched her from school at four o'clock, I noticed from her body language as she walked towards the car that she was in a totally different headspace and that she was, in fact, relatively cheerful.

She started off telling me, 'Today was really hard.'

'Yes, babe, I know, but it seems that something perhaps helped to change things in the second part of the day.'

'Yes, it was my lovely French teacher showing us a video of a sailing trip he did in the holidays way out into the sea. He's just lovely. Then I went to book club at lunchtime and we had such good chats. The girl who runs it is in Year 11 and she used to be at a selective girls' school and she was telling us how they aren't open there and even often anti-gay. We talked about our favourite books. She said she's going to get us reading Jane Austen. She seriously loves books – I was listening to her talking to one of the other Year 11 girls…'

And so she chatted on and on, and just got happier and happier as the afternoon went by. She diligently did her homework and played *Fortnite* with Stirling. After dinner, for the first time ever, she voluntarily phoned someone to chat: she phoned her trans friend, Mia, and they chatted and made plans to meet on the weekend. She came and asked me if she could get the bus on Saturday afternoon and go to the markets with Mia. Astonishing. Even if none of these plans materialised, it felt like progress that she could even be considering going out on her own on public transport to meet up with a friend.

Later in the evening, when I was working in my study, she came in to chat and told me that she had been thinking about how she could calm herself down during the school day and she had decided that she was going to take a notebook to school so that she could write and draw when she was feeling particularly stressed or sad. I told her how hard it had been for me when she had been texting me all the time and how stressed and scared it made me, and she said, 'I know, Mum, and I'm sorry.'

And then, when she was beginning to have long periods of time – more than a week – when she felt quite obviously happy and settled, it was time for another visit to the endocrinologist. When we had seen him in January, Liv had barely looked like a girl but by this stage she was living and presenting full-time as a girl and, thus, she hoped that he might be more open to giving her oestrogen. I knew that this was unlikely and I was worried about how she would react when he said no, so I had emailed him in advance to ask him if there was any chance he might give her hormones. His reply email did not give me any reason to hope.

I am sorry that Olivia has had a difficult time but I am pleased to hear that the situation is sounding better now. We can discuss further on Saturday but starting oestrogen at this age is not within our current framework of practice. One of the purposes of Stage 1 therapy is to allow time to assess psychological and practical adaptation in the affirmed gender role while preventing further puberty changes, before considering potentially irreversible changes with cross-sex hormones.

While the Family Court has removed the need for court authorization of stage 2 therapy prior to age 18 years, the psychiatrists in our team are still advising that young people are incapable of reliably understanding and making decisions about stage 2 therapy (i.e. achieving Gillick competence) until at or near 16 years. This ability is often further compromised by anxiety, depression or other mental health issues. For those that may achieve this earlier, we refer for adult endocrine advice about stage 2 therapy from age 15, so that may the best option of Olivia.

I decided that I would try to put a back-up plan in place in the likely event that the endocrinologist didn't give Liv hormone therapy. I took her to a friendly GP practice in Darlinghurst because I had heard on the trans grapevine that they helped clients access cross-sex hormones. The doctor Liv and I saw was new to the practice and he referred us to a different psychiatrist and endocrinologist to discuss hormone therapy with them. When we left his clinic and I phoned for appointments, it turned out that both the psychiatrist and the endocrinologist only saw teens over seventeen. So that appointment had been a waste of time.

On the way home, there was a real heaviness in the car as Liv and I talked about how desperately worn-out we were from telling her trans story to medics. She said that she was too tired for more appointments and that we should give up on trying to find someone to prescribe oestrogen for her and just wait until she is fifteen or sixteen years old, when it might be easier to get the oestrogen. Deeply despondent, we went home and, in a vain effort to cheer ourselves up, we shared a giant dark Lindt chocolate bunny and watched endless Netflix movies.

As predicted, our meeting with Liv's endocrinologist that Saturday did not go well. This is what I wrote on the closed trans parents website after the appointment

My husband and I took Liv (14) to see her endocrinologist this morning. Liv went in on her own to talk to him, then it was our turn. My husband, a lawyer, tried to argue with him legally, telling him that his protocols around when to give cross-sex hormones are based on the arbitrary chronological age of 15 and 16 (and these protocols are different in different parts of Australia and the world, hence they are especially arbitrary) and we feel that our child is mature and ready for oestrogen now at 14.

Then, since I trained as a psychologist, I tried the developmental psychology approach, saying that it would be developmentally healthy for my daughter to go through puberty as her authentic self with her girl peers (especially given how difficult being trans is at a developmental level generally, for example, around individuation and separation from parents). I also tried the medical argument that since the only irreversible impact of taking oestrogen is the formation of breast tissue, this is not actually irreversible, as medical technology will facilitate the removal of this tissue if there is a change of mind. In addition, there is some evidence that taking oestrogen reduces further height growth (Liv is just under 6 feet now, at 181 cm).

The doctor said, 'I hear you but this is our protocol and we have to draw a line in the sand somewhere, and that is at 15 at the earliest, particularly since it is most often between 14 and 16 that some kids change their mind about being trans.' He said he would be happy to refer Liv to a young adult endocrinologist when she turns 15 (and he, as a paediatric endocrinologist, is no longer appropriate) in March next year and this new endocrinologist will give Liv oestrogen – assuming the psychiatrist says that she is definitely gender-dysphoric.

Even though we all knew this would be the likely outcome of our meeting with him today, we are all still pretty devastated. Liv says she is so weary of medical appointments that she isn't even prepared to go to see a different psychiatrist and endocrinologist for a second opinion. I am hoping she changes her mind on this one. She also says she won't take oestrogen without an endocrinologist being on board because of the potential medical complications with taking hormones that aren't well regulated and monitored by an endocrinal expert. She has read so many horror stories online about the issue. It's been so tough, since Liv really wants the oestrogen, but she is tired now of fighting for it, so we will leave it for a while and see if she asks us again to get involved.

She is a sensible, socially conservative and rational young person – and I am often none of those things (I am more of an impatient activist, social progressive, action taker!) so I do need to let her make this call. She came home, sat down at her computer to do her assessments and isn't really talking to us much.

A week later, I saw and felt the heaviness settle about Liv. She refused to go walking the dogs with Angus when she woke up, she didn't want to eat breakfast, she was very reluctant to go to her dance class. Ultimately, she did go to dance because, she said, 'You've already paid for dance for the term, so it's a waste not to go,' but when I fetched her from her class three hours later, she looked ragefully sad. I had to take her from dance to therapy and she was rude and dismissive towards the therapist, refusing to engage with him and leaving the room partway through. I had to go in and chat to him and felt quite embarrassed by her behaviour. He said she should only come back to see him if and when she wanted to. It seemed likely that this was the end of another therapeutic relationship for her.

That afternoon, we were due to go on the ferry to meet Mia and her mother in the city to see the Vivid lights. Liv didn't feel like going out but she didn't want to disappoint Mia either, so we went. Throughout the evening, she was rude and offhand to Mia and her mother, who were being kind and friendly, trying to cheer Liv up. She was moody, disengaged, walking ahead, insisting only on eating but not communicating or checking out the lights. It was so awkward. I realised that we should never have come, that it would have been better to cancel the arrangements at the last minute, because I had known that it would turn out this way, given her mood and her general discomfort in big crowds.

As we walked back onto the Circular Quay ferry wharf to go home to Balmain, she started crying and when I asked why, she said that she was having a breakdown. She calmed herself a bit on the ferry ride home but when she walked through the front door at home and Stirling asked her how Vivid was, she swore at him and stormed off to her room. She sobbed hysterically for ages, especially after I chastised her for being so awful to Stirling. Eventually, I managed to get her to calm down and I went to watch a TV movie with Angus and Stirling and she watched videos on her iPad. By the time we went to bed, we were all traumatised. This mood continued the following day. At one point, I found Liv lying in the lounge room under a blanket, her head crushed into the sofa cushions. This is more or less how the conversation went, and how it often went in these situations.

'Liv, please turn round and let's talk about why you're feeling sad.'

(Silence.) 'Please, Liv, turn around and look at me so we can talk.' (She turns round reluctantly.) 'What's up, Liv? What precisely is making you sad right now?

'I don't know.'

'When did you start feeling sad?'

'Yesterday.'

'What prompted it?'

'I don't know. It just comes and goes. Sometimes it's a week or a day or a month and I don't feel like this and then it just comes.'

'Can you think of anything right now that might make you feel a bit better, even if just temporarily?'

'No.'

'Watching a movie with me and Stirling? Going for a walk with the dogs? Eating some of last night's leftover cottage pie? Reading?'

'No, I've got no energy to do any of those things.'

'Are you feeling depressed because of anything in particular?'

'Home, school, life.' (Tears.)

I felt utterly helpless and hopeless and gave up trying to get her to talk. I hugged her and scratched her back. Eventually, she said she was going off to look for something to do and she went to her computer and got into some gaming. I knew its wasn't necessarily going to make her feel better and also that this was not part of the allocated time for gaming that weekend but I just didn't care, I just wanted to be at my computer, hiding out from the sadness, trying desperately to sort myself out, knowing that I didn't I have the energy to cope with a full-scale emotional storm. I wondered too how often this would happen, when and if Liv would get over these storms, how many more months and years they might be with us, whether it would make a difference once she was on oestrogen, and so on. I felt totally drained and exhausted. These storms were so frightening and overwhelming and they weighed all of us down so heavily that I felt we were completely mired in Liv's pain. Sometimes I felt the heaviness so tangibly that I could barely walk, talk, breathe, think or be.

On nights like this, I said to Angus, a few times, and amidst many tears of my own, that I didn't know where I would find the strength to carry on with holding and containing so much trauma in Liv and the rest of us. One day when she sent me a text from the school bus saying, 'Screw this' (life, I guessed), I typed back, 'Yes, my views exactly today – screw this,' I nearly pressed 'send' but I didn't. I chose to say nothing, and a while later she texted again saying, 'I love you,' and, in return, I sent her the emoji with the heart-shaped eyes.

One particular change that helped us was that Liv's school banned the use of personal mobiles during the school day, so suddenly she couldn't text me any more. This meant that if she felt sad or low, she had to sit with the feeling – not project it into me – and she was then usually able to process her intense feeling and move on by the time I saw her later in the day. In this way, she was learning some self-management and self-containment – and I was not left dealing with a secondary, vicarious trauma during her school day.

As I have said before, this journey with Liv has been traumatic in unexpected ways. Stirling was happy when he went off on a Friday night to sleep over at his friend Max's house, where he could escape the home dramas. I really worried about him. It's hard as a mother to try to protect one child from the trauma of the other. They were desperately hard times for all of us. Most of the time, I felt sad and flat and lost. Angus and I tried to talk about what was going on but what was there to say? I felt trapped and unable to follow the normal rules of parenting with Liv because she genuinely had a 'crap deal,' as she put it: she lived with terrible gender dysphoria, she hated her body, she desperately wanted to be a girl physically, she hated being trans, she lived in a transphobic world, she had Asperger's and she was in the midst of adolescence. That all seemed a lot to deal with; no wonder she was so often miserable, rageful, despairing, tearful and hostile. I got that, and I did whatever I could to support her, change her world, find help for her, move her gender journey on as much as I could, as quickly as I could, but sometimes I felt as though my interior world was black and blue, scarred and bleeding, numb and silent.

And I didn't have any sense if and when this trauma would end. A significant part of our family suffering at the time was the constant expectation that Liv was going to fall apart, even when things were going well. I began considering that perhaps we needed to go to family therapy, but much of me felt as though Liv herself could commit in therapy to being more accommodating of the rest of us but when the tsunami began inside of her there was nothing to do but let it build up and wash over the rest of us. Even she seemed to have no power to stop it once it had begun.

Eventually, I decided to try to get an appointment with an endocrinologist who is known in the trans parent community to be more supportive of hormone treatment for genuinely gender-dysphoric teens under sixteen. When I phoned his rooms, we got an appointment for six weeks later, and that gave us some hope and something to look forward to.

Despite the many dark days, there were regularly light and less intense days for Liv. She often enjoyed her school day and was doing well there. On many days when I fetched her from school, she was cheerful and gushing with details about her day.

'I love recess so much, Mum. I just sit in the group in the weak winter sun and I slowly eat my sushi and make it last as long as I can and I savour the soy sauce and I don't talk much to the others but that seems OK… I was in the woodwork group at lunchtime and I had so much fun designing my wooden computer box and my lovely teacher, the one I really like, was so excited at my design and showed me lots of other interesting ideas for this project…then I went to French and we got our tests back and I got 21 out of 25, which was the top mark in my class… I really love Chinese writing and I'm getting better at it and I've found a way to record all the new Chinese words that I'm learning so that I can access them easily to learn them. I can really understand why people like calligraphy, because it's like Chinese writing, so beautiful, and I love too how Chinese writing is coded to cue the reader about the meaning, for example, by having a person sign in it so you know the word references people in some way…'

And on and on. I listened to monologues like this with so much joy because she was so engaged in life and learning at these moments. Indeed, school seemed to be the most positive space in Liv's life. I wrote to the principal to tell her what a positive experience the school has been.

I wanted to let you know that our daughter Olivia, who started at IGS this term in Year 8, is very happy at the school.

Liv says that the school is incredibly inclusive, that there are quite a number of kids there who would be bullied or treated as different (in a bad way) at other schools but that at IGS the teachers and students include and accept them and don't judge them. This is obviously a very important experience for Liv as a trans girl. She has found it very validating that there is a teacher in the school who is transgender and non-binary. Although the teacher doesn't teach her, they have made a special effort to seek her out and check on her and that has meant a lot to Liv too. There is also a trans student in Liv's tutor group who has been wonderful with her, giving his phone number to her and asking her to call any time she needs to, making a special effort to talk to Liv and include her. This is so significant for her in so many ways – not least because it is such a validating experience to see another trans teen who is so open, self-confident and so accepted by the others. The tutor system across the years is really effective at creating cross-year alliances and support systems.

There have been some difficult days for Liv in the first few weeks, as she has still been struggling to get over the awful bullying that she experienced at her last school and so she has been quite down on some days. The teachers have shown concern and support and seemed to be able to cope with her heavy moods, continuing to engage with her as she passed through these dark moments. As a trans teen, she is likely to feel down occasionally, so it is a relief that this is OK at IGS. She does go to therapy weekly and is feeling stronger and happier now, and much of this is to do with how happy and stimulated she feels at IGS.

As you can imagine, all of this is an enormous relief to us, her parents. It is truly wonderful to see her engaged with life and learning again.

The principal's reply confirmed my sense that this was the right place for Liv.

> Your beautiful email is music to my ears! Thank you so much for taking the time to send it to me. I hoped that IGS would be all the things we believe it is and I had a very good feeling when I met your amazing daughter but I'm absolutely thrilled that this has been the case for Liv since her arrival... academically, socially and in the ways that you describe. I am so glad that Liv is now an IGS student and we have wonderful things in store this year and beyond.

And so we inched slowly forwards, sometimes backwards, then once more slowly forwards.

At that time, one of the parents in the trans parents online family very generously started blogging (anonymously and confidentially) about her daughter's gender affirmation surgery in Melbourne so that other parents could learn about the procedure physiologically, logistically and psychologically. It was a remarkable journey for this mother and daughter pair who spent three weeks in Melbourne and then, when they went home, the young girl had a new, soon-to-be fully functioning vagina – and a new life. Their story made the whole gender affirmation surgery process seem, albeit bloody and invasive, definitely accessible, doable and feasible.

I showed Liv the blog and she read it very slowly and then, when I went to kiss her goodnight that evening, she told me that the blog had made her feel hopeful. I thought about how shocked I would have been just seven months ago to read the gruesome and gory medical (and emotional) details of turning a penis into a vagina and how now I was simply curious to learn how it all worked because I knew that this is likely to be our journey pretty soon after Liv turned eighteen.

One thing that did sometimes work to cheer Liv up if she was feeling low, was talking with her about her goals and how to achieve them. We did this one maudlin and mad Monday morning when she didn't want to go to school.

'What do you want most, Liv?'

'To be a girl in my body.'

'OK, we're going to get you oestrogen for that, hopefully before you turn fifteen, but, if not, then at fifteen. And we'll support you through gender confirmation surgery when you're eighteen if that's what you want. OK, what else?'

'I want to be less Aspie.'

'OK, oestrogen has been found to help with that to some extent – taking oestrogen can make Aspie kids less Aspie. And we'll continue to work on your social skills at home and in therapy. And once you're really living completely authentically, you may find it easier to communicate and connect. OK, what else?'

'That's all.'

'OK. Can you get going to school now?'

'OK.'

This conversation probably sounds a lot less traumatic than it actually was but, after this interaction, Liv did go off to school relatively willingly, after a weekend of trauma, and she had a great week at school.

She did have one difficult day when she and her friend Ciara were playing Truth or Dare with some other girls and, when it was Liv's turn, she choose Truth and she was asked by one of the girls, 'How long have you known that you're a girl?'. Liv says that she was initially upset at the question because, it turned out, she hadn't told anybody at school that she was trans and so it was a shock to her that her being trans was so apparent to others. I can see why the question was hard for her but I did also really appreciate that the premise from which the questioner was operating was good: she asked the question of Liv as a girl.

While she has become accustomed to being asked questions her, as she explained to me one day. 'One of the girls asks me heaps of questions about being trans, which I don't really mind but what I do mind is that some of the questions seem to assume that I'm not a girl or a boy but something else, a trans girl perhaps. It certainly feels like what underlies her questions is the belief that I'm different from other girls and that feels so hard.'

At that time, Liv was off school quite often because she had been feeling sick a lot. She is not a hypochondriac and so I take her ailments seriously. She had been feeling really nauseated often and had had a really bad cold, which she seemed to have only partially shaken. She had a few nights when she lay in bed with rigors (tremors), which is what used to happen when she was a child and had a very high temperature. The odd thing, though, is that she wasn't getting a temperature this time. I thought that perhaps she was not getting over her cold, so I took her to see one of the lovely GPs at our local practice. Gerald checked her very thoroughly and then suggested to us, while doing his very gentle, kind and intense interaction, that the rigors she was having at night, and the nausea, were perhaps side effects of the puberty blocker, Zoladex.

While Gerald was chatting with Liv, I googled the side effects of Zoladex on my mobile and there they were: hot flushes, sweating, headache, dizziness, mood changes, nausea, diarrhoea, sleep problems. I fixed on mood changes, googling that further and this is what came up pretty soon: psychiatric side effects (of Zoladex) including emotional lability (47% to 60%) and depression (40% to 54%) have been reported.

I felt the world stop still for a few seconds as I processed this potentially significant data. Was it possible that the emotional storms that Liv had been experiencing in the last few months had been caused by Zoladex? I asked Gerald this and he said possibly yes. Relief washed over me at the idea that this intense moodiness, rageful sadness and the terribly traumatic emotional times that Liv had regularly been going through were perhaps largely caused by the drugs. I felt immediately so much more hopeful because these feelings and reactions would presumably disappear when she stopped the Zoladex and started taking a testosterone blocker or oestrogen, which could be as soon as the end of July, when we were due to see the new endocrinologist. I was relieved to consider that her moods might not be a reflection of a crushing, innate despair and unhappiness, but a reaction to the medication. It made more sense to me because, even in her saddest moments in the last few years, I had not experienced the traumatic intensity that was present in these emotional storms since she had started the Zoladex in January. I felt the possibility of our world coming together again, just a bit.

So, despite the darkness, there was some light for us and, as was often the case, my dream life reflected what was going on for me. I dreamt that Angus and I were throwing away all the rotten fruit and veg from our fridge, strawberries with webs of mould growing over them, and so on. I put all the rotten food into the bin and then the bin was overflowing and smelling terrible, so Angus whipped the bag out and started the very long walk to the bin. There was a running race going on outside, so there were people everywhere and lots of the routes to the bins were blocked, which meant that he had to walk and walk a very long route to the bin. When he finally got back to the house, we were relieved that all the rotten food was gone.

I had a strong sense that this dream reflected, in part, how overjoyed I felt that perhaps we would be able to get rid of the Zoladex sometime and that there would be much relief for all of us. I knew that we couldn't stop Liv having the Zoladex: it was essential to her because it held her (male) puberty in abeyance. She was absolutely terrified of developing more male secondary sexual characteristics.

Since the Zoladex side effect information came to light, I started to sleep longer and more deeply for the first time in a very long time. There were even days I didn't wake up once from the time I got to bed after ten o'clock. and the time that the dogs woke us up at six for their breakfast. Sometimes when Liv said to me, 'I feel sad,' I still had what my friend Jacqui calls my trauma reaction: freezing and panicking and expecting the worst, but most often her mood just stayed at sadness, and the devastating tsunami didn't arrive. A few times, Liv did have a minor meltdown but mostly things were easier and calmer and she usually got up and willingly got dressed and headed for the school bus every morning. There was relief all round in our family when this happened.

And then, slowly, I noticed that I was changing too. I noticed this one evening when Liv and I were eating at our favourite sushi train in Balmain. It was family dinner time, so there were lots of parents and kids sitting around the train. As we arrived, Liv went off to the toilet and I sat down, and I hypervigilantly noticed the woman over the train from us, turning around and staring at Liv. Immediately, I felt hostile and defensive and decided to move to the other side of the train so that she couldn't stare at us through our dinner. As we sat down at this new spot, Liv, very excitedly, started telling me the details of her afternoon with Fin, Stirling's friend, who had built his own computer but hadn't been able to get it working properly and how she had been able to help him by rewiring it, showing me the photos on her phone of what she had done to get his computer working again.

All this chatting was going on while we were just settling down at the train, choosing our meals, when I noticed a young girl – about ten – staring at us a lot, then a father with his three kids doing the same. I started glaring at them, feeling as though I was batting away the stares from both sides with my eyes. All the while, Liv was chatting animatedly,

'At the arts festival today at school, when our house got onto the stage to do our dance and narrative, and the Snoop Dog song came on, the hall erupted, and then we did our dance and won the house competition…and when people asked me which icon I was dressed as, I told them I was Edward Snowden and some people were like "Who?" and others were like "That's so cool" and Ciara looked so brilliant as Dora the Explorer, she *was* Dora and she had a Dora backpack which had an iPod in it that kept playing the theme song for Dora…'

Suddenly I started to imagine that the young girl who was watching Liv was noticing how brave she was because she was so confident and out there in her differentness. I figured that Liv was a powerful role model for young girls like this to be their authentic selves, to take chances, to care less about what people thought of them,

176

and maybe even find their own confidence and follow their dreams to be who they really wanted to be. I watched the father with his three young children: he was holding his beautiful two-year-old son on his lap at that stage, holding him tight and close while looking into the distance at the cherry blossoms painted on the wall, seemingly quite melancholic. I thought to myself that perhaps his staring at Liv had been laced with envy at her ability to live her true and authentic self, her bravery at living so boldly in the world, that she could be seemingly genuine and at peace with herself being other and different.

And so that night I began to shift my perspective, reframing the glances Liv encountered out there in the world, assuming that people were repeatedly looking at her because they admired her, envied her, were entranced by her, wanted some of what she had: the extra-ordinary courage to live without really noticing or caring that people were observing her, not wondering if their noticing was good or bad, kind or cruel, but just living her own reality.

When we had nearly finished eating at the sushi train, she was engaged in a long monologue about what she admired and disliked about the Apple company and their 'beautiful, overpriced, under-powered, trendsetting' products and she was talking expressively with her hands and body, deeply unaffected by what was going on around her in the social dynamics, looking so beautiful in her profound engagement with life.

Later on that evening, Angus and I took Liv to her one-on-one ballet lesson with Vanessa. It was raining hard but, after dropping Liv with Vanessa, Angus and I walked close together under our Bunnings umbrella to a trendy, local bar of inner west hipsters. While Angus had some craft beer and I had two glasses of Pinot Noir, we talked about him becoming head of chambers the next week and how he would manage that, about the building project for our new house and how we would have to get on with that. I told him about Liv's art festival that day and how much fun she had had.

He asked me hopefully and tentatively, 'Do you think that we could have reached a turning point with Liv? When did she last have a meltdown?'

'Yes, I do. Two weeks ago was the last time'

And I felt our joint hope swell. Maybe, maybe.

Then we wandered back to fetch Liv from her ballet class and she had that light in her eyes that she gets when she has been doing ballet with Vanessa. As she told me we needed to get new ballet shoes because hers – only six months old – were too small already, I recognised that, unusually, there was no drama in her talk about how she had grown. When we got home and the four of us had foraged in the kitchen for a second dinner, we sat down and watched many episodes of *Brooklyn 99* and the wonderfully irreverent detective Jake Peralta, another person who really lives his authentic self.

There was no tsunami trauma that weekend. It did feel tenuous but also such a huge, huge relief.

On the Sunday morning, I asked Liv rather tentatively, 'How are you going on the transitioning journey?'

'OK. I don't like my body still, but socially I do feel much better.'

Then Stirling woke up and the first thing he said was 'Where's my sister?' because he wanted to play *Fortnite* with her. Much as I don't really like the game, I do really like how it connects them.

Stirling, too, had made great progress emotionally. For example, one night when I fetched him from his therapist, he got into the car quite euphorically and said to me, 'Let's go, Mum. I'm hungry and I need to play Fortnite with my sister and I'm happy… Danni and I are friends again, there aren't any problems at home any more…'

I have to say that we have made concessions for Stirling that are, in effect, a way of compensating for the various difficulties he has encountered since Liv identified as transgender. For example, we let him have the dogs sleep in his bed (instead of beside it). This appears to have made a very significant difference to his state of well-being – he tells us most nights that cuddling the dogs in bed is the highlight of his day. In many ways, the dogs have been an absolutely vital part of our lives over this year: there are many times that I see either Liv or Stirling curled up with a dog in their arms, clearly deeply soothed and comforted by the presence of the lovely, furry beasts.

There are other small concessions we have made for Stirling: we often let him have Nutella on white bread toast for breakfast (instead of healthier options like sourdough toast and eggs and fruit), we have allowed him to play Fortnite with Liv every evening (instead of only on the weekend) and we let him have as much chaos in his room as he likes (as long as it's tidied up before the cleaners come on Mondays). As I have said before, this time in our life has been completely uncharted. Nothing has prepared us for it and so often we have been at sea when making parenting decisions, big or small, with nothing in our previous experiences on which to draw. Our decisions are now often made on the basis of gut feel.

For Angus, his transitioning with Liv was slower than mine. He reads many papers every day and has managed to find almost an article a day about transgender research and issues and when he sent them to me, then I knew that he had been thinking about Liv and worrying about her. At other times he just sat with Liv when she was sad, hugging her and being present with her. Still he did say, at this stage, that he felt as though he wasn't managing his relationship with her well and that he just didn't know how to support her. I learnt how vulnerable and fragile he was feeling when I asked him to stand in for me when I was asked to speak as a trans parent at a Trans Pride forum. I couldn't do it because at that time I was due to be in South Africa, attending the wedding of our surrogate Brigitte and her partner Jackie.

Tears filled Angus's eyes immediately. 'I can't talk about Liv publicly without tearing up and I don't want to do that because people will assume that my tears indicate that I'm ashamed of her being transgender when I'm not. I'd be crying because I feel so much loss about her future, so sad and worried that her life might be terribly complicated and hard.'

I spoke to Justine, a psychiatrist friend, who referred us to Belinda, a family and adolescent specialist psychologist. As we sat in Belinda's fourth-floor office in Bondi Junction for our first session, the sun streamed onto the couch where we sat together, and we detailed for her our own experiences of being parented. I felt relief wash over me as we talked and as Belinda talked; it felt as though we were doing something to work out a way of jointly parenting our troubled teens. Belinda said she could work with us to develop a positive, conscious and proactive approach to parenting, emphasising that how we managed the next few years would make a critical difference to Liv and Stirling's futures.

We didn't have time in that first session to talk about how Angus, Liv and Stirling were going to manage while I was in South Africa for six days to attend Brigitte's wedding. Brigitte had been diagnosed with a malignant brain tumour and she was appreciating every moment of life with the great intensity that comes to those who are, suddenly and brutally, reminded of their mortality. It was very important to me to be there for Brigitte, but I was also rather anxious about leaving Liv, which is why I was only going for such a short time.

I need not have worried, because it turned out that Liv managed fine without me. She willingly went to school each morning, came home in the afternoon and did her homework, played Fortnite with Stirling, walked the dogs, cooked dinner with Angus, and watched comedy shows on TV with Angus and Stirling every night. No tears, no slammed doors, no throwing herself onto the couch in a heavy fugue of despair. Angus wrote in a text to me that it was the best time he and Liv had had together since she had come out as trans.

When I came through the arrivals gates at Sydney Airport, hoping to see Liv looking cheerful and welcoming, she was already looking slightly downcast, and by the time we arrived home, she was tearful and tetchy. When I asked her why she was like this with me and not with Angus, she explained that she hadn't wanted to stress Angus out because he had so much work to do and she also hadn't wanted to give him anything that he couldn't deal with. She added that she had suppressed a lot of her sadness while I was away.

For the next twenty-four hours, she was in a state of mini-depression, not wanting to get out of bed, not wanting to dress, not wanting to go to school, texting me from school telling me she was sick and sad, walking heavily and slowly about the house, lying under a blanket on the couch, clearly communicating her distress to me through her behaviour. She was like a young child who, when their mother returns from being away, suddenly realises that she has been left by the mother and is furiously sad about that (retrospective) absence.

I emailed her endocrinologist to ask if he thought the Zoladex could be causing her depressive symptoms and he said he didn't think so as she hadn't had those symptoms when he had seen her in May and she had been on the Zoladex since the end of January. He suggested that she have a psychiatric and psychological intervention and a series of blood tests to check for various medical maladies.

So I organised for her to see her gender specialist therapist and that helped significantly to settle things. I also took her to see the GP and he did a range of blood tests to assess if there was a medical cause for her fatigue, aches and pains, nausea, general body weakness and headaches – and there wasn't.

Slowly as the days progressed, Liv brightened and was, in fact, often cheerful, engaging and helpful. 'What else can I do for you, Mum?' was her constant refrain. She brought in all the clean washing from the line, folded it and put it onto the relevant beds, she cooked the dinner with me, laid and cleared the table, ate all her dinner, and went to school relatively cheerfully. After dinner most nights, the four of us watched *Brooklyn 99* and Liv watched with good grace and humour, rather than reluctantly, as had sometimes been the case in the past.

One afternoon when she came home from school, she monologued endlessly in a free association about her day in such a way that I knew she was finding great pleasure in life again. 'Our science lesson was really great today. We dissected a lamb's heart and lungs and on Friday we're going to dissect a lamb brain, so that will be really interesting...Ciara and I had so much fun at rock climbing, I was thinking that maybe I should see her in the holidays. She likes gaming and lots of other things I like and maybe she and I could go for a walk and have some sushi and a chat… I really tried hard to enjoy rock climbing, I thought about how the doctor said yesterday that it doesn't matter how weak I feel, I should try to do exercise and that will make me feel stronger and it worked well… I didn't feel weak or sick today, just a bit sad at one point because some girls in Year 2 asked me if I was a boy or a girl and if I was wearing a wig. I wanted to tell them off but I didn't because they're young and they don't mean any harm, but still it made me feel bad about myself. I just ignored them and soon they stopped. I know Mrs Colnan says I should tell her about any bullying but they didn't mean anything bad, so there was no point… I was reading on the internet today about a study done with twins and relatively often one of the twins is transgender, or even both of them, so maybe there's some biological basis for being trans… History was amazingly interesting because the teacher showed us the writings of an author who said terrible things about Aboriginal people, like that they weren't killed off by white colonials. She was showing us how subjective history is and how we have to think carefully and critically about everything we read…'

The next day, she came home with her school report and, given the storms we had endured that term, her results were really quite a remarkable feat: an A for Maths, English, History, Technology and Visual Arts; a B for Science and PDHPE; a C for French and Music and a D for Mandarin. She hadn't studied French for a long time, so she had to catch up a lot, and she had never studied Mandarin before, whereas most of her peers have been studying French and Mandarin for years.

The report comments from her tutors and teachers were uniformly positive, like this one from her home room tutor:

Olivia is an exceptionally polite and respectful student who engages meaningfully and sincerely with her peers and tutors. Starting a new school is always a daunting prospect, but Olivia has settled in very well to IGS and brings a positive and enthusiastic attitude to tutor group every morning. She is well-read and informed and brings a wealth of insight and reflection to her conversations with others. Academically, Olivia has made an impressive start to her studies. Across the board, her teachers have recognised her motivated, diligent and hardworking attitude.'

Astonishing. We were so proud of her.

8

What would love do?

I dreamt that I was going swimming in the ocean with one of my oldest friends, Jono, who works as an international human rights campaigner fighting for the marginalised in society, including trans teens. The waters were choppy and we were swimming near the rocks which was really quite dangerous but we were managing well enough and having a good time, diving down and seeing the amazing and vibrant ocean life, a world that I had never seen before. Just then we become aware that some human activity – perhaps a ship – had created a series of massive waves that were rolling towards us. We knew we had to get out of the water immediately, as we couldn't possibly survive these waves if we stayed in the sea, so we scrambled madly up the rocks and onto safe ground. Halfway up the rocky mountain, we realised that we had both left our glasses on the rocks and so we could hardly see anything. Our vision was seriously impaired and I didn't know how we were going to get anywhere. Then abruptly, in the next dream frame, we were in dry clothes and our vision was restored.

One day, Stirling and I were driving home after he had been in therapy, and he commented to me, 'You know, Mum, I can't even remember Liv as a boy. It feels so wrong to even think of her that way now.'

'Me too, Stirlo. I don't really even remember that person. It feels so long ago that we got to know Liv but it's only been about seven months.'

I was remembering this conversation as I drove to the monthly trans parenting support meeting at the Gender Centre. I reflected on how it seemed literally years ago, rather than seven months, that I had sat in my first support group meeting and I had cried and asked those in the group for advice on how to transition myself, how to learn to see my son as my daughter.

As I walked into the Gender Centre this time, I felt relaxed and at home. After I had greeted Lee, I asked her if I could go to the kitchen to make myself a cup of tea. I stood there waiting for the kettle to boil and thought about how the centre felt so much more like my place now. Then, while I was waiting for the meeting to start, I collected a pile of olives and Brie cheese from the table, and looked around the room at the assembled group. I didn't recognise many of the people there that night and, as we went around the group doing our personal mini-inputs about our trans children, it became apparent that, for some inexplicable reason, very few of the experienced trans parents were there that month. This meant that most of the parents present were first-timers radiating the trauma of troubled, sad and/or angry new trans parents, either subtly or not so subtly, consciously or unconsciously, struggling to accept the transitioning of their child.

The first set of parents who spoke were stiff with tension: they looked as they though were literally struggling to breathe in and out. They explained to the group that they didn't feel that their sixteen-year-old child was sure about transitioning and so it was particularly difficult for them to use their child's new name and chosen gender. They wondered perhaps if the child was just going through a phase. While they talked about their trans son, it was apparent from their anecdotes that they were misgendering him, not just when talking about him, but also when talking to him. They spoke about how withdrawn 'she' was, and how 'she' didn't want them to come with 'her' to appointments to the psychologist.

One of the more experienced parents asked them a rather ordinary question about whether the child was seeing a psychiatrist or not, and in the process asked the parents a side/sub question, very tactfully, 'What pronouns does the child want you to use?'

'Male ones, he and him,' said the parents.

The experienced trans parent then continued to ask the parents the question using the correct pronouns he/him when talking about the child. 'OK, so your son has been to see a psychologist but not a psychiatrist yet. Does he like the psychologist?'

Another parent then also asked a question, also using the correct pronouns, 'How does he explain to you how he feels about being trans?'

It seemed to me that this gentle intervention in using the correct pronouns and referring to their son must have had some impact on these new and struggling trans parents, hopefully making it more possible for them to begin to accept his transitioning.

Then one particularly well-heeled and articulate new trans father with a sixteen-year-old trans son, much more languidly relaxed than the tense parents who had just spoken, tried to persuade us (and himself?) about the dangers of taking hormones for life, using scientific and medical terminology to explain that his concern was that there were no long-term studies about the impact of these medications.

I found myself speaking up, being as diplomatic as possible (generally not my strength!), empathising with him (because I too had been a first-timer overwhelmed by the idea of having a trans child) and then talking about my own experiences. 'I hear you. It's hard for all of us to realise that our children will be taking these medications for the rest of their lives. I guess that, for me, it's worth it because I know that it will make all the difference in the world to my daughter. I know that, for her, being able to take oestrogen and chemically transition to being her true self is likely to be life-saving. So, I guess for me, for our family, it's been about weighing up the costs and benefits. For us, it's safer for her to take the hormones than not. And there are a lot of scientists now who are finding that actually taking them is not a medical problem for our trans kids in the long term.'

Then two mothers spoke, one after the other, about their trans children, one aged four and the other five, and how certain these children had been about their authentic gender from the time that they could talk. Both of the women seemed delighted to have found each other and were making plans to meet up outside of the meeting to share their very particular and early trans parenting journeys with each other.

One of the more difficult stories for me was told by a mother of a six-year-old child, born male, who had always wanted to dress as a girl and who went to school presenting as a girl but wanting to be called by a boy's name using boy pronouns. I would find that pretty confronting because it is confusing and doesn't conform to gender binarism. In situations like this, Lee is good at talking with us about accepting our kids as being gender fluid, gender expressive, gender creative or gender non-conforming.

There was one parent story that I loved because it gave me hope for Liv's future: one of the fathers talked about his trans daughter who was at university and who had been transitioning socially and medically for a few years. She lived at home, and she now had a partner for the first time, a cis man, who was also living with them. The dad spoke about how well the relationship was working out. This was so reassuring for the trans parents because, of course, this is every trans parent's dream: that their child will be able to have a happy and successful love relationship – and all of this while going to university and studying and building a life. This young woman is soon going with her parents to have gender confirmation surgery in Melbourne and while I listened to the father talking about that, I wondered what her boyfriend made of it all and I marvelled at how this younger generation obviously had much less fixed views about what constituted gender, sex and sexuality. Thank goodness.

This discussion brought to mind a conversation I had had with my friend Jacqui's very mature eighteen-year-old son Thomas when I had been having breakfast with them. I had asked Thomas what he knew about the sex life of trans women and he had explained that his generation, when compared to mine, had a much, much broader interpretation of what constituted sexual activity and how it could be done, including with various sex toys or aids. It was an elucidating, if not completely comfortable, conversation, in which I learnt a great deal, and which has left me committed to being more open-minded about sexual matters.

Back to the parenting group. There were a few experienced parents talking about the more advanced trans parenting dilemmas that night: how to most efficiently change their children's names and genders on birth certificates, passports and Medicare cards; how to decide where to go for medical transitioning; how to help their young adult offspring transition into the adult world of work; how to help their youngsters negotiate relational difficulties, and how to work out what role to play if their child was not being compliant about taking their trans (or mental health) medications.

But, despite this limited input from more experienced trans parents, for much of that session Lee was having to do intensive psycho-education with the new trans parents about the importance to the trans child of not being misgendered and of being called by their chosen name and correct pronouns. She told the group of the research that showed that trans teens with supportive parents were likely to have practically the same relatively low levels of long-term mental health concerns as their cisgender peers, while those trans teens with unsupportive parents had a 70% chance of having serious long-term mental health concerns.

While I watched Lee so patiently empathising and working with the new, angry, hostile, sad and/or reluctant trans parents, I thought, with the deepest gratitude and respect, about how hard she works to keep trans kids alive. She is literally a life saver. Such a huge responsibility for her.

These differences between the less and more experienced trans parents were also evident on the closed trans parents' website that I accessed every day, many times a day. I often posted questions there, engaged in discussions and read other parents' problems and suggested solutions, learning so much in the process. It was a similar experience in some ways to my fertility struggles when I had felt, undoubtedly, most comforted, supported, heard and understood by other women who were also having fertility problems. I do sometimes feel that only other trans parents can really understand the trans dilemmas, debates, discussions and difficulties that arise for trans parents, especially because there are so many ground-breaking developments in the world of trans kids in Australia. For example, it was only in 2017 that medics could dispense hormones to trans teens without a court order and it was only in 2014 that they could do so with puberty blockers. So it is only now really feasible for kids to transition earlier and this brings with it many challenging, uncharted physical, medical, legal, social and psychological dilemmas and dynamics. The parents on this online page are at the forefront of knowledge about these changes and challenges and the administrators of the page function as leaders, guides, mentors, counsellors and supporters for all of us who are struggling every day to work out how to chart a safe and positive path forward for our trans offspring.

One of the very useful aspects of the online page is that parents offer up all the information that they have discovered, so for example, if I take Liv to the endocrinologist and learn new trans-related information which may be relevant to the other parents on the page, I post all the details and then people comment on them, and we debate and discuss the issues. If someone has worked out an effective strategy for helping their kid's school to adopt trans-friendly practices, then this parent is likely to share the information for other parents to try to have introduced at their kid's school. If a parent has a terribly difficult and sad exchange with their parents or in-laws who refuse to accept their transgender grandchild, then this parent can post about it, and get support and care and advice and a sense that they are not alone in their loss, anger or sadness. When a parent needs to know how to accept their child's new authentic self, then he or she can reach out to the parents on the page and we are all, firstly, empathic and supportive, and then we offer up our own stories about this experience of our transition. Whenever I have had a dilemma that is trans-related in any way, I have posted about it and found very useful ideas, answers, suggestions and advice. This e-family of trans parents has been an absolutely invaluable source of information for me because I have come to recognise that, in the controversial and ground-breaking context of the medical trans- itioning of trans youngsters, trans parents have to manage their child's transition – it is not possible in this instance to rely solely on the medics.

I am also enormously grateful to those parents who have been through the wars of gender dysphoria and come out the other side, and who show us what the other side looks like, into more of a gender euphoria when the grass is greener. A while ago, one of the parents on the trans parents website posted a picture of her gorgeous (trans) son, currently sitting his HSC, and she spoke about how he was really thriving despite Year 8 being a near complete write-off for him because his gender dysphoric depression and suicidality had been so over-whelming. An even more encouraging post from one of the other mums was a story and photos of her very handsome trans son getting married to a lovely and kind-looking woman. Those posts give me such a significant injection of hope that I regularly promise myself that one day, when Liv is living easily, happily and authentically, I will write these kinds of inspirational posts on this page in order to help to sustain the next generation of trans parents.

While I spend a lot of time trying to protect Liv from the trans-phobic world, I try, in various small ways, to change the world so that it is less transphobic. For example, I volunteered to talk on ABC radio in a show about transgender teens and whether they should be allowed to transition medically whilst they are amidst the vagaries of adolescence. When I got into the recording studio with the program host, Josh Szeps, and the two men who were intended to represent the voice of the people, I was very nervous, wondering if I could do justice to those trans teens who wanted to take hormones and, in so doing, become themselves.

Soon after I met the other guests on the show, I learnt that one in particular – a young man in his late twenties – held the relatively common view that transgender teens are confused and having an identity crisis from which they will recover post-adolescence 'when they will then realise that they are not actually transgender'. While talking on air, I tried to make it clear, using Liv's experiences (anonymously) as examples, that for the majority of trans teens, being transgender is a permanent state of being and that, as her parent, I know that Liv is 100% transgender, and always will be, that this is not a choice that she is making but simply *who she is*. In fact, she has made it clear that she would never have made a choice to be transgender – if a choice had been involved. I was quite shocked by the conservative views of the young man who implied that trans teens could choose not to be transgender. Of course, it followed that he was resistant to the idea of trans teens being able to take hormones to medically transition.

The other citizen on the program was a mental health nurse, an older man who, over a few decades, had been a close witness to the transitioning process of a friend's daughter, and who strongly advocated that trans teens who were sure of their trans status should be able to choose to take hormones. The show host, Josh, then dialled in experts from various universities who provided evidence and statistics for the positive impact of hormones on the mental health of trans teens.

One of the other things that I do as a trans ally and advocate for trans change is to talk openly about Liv being transgender in the most 'normal' ways that I can with as many people as I can. When I do this, I make it clear that, while this has been a tough journey, it is tough mostly because society does not accept transgender people for who they are. This is a relatively regular topic in the parents' online group and at the Gender Centre group: if an acquaintance asks after your child and they use the wrong gender because they don't know that your child is transitioning, what do you do and say? Some parents believe that it is not the business of the person inquiring to be told that the child is transgender and no longer a girl/boy.

Personally, I have a different view: I believe that it is vital to answer the question put to me so often, 'How are your boys?' with the explanation that 'Stirling is fine. Our other child is transgender and is transitioning. She is now Olivia and we are entirely supportive of this change.' I think this kind of brief, frank answer conveys to the person asking about my children that I am fine with Liv being transgender, and it models to the other person how to act around Liv – and maybe other trans people. As I said, I see it as my responsibility/duty to be open about having a transgender child in order to normalise it and to (hopefully) contribute to broader social change and acceptance for trans people.

One example of this happened during one of my work projects. This project, called Weaving Bridges, entails facilitating Aboriginal women weavers creating a massive woven art work that is displayed annually on the Stuart Somerville Bridge in Queenscliff during Naidoc week. We do this with the help of local northern beaches non-Aboriginal women who come along once a week for about two months to do the weaving with the Aboriginal artists. During the 2018 weaving project, I was sitting next to a woman, Meg, whom I had never met before, and we were chatting as we wove. She was about sixty-five years old. As part of our general getting-to-know-you conversation, she asked me about my children and my answer included telling her about my transgender daughter. As always, I wasn't sure about talking to a stranger about it but my answer was part of my general commitment to destigmatising being trans. After I had explained to Meg about Olivia and our journey with her, she was quiet for a bit, and then she told me that her twenty-year-old grandchild had recently identified as transgender, also as a transgirl.

Meg and I chatted for ages about our trans family members and I showed her a recent photo of Olivia. It was amazing serendipity that we should be seated next to each other in this group of women. I recorded her email address and sent her information about various trans resources that might be helpful to her family and she wrote me the most beautiful email in reply.

I thoroughly enjoyed meeting and talking with you. Thank you for sharing your life events with me, it was most opportune for me to experience another parent's journey.

I did think that Olivia had the most beautiful face and I still see her, what seemed to be dark brown eyes, looking at her mother. She is blessed to have a mother that realises the importance of hormonal treatment now which, I believe, will see her develop into a gorgeous young woman. My son is currently overseas and I will pass on your information, which I appreciate you sending. His brother, our eldest beautiful son, died a few years ago and in those dark days I would often meet him at 5.30 a.m. for coffee and he would say, 'What would love do, Mum?' And so, it is not always easy but it is what we do, isn't it?

When I read Meg's email, I was in tears about her loss and about my sense of our shared humanity and connection and about a shared acceptance and a recognition between Meg and me that love is what life is really all about.

Within a few days of that email, the mother of one of Stirling's cricket team mates wrote to me and asked if I would talk to someone that she knew whose child had recently identified as transgender.

I sent her an email that she could send to the person she knew

My name is Lyndsay and I have a transgender daughter, Olivia (14). We learnt in October last year that our son was actually our daughter. It was completely unexpected and a great shock to us. It was really hard to adjust to this idea at first but we (my husband and I and Olivia's twin, Stirling) have all come around and accepted Olivia being transgender – which is not to say that we are all worked through about this but just that we have come to terms with it to a large extent.

Psychologically, being gender-dysphoric is pretty traumatic so life isn't always easy but, on the whole, Olivia is much happier being out. In the two years or so before we learnt that she was trans, she was deeply depressed and even suicidal at times so we are really happy that she is much more stable now. Socially and educationally Olivia started at the International Grammar School, Ultimo, this term and it is the most wonderful, accepting, diverse, academically sound and inclusive school and so she finally has a place where she feels at home. Medically, she is currently on puberty blockers (administered by an endocrinologist) but, like most trans teens, she wants 'cross-sex' hormones as soon as possible.

I have found great support in the trans parents' community, both the closed online page for trans parents only, and the monthly parents support meetings at the Gender Centre in Annandale. I will send you all the links to the relevant websites where I found very useful resources.

When I was very new to this trans parenting business, I met with a few trans mothers (friends of friends) and that helped me enormously. I also emailed with other trans parents and talked on the phone with a university friend who too has a trans daughter. I have often felt that it is only trans parents who can really understand this journey. So, I am happy to pay it forward and meet or chat or email, whatever would work for you. I know how lonely and tough this journey can be.

I have collected the resource information into one document now, because I regularly get the opportunity to forward it to someone who needs it. It happens to me relatively often that people will respond to my story with information about a transgender person that they know, or know of, in their community, their family, their town, or somewhere else in their world.

There are varying statistical estimates about the numbers of transgender people in our society today, most of which have been found to be underestimates because there is such a taboo about being transgender that most people actually choose not to come out as transgender. The figures range – depending on the sources/researchers – from 0.5% of the population to 7% of some populations (for example, Thailand). Lee says that a recent study of high school kids in Australia found that 1.3% of them identified as gender diverse.

So I wasn't surprised when a young work colleague, Claudia, whom I didn't know well but who had had heard me talking about Liv, came to me to talk about her transitioning sibling, Saffron, who was in her early twenties. I could tell how much Claudia was struggling to cope with the confusion and chaos that often accompanies gender dysphoria, because Saffron sought to find the courage to really fully come out as a man to everybody, and to live fully in his authentic gender all the time. Saffron hadn't been able to settle on a male name yet, yet he was taking testosterone and his voice was breaking, so for Claudia she lived with her sibling somewhere 'in the interregnum', which she found confronting and confusing. Perhaps what was even harder for Claudia was that Saffron, like so many transitioning young people, was wracked with a sad-anger that was often vented against Claudia. Indeed, Claudia described herself as frequently being Saffron's emotional punching bag.

Another work colleague, Sarah, whom I told about Liv's transitioning, spoke to me about her trans sister who was in her mid-thirties and who was still living at home after having done all of the medical transitioning procedures. Even though Sarah's sister completely passed as a woman, she was not feeling confident enough to move out independently into the world to live as a fully functioning adult. She felt trapped and angry at home, yet frozen and powerless to be able to move forward with her life. Sarah said her sister often treated her mother badly despite her mother having been entirely financially, psychologically and logistically supportive of her trans child over the years.

I have seen this relatively often in the trans parenting community: transitioning youngsters, often feeling rejected by transphobic elements in society and fraught with internal rejection of themselves as a consequence, strike out against their closest connections. Perhaps they do this because it is psychologically safe to do so, given the expectation and experience of unconditional love in most of these families. Ironically, however, this often creates tension and alienation when the transitioning person most needs the love and support of these allies. It's a complex situation.

What I seek to do in situations like Claudia's is to share my stories of struggle with Liv and her gender-dysphoric behaviour so that Claudia can perhaps feel a bit less alone with her difficulties. Then I try to encourage Claudia, or anyone else in this situation, to keep loving and supporting the trans person, given how tough the world is for trans people and how much they need support. I know it isn't easy to do, though. I have had my own experiences of Liv raging at me so much that I just want to keep my distance from her fury. I have learnt too, when things feel particularly tough and fragile, that it is essential for me reach out for support from others in the trans ally community.

I gave Claudia all my contacts and encouraged her to seek out a therapist for herself as a way of psychologically surviving her sibling's transitioning process.

My attempts to challenge and change the transgender world are not uniformly gentle and strategic, I am sorry to say. I have to confess that I have had a few aggressive moments when I confront people furiously about their transphobia. The parents on the online page refer to these kinds of moments as 'Mumma Bear' experiences. For example, one evening when Liv and I were heading onto the wharf to get the ferry to Circular Quay, the 'Balmain Bruiser', the very worst bully from her old school was at the wharf, sitting on the railing with a friend. When he saw Liv, he turned to his friend and said something and the two of them looked at Liv and laughed loudly at her. I saw red and walked up to him, standing very close to his face and asking him threateningly, 'What's so funny? Are you laughing at my daughter? Beware. I'm onto you.'

Despite the lameness of my threat, he stopped laughing and just stared at me and then turned away. With my heart literally pounding, I went to sit down on the wharf bench next to Olivia, who had hidden her face inside the hoodie of her jumper. I just kept on glaring at the bully, radiating hostility at him. Then something unexpected happened: he came over and said to me, 'I wasn't laughing at *her*... appearance, I'm sorry if you thought I was.' All I could say was, 'OK, but I'm still onto you.' Not very articulate or forgiving, I know.

I have no idea what the other ferry passengers made of our interaction that night but I did not care. Engaging in this level of conflict is not something I would ever choose to do but that night I didn't choose it: it was an instinctive protection of my child and a resistance to the boy's devastating bullying behaviours for so many months.

Liv is not an activist, so this engagement was really difficult for her. She does, however, regularly post answers in the trans section of the website Quora, a question-and-answer website where questions are asked, answered, edited and organised by its community of users. When I asked her what she posts, she told me that she mostly posts encouraging responses to people who are struggling with their experiences of being trans or coming out as trans, trying to give them a feeling of hope about their future. And thus, Liv has developed her own form of trans activism.

9

Are we over the hump yet?

I dreamt that Angus suggested to the kids and me that we give up living in a house and head off for an adventure living on the street, without any possessions. We agreed and off we went to live on the street, happy, close and connected, engaged with each other, not distracted by daily life (phones and so on). Amazingly, when life became hard on the streets for us, then something good would work out for us. For example, on our first night of being homeless, we were wondering how and where we would sleep outdoors. We were in a park with lots of other people and suddenly it was apparent that there were four black fleecy swags for us to sleep in where we could be warm and comfortable.

One of the difficulties of being on this trans journey has been an increase in my sense of not living life in the moment, but living for some time in the future, a time when, for example, Liv has oestrogen, a time when Liv has gender confirmation surgery, a time when it will be easier for Liv to be invisibly female, and so on. This feeling of not living in the now sometimes makes me feel that I am, we are, wishing our lives away. In the last few decades, I have worked hard to rid myself of this feeling of living for the next thing to happen, but I don't know that we can escape it in our current situation with Liv. I look forward to the day when we forget about her being trans and we are all, in our family, just living our lives in the moment, and Angus and I can be confident that she and Stirling are doing fine and are at peace with themselves and the world. I do wonder if and when this will be possible.

There are so many hurdles ahead. For example, we are going to have to support Liv extensively through the gender affirmation surgery that she wants to have at eighteen. The trans parents' website has had a few people go through this with their trans girls, some in Melbourne here in Australia, some in Thailand, and it's pretty enormous and onerous for about a year before, during and after the procedure. It's developmentally odd for me to consider just how involved we are going to be with Liv for years to come and how she is likely to be closely dependent on us for support given her gender dysphoria and the transphobia of the world. It's tough on her and it's tough on us. But at least technology and medical advances are on her side.

Advances in technology are also likely to make it possible for Liv to find love, as it seems most likely that, as with so many in her generation, she could meet her lovers online. This certainly seems to be the experience of most of the older trans teens that I read about on the trans parents' page and hear about at the trans parents support group. Liv is also open to much more fluid interpretations of how her life will work out. A while ago, she told me about a couple, a trans woman and trans man, who had a baby together and how some people were hating on them online but, in her view, it was really a sensible thing to do.

One of the advances we have made use of has been the modern advances in voice therapy. I have been taking Liv to Rosie, a speech pathologist who is helping her to feminise her voice. This amazing woman is about twenty-eight, a beautiful redhead with a big personality, a quick wit, sharp brain, and a warm heart. From the way she talks to and about Liv, it is apparent that she is a trans ally. In Liv's first meeting with her, they were sitting chatting, Rosie asking questions and Liv answering in her quirky way, and they were finding each other funny and clever, and they were having a very good time together. I loved that I was on the outside of their interaction, watching these two clever, young people enjoying each other's company. I felt as though I had a brief glimpse into Liv's future, a future where it was possible for her to interact happily, normally and easily with other young people, interactions which weren't shaped by her being trans or Aspie, just by what she and another person together found interesting, funny, and worth talking about. I wanted to hug Rosie when we left her rooms but, of course, I didn't – I knew it would embarrass her and Liv.

The July holidays were quite different from the April holidays. because Liv seemed to have made some significant internal shift that was solidifying into a situation where she was most often happy, and where she was able to conceptualise a future for herself. One morning, she and I were walking the dogs and her monologue suggested that she felt hopeful about her future.

'I was watching a video this morning on a series that I follow about child prodigies and the one I was watching today was about a girl in Sweden who is an artist prodigy. She's being home-schooled and only does art. Her mother says she wakes up and starts painting and just paints for six or eight hours, sometimes twenty if she's working on a big art work.'

'Did you like her art, Liv?'

'Well, she's very religious so her art is pretty religious but it's amazing. My favourite is an artwork she did of a huge baby with its arms open up like Christ on the cross. The detail and colour are amazing... One day I would like to live in a penthouse apartment with a grassy area for all my dogs, and you and Dad can live there with me if you want to and I'll make you eggs for breakfast every morning and I'll do dance training for two hours then I'll go back to my home studio where I'll work. Really it'll be a study but I prefer to call it a studio because I'll be creating in there, and I'll have everything there that I need and I'll work really hard, and maybe in the evening I'll socialise at a party or a pub for a short while with my friends, and then I may go to a dance class before going home to get to bed early so I can work well the next day...'

On and one she went, entertaining me with her soliloquy, her dreams for the future making my mother-heart so very happy. As we walked and I listened, I smiled at all the other dog walkers and greeted them warmly. After a while, I realised that I wasn't looking to see if they were clocking Liv as trans, I was just taking them at face value as good and kind, accepting and tolerant. I was no longer searching for discriminatory stares. It was extraordinarily liberating for me.

There was also hope on the horizon because Liv's appointment with a new endocrinologist was in sight. I was working hard to get together as many reports as possible to send to him before the appointment. Depressingly, the psychiatrist that Liv saw every few months was clear that she would be telling the endocrinologist that, even though she was certain that Liv was gender-dysphoric, she believed that teens are not ready to have hormone therapy until they are sixteen. Fortunately, Liv's gender counsellor, Anthony, sent this very supportive and insightful report through to the new endocrinologist.

Experience of Gender Dysphoria & Social Transition

As is a fairly common experience amongst transgender individuals, Olivia describes experiencing significant distress when the emergent physical changes of puberty started to take place early 2017. This was characterised by a worsening depression and anxiety caused by the conflict between her body developing male sex characteristics and her desire to be seen as and knowing she is of female gender identity. She describes feeling 'disgust' at her male features and struggles significantly with this.

In October of 2017 she came out to her parents and twin sibling, receiving both their acceptance and support. Olivia then made the decision to transition socially and change schools for 2018 to facilitate this process and commenced studies at a school in the inner west. Despite the presence of an LGBTI program within the school, Olivia was bullied by some students both at school and outside, with transphobia being the main component of the bullying. This was understandably traumatising, and much of the counselling with myself focused on Olivia processing and overcoming these experiences. To her credit, Olivia has shown genuine resilience in not allowing this to deter her authentic gender expression on a full-time basis.

Subsequently, Olivia transferred to the International Grammar School as a means to avoid transphobic bullying and reported, despite her initial concerns about the possibility of being bullied, that she was having a much more positive experience. Since counselling with me ended, her mother Lyndsay has advised that her grades are good and she is enjoying her studies far more now. Her teachers report she is motivated and hardworking.

Olivia presents as an intelligent, thoughtful young woman who is capable of significant insight not usually observed in people her age. Although initially quiet, she began to express herself more freely and display maturity beyond her years as the counselling relationship developed. Whilst some self-expressed difficulties around finding a peer group and friends is in-part linked to the presence of mild autism, she is able to persevere in seeking connections with others and succeeds in doing so. Olivia began to communicate her own desire for more space to individuate herself, which is a necessary component of teenage development into adulthood. Her mother has indicated a willingness to support this process and to negotiate this with Olivia.

Current Issues

A significant component of the counselling with Olivia involved supporting her around the significant depression and anxiety she experiences in relation to having to wait until age 16 to commence hormone replacement therapy. In our final session, I did seek to support Olivia with regards to this and the likely scenario that she would be denied access by medical practitioners to this treatment until age 16. She was significantly distressed during this process and this is understandable considering the level of emotional pain she experiences in relation to the physical changes associated with puberty.

This presents a challenging situation for both Olivia, her family and care-team. Olivia's presentation and identification as female has been consistent without any valid indicators to question the authenticity of her gender identity. The ongoing delay in the commencement of HRT is likely to continue to cause

Olivia significant difficulties with regards to her mental health which are self-explanatory. I consider it unlikely that anyone of significant expertise in the area of gender diversity would disagree that at a minimum, puberty blockers are appropriate for Olivia.

It is also worth noting that on June 18 of this year the Royal Children's Hospital service in Melbourne released guidelines on treating gender diverse children. These guidelines move away from the idea that access to hormone treatment should be based on chronological age, instead suggesting that the transition to treatment should depend on an individual's ability to make informed decisions, duration of puberty suppression, any coexisting health issues, and the level of family support. I am of the opinion that Olivia would benefit from such an approach.

As I read this supportive and thorough letter, I thought about how there is such a difference in what the medics choose to focus on when they see Liv, and hence how they treat her, and consequently how she feels about herself. The psychiatrist's report pathologises Liv as emotionally immature and focuses on the fact that she doesn't have much of a social life at the moment. Her gender counsellor and the lovely psychologist she now sees, a specialist in gender and sexuality, both focus on and encourage Liv's strengths. When she came out of the last appointment with the psychiatrist, she was depressed and angry. A day later she saw Kerrie, her psychologist, and she was, literally, skipping her way to my car after this session, a light in her eyes, her confidence peaking as she told me what she was planning to do to make our upcoming family holiday at the youth hostel in Pittwater a good and positive experience.

Liv was buoyant and hopeful that the new endocrinologist would give her testosterone blockers or oestrogen, telling me, 'I know the psychiatrist says I shouldn't rush into taking hormones but she forgets that I've thought for years about being transgender. It hasn't been an easy journey. I haven't just flippantly woken up one day and said, "Oh, I'm trans, I want hormones." It's been in my head for years now. And, for me, taking hormones isn't nearly as serious or difficult as having to keep starting at new schools because I've had to deal with bullying or rejection for being trans. That stuff is really hard. Taking hormones is just something that I have to do now.'

When the day of the appointment arrived, Liv got up early, showered and did her hair and make-up carefully and neatly, even allowing me to help – which doesn't happen often. Then she went to her room and put on her girliest clothes – pink camo pants and a feminine green T-shirt. I dressed to look as normal as possible – skirt, stockings, pretty pink shirt, ballet pumps, lots of make-up, trying to neaten up my short spiky haircut. Probably irrationally, I hoped that looking very normal and feminine would add credibility to our request. I guess I was operating on the probably faulty principle that if the endocrinologist saw me, not as an off-the-wall, radical parent, but as a very ordinary, middle-class mum who had accepted that her daughter was transgender, then we might more readily get a script for oestrogen! And so, hopeful as could be, we set off to across town for the appointment, looking as conventional and girly as possible.

On the way, we stopped off along the way for me to briefly meet with a work colleague. When she offered us tea, the three of us sat at her kitchen counter drinking tea and chatting and Liv was utterly charming and engaging – which was rather surprising to me given how anxious she was about the impending appointment. I guess the one sign of her anxiety was that she kept doing her strange 'sad whale' voice exercises that the speech pathologist had given her to do many times each day.

Once we were on the road again, I mentioned to Liv some of the possible questions that the endocrinologist might ask her, hoping she could try out answering them with me, but she said she would think about them, and then she turned the volume on the radio up so that there was no space to chat further.

We arrived at the endocrinologist's rooms early and so we headed to a café for lunch and tea. As we sat on the wooden bench in the glorious weak winter sun, waiting for the tea and chicken salads to arrive, Liv read her book very intently, clearly avoiding any conversation with me.

Before we ate lunch, we had scouted out the exact location of the doctor's rooms so we knew exactly where to go when the time was right. Even so, we were still a few minutes early through his doors. The family before us – a dad, mum and young trans woman – were just paying the receptionist for their appointment when we arrived. The parents looked even more mainstream than me. They also checked me out as I did them, probably, like me, mildly curious about each other's experience of having a transgender child given that it is a rather unusual familial situation.

The doctor called us in promptly at two-fifteen. His office was simple and modest and he sat behind a large desk with a very smart laptop dominating the space. As he introduced himself, I was struck by how diffident, quiet and shy he was. This was unexpected for me, given how large his reputation was in the trans community. He had Liv's file in front of him and he referred to it as he asked her a number of questions. It was apparent from his questions that he had read the many documents and reports that I had emailed to him.

A few questions in, I couldn't help myself and I started on my advocacy campaign. 'My husband and I are very certain that our child is gender-dysphoric. So are all the medics she has seen. We feel that it's important she's able to medically transition as soon as possible and that she goes through puberty with the girls in her age cohort. There have been so many medics in our journey, including psychologists and counsellors, as you'll see from the reports, who agree with us. We've heard the argument from a previous endocrinologist and psychiatrist that she's only fourteen and she should mature further, and do more therapy, and live as a girl for longer before she takes hormones, but we don't see the sense in that. The same medics have said that they too are convinced that she is gender-dysphoric and that she's not one of those teens who's going to change her mind, but they assert that their protocol dictates that Liv must wait until she's sixteen to have hormone treatment. We're of the view that such a position is irrational as it assumes that all people develop in the same way and at the same time.

We believe, in line with much international research, that chronological age is not an adequate measure to judge readiness for hormone therapy.'

I was obviously sounding too argumentatively persuasive, because Liv put her hand out to me and suggested that I needed to calm down a bit, Mum. That didn't stop me but when I paused for breath, the doctor, who had been intently focused on listening to me, said, 'I really can't see why Olivia shouldn't have hormone treatment.'

That really stopped me in my tracks. 'Really?' I asked him, the wind taken out of my sails.

'Yes,' he said. 'Come over here, Olivia and, if you don't mind, I would like to do a physical examination.'

As he examined her, I felt my body relax and I felt the tears well up in my eyes. As he measured her height and noted that she was 182 centimetres tall – nearly six feet – he commented to her that oestrogen would potentially inhibit further height growth. When they sat down again, he began to explain some of the possible hormone options for now and in the future.

Then, bizarrely, Liv set about working to persuade him that he should be cautious with what he prescribed to her. 'For years I've read about hormone treatment on the internet and I know that these drugs can go wrong for people and that it's very important to start off slowly and carefully, with regular tests to see how the body is reacting to the medication.'

I looked at Liv in shock and surprise, thinking that she might convince him that she didn't need hormones. As he started to talk about all the precautions that he would take, I realised that probably she had been more persuasive than me in convincing him that she was a sensible, thought-through, and cautious person who wouldn't be asking for hormones lightly.

We agreed on a protocol for the way forward: starting immediately, Liv would take a two-milligram oestrogen (Oestradiol) tablet three times a day after meals, and in five weeks she would have a blood test to see how she was processing the oestrogen. The doctor asked us to see him again in six weeks to discuss the way forward based on her blood tests and her response to the oestrogen. He added that, at that stage, he might need to add testosterone blockers and/or progesterone to her chemical concoction and that, once she had settled on the oestrogen, it would be safer for her to have it administered as an implant every few months because then the oestrogen would not be processed via her liver, as the tablets were.

And that was it. We walked out of his rooms with a script and a path lab request form for a blood test to be done in a few weeks. As we were paying the receptionist, she commented that it was a while since she had seen people smiling as widely as Liv and me. I could not believe that finally we had managed to secure the oestrogen for her. I was practically skipping down the street towards the car-park, not even caring how much I was embarrassing Liv with my child-like behaviour. The world immediately seemed like a better and kinder place to me.

On the way home, we stopped off at Westfield Mall to have Liv's ears pierced again – the last piercing had gone sceptic after she wore cheap earrings and she had had to let the holes close over. The young woman who did the piercing was lovely, although she did think that Liv was transitioning from girl to boy, a mistake which Liv felt ambivalent about! We filled the oestrogen script at a pharmacy in the mall and Liv took her first oestrogen pill on the way home. It was a momentous occasion.

Liv was very responsible about regularly taking what she called her 'booby pills'. She seemed more hormonal and grumpier at times and I wasn't sure if it was caused by the oestrogen or by her being fourteen years old. However, after a few weeks on the tablets, she started feeling really nauseated and having headaches most of the time too. I felt sorry for her, desperately wishing that I could do something to take away the nausea and headache. I know what it is to feel the physical side effects of hormones.

Ironically and unhappily, at that time when Liv started on

oestrogen, she was misgendered more than usual. For example, when some very sweet men were doing some work at our house and one of them addressed Liv and Stirling with 'Hello, boys' and the manager at the Pittwater Youth Hostel said to them, 'Boys, please collect some wood and make a fire in the lounge room,' and then the ferry man said 'Jump aboard, boys.' This happened over and over. Even more than usual, I consciously sought out opportunities to mention to people whom we encountered for the first time, 'This is my daughter, Olivia,' in order to cue them to recognise that she was a girl and thus ensure that they didn't misgender her.

It seemed possible that misgendering was happening more at this time because Liv had had her hair extensions removed in the first week of the school holidays. The extensions had become awful and messy and looked really artificial, so they had to go. Having a relatively short bob-style haircut meant that there were less cues to others that she was a girl – hence the misgendering.

I knew that Liv was feeling apprehensive about starting term 3 at IGS with her shorter hair and was worried that she might be misgendered more, so I was working hard to convince her to wear a skirt to school and wear make-up every day. She was not keen on these suggestions, though, telling me that she wasn't feeling confident enough to wear a skirt to school again but that she would be wearing the girls' sports uniform and girls' school pants. It was such a terrible catch 22 situation and was making her moody and miserable, often reluctant to venture out of the house and see people. There were times when I colluded with this choice of hers: I couldn't bear her being misgendered, so sometimes I avoided taking her into situations where there was any chance this could happen.

Angus and I were talking about this difficult issue in our parent therapy session and Belinda, our therapist, argued strongly that we had to explain to Liv that she can't have it both ways: she can't be sensitive to misgendering and really angry when it happens if she is not prepared to try to feminise her look. She also said that Liv can't blame others for misgendering her and that she shouldn't be angry with anyone who does misgender her accidentally, because it is not their fault and that we need to help her to see this.

While Belinda was talking, I realised that underlying this proposed discussion with Liv was the implicit suggestion that she didn't yet pass completely as a girl, something that she would likely find very hard to hear from us. Belinda said that we should not worry about it as Liv was likely to be fully cognisant of the painful reality that she didn't really pass (yet) and that it was vital that we were authentic with her about it.

As I have said before, this is a difficult issue for Angus and for me because we don't like the idea of policing her feminising process, especially as we believe that women should be freed from the unfair pressure of working hard to look good and being judged primarily on their appearance. Liv should be able simply to dress as she pleases; she should be able to refuse to be confined by binary identities and gender stereotyping.

A friend told me how, at a conference she had attended, there had been a participant who looked absolutely male in all physical respects including clothing and so on, but, when she introduced herself (with a deep, male voice), she had explained to the group that she was actually female and she wanted to be addressed using her female name and with female pronouns. She made no effort at all to feminise and explained that she had no intention of doing so. The person telling me this story had spent a day in the group with the same group members and she said that all day she had struggled with recognising and identifying this participant as female. I could empathise. I believe that there should be more freedom for people to identify and present exactly as they wish, but we live in such a binary and genderised world that it just doesn't seem feasible – here and now, anyway. Maybe in the future, it will be possible.

Around this time, I had a dream that Liv went off to camp and, somehow, came home on her own before the camp finished. When she walked in the door at home, she said to me that she didn't want to go back to camp because she didn't want to conform by doing the same thing as everyone else. I disagreed with her, as I thought the camp would be fun for her. I drove her back to camp and left her there. She returned home again before camp was due to finish. This time she returned with a bunch of other kids, and they were all cheerful and confident, telling me that camp was not for them and that they were not going back. I think the dream is a reflection of how Liv chooses to be in the world: fiercely independent and uniquely different, and this is evident in her approach to being a girl/woman too – and it is something I need to accept.

Interestingly, when school resumed, Liv's peers gave her many compliments about her short hair (with the extensions now removed).

She told me after day one of term 3, 'People really liked my haircut. The other Olivia in my class was telling me how much she liked it and I said to her I was aiming for the bad ass look and she laughed and said that I didn't really succeed in getting that particular look, but my hair looked really good anyway.' Liv was clearly very pleased with these compliments, as she mentioned them often in her stories about her school day.

She and I also had an interesting discussion about her current studies in the subject personal development, health and physical education (PDHPE).

'In PDHPE today, the teacher showed us a video about gender and it was OK, not that good, but still it was great to talk about the issues, even though I know all about them. He asked if anyone who has experiences with LGBTI would talk about them to the class to help everybody understand and I think I'll do that so that people can know what it feels like to be trans. Can you believe that some people didn't know what bisexual meant? They didn't know what intersex was either, but that's not surprising.'

'What would you say if you did talk to the class, Liv?'

'I'd explain the stages of transitioning and how the medical and chemical processes work.'

'What about telling people about the social and emotional aspects? Perhaps you could tell them about how you came to realise that you were trans, what the social transitioning process has involved, what's been good about transitioning, what's been hard.'

'Maybe, but I think they'd be most interested in how it all happens. Anyway, I'm not sure that I'll do it. I'll see.'

In the end, Liv didn't speak to her class about her experiences of being transgender but, for their term assessment in PDHPE, the students had to choose to do a presentation on 'A significant Australian woman' and Liv chose to do hers on the remarkable transgender activist, eighteen-year-old Georgie Stone, Young Victorian of the Year in 2017. At the age of ten, Georgie was the youngest person to receive hormone blockers in Australia and eventually campaigned to change the law requiring transgender children and their families to apply to the Family Court to access this treatment. At the time that Liv spoke about her, Georgie was in Year 12, school captain at her Melbourne school, and bravely speaking out on transgender rights in many public forums. Georgie also spoke with Prince Harry and Meghan Markle about transgender rights when they visited Sydney for the Invictus Games. She explained to their Royal Highnesses that the message of community and determination to overcome obstacles, which the Invictus Games embody, was also inspiring for a proud transgender young person like her to be the best that she could be. She is an amazing young woman. I was so pleased that Liv chose to talk about Georgie for her assessment. It felt brave, healthy and good for Liv.

Over the term in PDHPE, the teacher continued to discuss gender differences with the class and, during this time, he was very clear about the significance of not misgendering trans people and always using the correct pronouns. Thank goodness Liv was in a school where the issue was taken so seriously.

Liv doesn't find fitting in at any school easy and, even at IGS, she is clearly quite an enigma for the other students, who really don't know what to make of her. It seemed to me that, at the early stages of her time at IGS, most students responded by keeping their distance from her.

This was apparent when, one day, after fetching her from school after a school excursion to the mangroves of Botany Bay, she told me, 'The excursion was so much fun, Mum. We got so wet and muddy wading into the water to catch fish with nets and we caught hundreds of little fish and even a squid that released red ink, which was scary because I thought we'd killed it but we hadn't. We released them all and then we waded in even further to look at the sea grass. I'm so tall that my shorts didn't even get wet. It was fun and exhausting. On the way home, nobody wanted to sit with me, so I sat next to a teacher who took up most of the seat, so that was a bit tough. On the way there, everyone was on their phones but I wasn't because I wanted to look out of the window and see where we were going because it was all new…'

On and on she went talking cheerfully about the day, but my heart had stopped at the point where she had said that nobody had wanted to sit next to her on the bus. Liv can be awkward socially but she can also be engaging with the right kind of person – for example, someone interested in ideas and innovations, technology and books, and in the world beyond pop culture and celebrities.

Belinda, our parent therapist, had been clear to Angus and me that Liv not having much of a social base at school was a big issue that needed attention. Belinda's view is that, for a fourteen-year-old girl, winning is belonging and we had to help Liv find ways to truly belong at IGS. She suggested we make an appointment to see the school psychologist to discuss how the teachers could support Liv to establish strategies for her to feel more included and more connected with other students.

I discussed these social issues with Liv and she explained to me that she was making an effort at school. 'I do try, Mum. On Friday at the excursion, I had your voice in my head and my therapist's voice too as I went over to talk to the groups of people hanging out together. I tried really hard to make conversation with them, even though sometimes it felt like they weren't interested. I know you have to just stick it out and keep engaging until you become friends. I find it easier to relate to the boys, as we have more similar interests and they're less cliquey and closed than the girls, who don't seem open to having new people join their groups. Most of the kids have been at school together since kindy, so it's especially hard to break into their groups. I'm quite friendly with a boy called Logan, who seems to like the same things as me. Do you know what I'd like even more than a friend? I'd like an associate, someone I could work with on big projects like coding or technology.'

I wondered, though, if her moodiness deterred the boys and girls at school from wanting to engage with her. At home, since being on oestrogen, she had become intermittently sulky, brooding and intensely hostile at times, storming out of the house one Saturday night while shouting at us, 'Screw you all,' and slamming the door after her, all because she didn't want to watch the film Stirling and his friends had chosen, and she was mad because she couldn't game on her PC in the same room. This was a new kind of rage and form of forceful hostility from her. Previously in her low moments, she had been deeply sad; now in her low moments she was intensely angry.

My research on the net said that this intensely emotional and hostile behaviour was a likely response to beginning to take oestrogen. There were some obvious signs that the oestrogen was working on her body so, of course, it must also be working on her mind and her moods. Knowing this helped a bit but really it was hard to live with so much anger being directed at us in her close family. If I let her game all the time on her computer and let her watch videos endlessly on her iPad, I think she might have been relatively happy (certainly easier to live with) but one thing I was really concerned about at that time was losing Liv to the world of virtual reality. It was already difficult for her to go outside and to engage with strangers – she didn't even like to go into a shop to buy a chocolate on her own – so allowing her to retreat full-time into the virtual world could not be good for her in the long term. She told me many times that she desperately wanted to turn eighteen because, for her, itn signified a time when she would be free of the constraints and strictures of school and parents, a free agent able to make all her own decisions.

At other times, she was just angelically lovely, waking up after a traumatic/dramatic night, friendly and talkative, willing to walk and talk with me for ages, being cooperative and helpful at home, and sociable and engaging with the three of us. Adolescence really is a bipolar state of being: so much up and down. So, after the initial exhaustion and misery when term 3 began, she was, by week four, coming home from school most days excited and cheerful.

'Today at lunchtime in Karaoke Club I finally sang my karaoke song with Mr Galea that he and I have been talking about since last term. "Never gonna give you up, never gonna let you down, never gonna run around and desert you." It was such fun. Everyone's scared of Mr Galea because he's so strict but actually he's really cool if you're good… Today during assembly time we had our elective presentations and the hard thing is that there are so many subjects that I want to do next year and the year after for my elective and I know that I mustn't do all the subjects I really like next year in Year 9 because I have to keep some of my favourites for Year 10… I'am obviously going to do maths and maths extension. I love maths and I'm sure I'll need it for whatever job I do, programming or being a surgeon or whatever…'

I loved this conversation because Liv was talking positively and purposefully about her future: next year and the year after, and even when she is an adult. And I had a sense of her life potentially being 'normal' and 'ordinary'. I also loved it because it indicated to me that she was happy and engaged during her school day and that she was finding joy and meaning in her daily life. This was a great relief because it was in stark contrast to some of her dark and desperate days in the last few years. When she talked in a rush like this, with a light in her eyes, full of excitement about the possibilities that life had to offer, I felt intensely emotional, full of relief, hope, and even joy, and I asked more and more questions because I did not want these life-affirming conversations to end.

One of the issues that was making Liv unhappy was that she had not transitioned legally. Every time we went to a medic, for example, her old name had to come up sometime, somewhere: when we filled in the 'new patient' forms, or when the nurse at reception was confused and couldn't find an 'Olivia' on her system because they still had the old name recorded there, or when we went to pay and I had to use our Medicare card with her old name, and so on. One morning when Liv was having blood taken before our visit to the endocrinologist, she had to sign forms and vials of blood to verify that her 'old' name was her name. She always came out of these situations fraught and angry because she had had to identify with her deadname. Changing her name is a very bureaucratic task which requires changing her name first on her birth certificate, then on her passport, then on our Medicare and private health insurance card, and so on.

On this day, on the way home from the blood test, she told me that she was going to investigate the process to legally change her name and get the process going – and she did. She found the forms online for the birth certificate process and we filled them in. We have now changed her name at Births, Deaths and Marriages NSW so she has a Change of Name Certificate with her new name recorded on it and we have moved on to her changing her passport and her Medicare card and private health insurance card.

After Liv's experience with nobody wanting to sit next to her on the bus on the way back from the school excursion, and our therapist Belinda's encouraging us to contact the school counsellor to see if she could talk to the teachers about facilitating Liv's connections at school, I got onto it. This wasn't usually the kind of thing I did – ask the school to help out with my child's social integration – but I did worry about Liv's social life at school so I went to IGS to see the very gentle school counsellor, Tamara, and Paul Galea, the deputy principal of the high school and the coordinator of extracurricular activities. After listening to my concerns about Liv making social connections, the deputy head l and I had this conversation.

'Is Liv happy here at school?'

'Yes.'

'Good. That accords with my experience of her. She seems settled and happy and involved. What does she like to do?'

'Technology. Dance. Reading. Unity and other forms of coding. Anything to do with computers or anime. She loves the school Book Club, Woodwork Club and Anime Club.'

'OK, I'll see if she can come and help out with the Unity classes for the younger kids. Would she like that?'

'Yes, I think she would.'

'OK. What about her joining the Robotics Club? They meet after school on Tuesdays. I reckon she'd find like-minded people there.'

'Yes, I think she would.'

'OK, I'll sort that out too. You talk to her at home and see if she'd like these activities and I'll talk to her at school and to the teachers concerned. Olivia is a really great kid. I make a special effort to see her as much as I can. I'll work with her and see how I can get her included but it's early days for her at IGS and she'll develop her own social world organically.' And off he went to supervise a Year 12 trial exam.

Within a few days, he came through with all that he said he would and he was right: organically, Liv was making social connections and engaging more with the others in her class and in her year cohort. She mentioned a number of the same students regularly, she had slowly found a small group to sit with at recess and, seemingly, she was at home in the clubs and societies that she attended each lunchtime. She was in a daily online chat group with some of the nerdy boys in her classes. She attended the Robotics Club after school and loved it. She and her friend Ciara spent quite a lot of time together and, she told me, they always have to hug each other when they first see each other 'as girls do'. She and her friend, Leo, were in the school's Inner-city Hiking Club together and, apparently, they chatted flat out for the hour and a half that they walked together around the city. So things were going well for Liv.

And then the hormone hurricane really hit us.

10

Hormone hell

I had a dream about being in a wheelchair on a complicated maze-like ramp and I couldn't seem to make my way down it, encountering blocked paths wherever I went. I was frustrated and felt trapped and helpless with no idea how to move forward.

After six weeks on the oestrogen pills, we went back to the endocrinologist for a check-up and there was good news and bad news. He showed us the results of the blood test that Liv had had a few days prior: she had almost no trace of testosterone in her blood at all. That was good news because it meant that the oestrogen pills were working. The other good news was that there was an alternative to her current pills, which seemed to be giving Liv terrible headaches and nausea: he prescribed oestrogen patches (100 mcg) to use instead of the pills, telling us that it was likely that the patches would stabilise the input of oestrogen into her body. The patches also meant that the oestrogen did not have to enter her body via her liver so this too should mean that the nausea she had been experiencing would be alleviated, and maybe even eradicated. The bad news was that Liv's emotionality and moodiness was, according to him, here to stay for some time at least, and was largely related to her being adolescent.

Over the next few days, it was apparent that the patches didn't reduce the side effects. Liv still had debilitating nausea, headaches and dizziness. She was even finding it difficult to focus during class. She told me that during a Chinese assessment, her headache had been so bad and she had felt so dizzy that she had no idea what she was writing and speaking. I felt sorry for her when I saw how much she was struggling physically and I felt desperate when she was sad, grumpy, angry and moody. I guess perhaps she was experiencing an exaggerated or intense version of the hormonal troubles many girls have during adolescence, particularly when menstruating.

These were the kinds of troubling texting interchanges that she and I had at this time.

'Mom, I guess that notifying you of my deteriorating mental state isn't a good idea right now.'

'Babe, I'm trying to take care of you the best way that I can. Can I make a therapy appointment for you?'

'Nope. Can you fetch me from school now?'

'Liv, I'm visiting Guy in hospital. I can't come now.'

'Well, thanks. Sarcasm. I practically had a mental breakdown in Chinese today. I was crying. I can hardly function right now.'

'Ah, babe, I'm so sorry. What do you want me to do?'

'Right now, nothing, as it seems you can't fetch me and take me home.'

'I'll be back in the city by lunchtime and can fetch you.'

'I'll be OK. It'll be too late by then.'

One of the very difficult aspects of Liv's transitioning was that her angry-sadness was most often directed at me. One morning I was at her school helping out with RUOK day activities, encouraging students arriving at school to draw positive and cheerful RUOK messages with chalk on the pavement outside the school. While I was doing that, ironically, Liv was inside the school building texting me about how miserable she was

'I feel very lonely. Screw life.'

'I hear your pain, babe, and I love you.'

'Do you? Do you? I've just had enough.'

'(emoji of crying faces)'

Every day during that terrible week – the second week of the 100 mcg patches – when she got home from school, she raged at me. Eventually, I could not take it any more and I explained the impact of her anger on me, how hard it was for me to feel her raging against me. She listened and then she cried like a child and held on to me, sobbing and saying sorry over and over.

I was reminded of my therapist saying to me that Liv's behaviour is the classic attachment behaviour of an infant who is furious with the parent for not seeming to meet all her needs, and then when the parents seems angry and alienated by the child's behaviour, she clings onto the parent, desperately afraid of having caused a potential break in their bond. It was absolutely exhausting. I knew that Liv was struggling massively and I felt terribly worried, sad and helpless. I worried especially because I knew that Liv had to have oestrogen in order to transition and I worried that maybe she wouldn't be able to tolerate it and then where would she be?

She was also not wanting to go to school, going to sick bay as soon as she was there and then asking the receptionist to phone me to fetch her – which I usually couldn't do as I was working. She told me that she could barely concentrate in class. One day she told me that in maths that day – a class that she loves and usually does well in – she had felt really dumb because she couldn't understand anything that the teacher was saying. This, she said, was happening to her in most of her classes at that time. When she spoke about it, I worried that the oestrogen might permanently and negatively impact an aspect of Liv's life that was good and positive for her: her academic interest and achievements. I felt that the oestrogen was changing an essential aspect of who she was.

There were days when I had to go to work and I would drop her at the school bus stop and she would be sobbing and desperately unhappy. There were other days when she said that she just could not manage to go to school because she felt so sick and sad and she just lay in bed. She missed a lot of school at this time and she told me that, even when she was at school, she often put her head on the desk or lay on the floor because she felt so sick with nausea, headaches, muscle weakness and vertigo. Angus and I worried that the more she didn't go to school, the more she wouldn't want to go to school. It was an overwhelmingly tough time. I realised that I had to give up focusing on how Liv was doing academically and just concentrate on her ability to go to school and get through the day without too much misery.

The irony didn't escape me that I was, at that time, developing and facilitating a well-being program for vulnerable Year 9 teens at high schools around Sydney. Some days, I would come home from working with seriously disaffected teens and then have to deal with my own very disaffected teen at home. I felt exhausted and deeply troubled, unsure of where to turn and how we were going to progress.

One evening she came into the study where I was working and put her head on my lap, and I could see that she had been crying. When I asked what was wrong, she told me she felt worthless. I know from the trans parents' group and online page that depression is a very, very common experience of trans youngsters, and that it often centres on the physicality of the trans kid, a physicality that they loathe. Liv, for example, had told me how hard it is to feel confident doing ballet when she feels herself to be so big and ugly. I wondered if this sense of worthlessness and even debilitating self-hatred is a response to how transgender people feel consciously and unconsciously rejected by large tracts of society. I wondered too if the dissonance between the body and mind, between the genotypes and hormones, between the inner and outer physical selves is a significant cause of these depressive episodes and associated sense of worthlessness.

Liv told me that she was having terrible nightmares most nights and that some nights she just didn't want to close her eyes and go to sleep because she was afraid of the nightmares beginning. The nightmares were usually about us enrolling her in another new school and her feeling absolutely unable to cope. Sometimes they were throwbacks to the bullying that she had experienced in her previous school.

Liv's physical and mental trauma after she began taking the high doses of oestrogen impacted on all of us. During this time, Angus and I were at a dinner party at the home of people we didn't know all that well.

The host, Sean, was having a getting-to-know-you conversation with Angus. 'So why did you leave Manly, Angus?'

'We moved because last year we came to know that we have a transgender daughter and there were more schooling and other opportunities for her in the inner west.'

'Wow, that's tough. It must have been a big year for you.'

'Yes, it has been.'

'What has been the hardest thing about your daughter transitioning?'

'I always thought it was going to be the social transitioning process but it turns out the medical transitioning may be the hardest because the oestrogen is making her so sick. I'm not sure what we'll do if we can't find a way for her to tolerate oestrogen. I also worry a lot because the oestrogen makes her so sick that she doesn't want to go to school and I don't know what that means for her future. The hardest thing for me is that there is no sense of when and whether this will ever get easier for her.'

Watching and listening to Angus talk, I could feel his heartache.

A week or so later, I was visiting our lovely GP, Simone, with Stirling, and after she had finished sorting out Stirling, I talked with her about the extreme oestrogen troubles that Liv was having. Simone researched the dose of the patches that Liv was on at that time – 100 mcg – and suggested that we move her onto the lowest dose of 25 mcg and see if she could tolerate that and then slowly move on to 50 mcg and 75 mcg and then eventually, hopefully, she could tolerate 100mcg. And that is what we did. Simone gave us a script for the very lowest dose and I went straight home and replaced the high-dose patch on Liv's lower back with the new one.

Within a few days, Liv was coping so much better. She still had a headache often, and nausea sometimes, but she could manage them and she even had moments when she was singing in the bathroom again – a sure sign that she was doing OK. She started to come home from school with stories again, stories about conversations with her friend Leo, and about how her friend Ciara was one of the best friends she had ever had, that she had really enjoyed maths class that day, that she was keen to go on the Gender Centre trans teens camp during the holidays, and so on.

When I took her for a check-up with the endocrinologist and we discussed her ongoing negative side effects from the oestrogen, he suggested that the headaches and nausea that Liv was still having might well be related to the uneven dose of oestrogen that she received from the oestrogen patches. He proposed that he gave Liv a very low-dose oestrogen implant because it distributed the oestrogen more evenly and steadily over time and hence could potentially significantly reduce her symptoms.

Liv and I discussed this option there in his rooms and she decided she would try out the implant. She went into his examination room and he gave her a local anaesthetic and then made a three-millimetre incision into which he inserted a 100 mg implant of fused crystalline beta-oestradiol. He put on steri-tape to close the wound and that was that. It felt quite scary that for the following six months we could not adjust Liv's hormone input because it was too difficult to extract the implant.

On this implant, Liv still has a few negative oestrogen side effects, but they are limited and irregular. She sometimes still gets headaches but they are briefer and not debilitating. She doesn't seem to have much nausea. I chatted with our pharmacist and she advised me to try giving Liv a supplement called Vitex which is made by a company called Bioceuticals. Vitex has been created for women with PMS – which, I guess, is what is happening for Liv but not just for the usual week a month but for the whole month. Vitex has made a big difference to Liv's ability to process the oestrogen and we hope that at some point her body is going to completely adjust to the influx of oestrogen and she will no longer have any side effects. Maybe when we do the next implant, six months from the time she had the first one inserted, we might consider her having only half of the capsule implanted, that is, 50 mg.

On an emotional level, Liv has begun to have very much milder storms. Although these storms don't come with much of a warning – her face will just crumple and tears will start to run down her face – they are no longer tsunami-level storms, and they pass relatively quickly. If she seems sad, we check in with her, asking her, 'What's up, Liv?' and she tells us that she feels sad and so we just love her and comfort her and try to distract her and the storm passes and soon she is cheerful again. I have come to accept that this will likely be a feature of her adolescence and that we need to be open to accepting it and loving her through relatively regular dark moments. Her emotions do build up and she has to release them through her tears and then, when the tears have passed, she often/usually comes out of the other side in a more positive and cheerful psychological and interactional space.

On most days now we have no sadness at all – just good cheer and positivity. For example, one Saturday morning when Liv woke early and came through to the lounge room in her pink pjs and giant pink fluffy gown, she lay next to me where I was reading on the sofa and, while I played with her increasingly wild and long hair, she cheerfully free-associated.

'Mum, yesterday we got our English writing assignment back and I got 18/20 and for my drama assessment I got 15/15... I want to show you the pictures of Bauhaus Ballerinas, I think that the Bauhaus Revolution is my favourite revolution because it really brought in modernism... I think the oestrogen is working now, which is good... I need to get a job so that I can give you and Dad half of my money so that Dad doesn't have to work so hard... I really like my mentor at school, the trans guy. He's just so casual about being trans – like yesterday he was telling us that Chemist Warehouse is having a sale on testosterone and oestrogen and that he hopes that sale is still on when he starts testosterone in a few months...'

On and on she talked and my heart contracted with love as I watched her and listened to her.

Later that morning, I was at my desk and I heard her in the kitchen chatting with Angus while he made us all coffee and pancakes. She told him about her French excursion, analysing in detail the French movie that she and her classmates had watched, explaining why she liked it and why she thought most of the other students didn't, then describing the galettes they had eaten at the French café where they all forgot to order in French and what she could have said to the waitron in order to practise her French. After the excursion had been thoroughly covered, she and Angus talked about the tools that they needed for the workshop and what they would be able to make and do. Their relationship has, of late, become so much closer and more connected.

And in those moments, on that Saturday morning in her interaction with me and with Angus, I could feel that Liv was much more at peace with herself in the world and that being trans felt, right then, incidental and marginal, maybe even insignificant, to her. She was just living life as an ordinary teenager. She was just Liv.

11

Futurists?

I dreamt that Stirling and I were going on holiday and that we had to walk to our holiday destination. We were walking and walking and it was raining some of the time and we walked past other people having happy and relaxed holidays. We passed a house where a young woman was sitting in the half-light on the window ledge staring out into the distance, reflectively, and we couldn't tell if she was sad or not, but we assumed that she might be. I kept thinking that perhaps we were nearly at our holiday destination but I was wrong and we had to keep walking round one bend after the other. The clouds were heavy and it was getting dark; it was nearly nightfall. Stirling saw a triple bunk bed in a house near the road and asked if we were staying there. No, I said, we have to keep going. I kept thinking our destination was closer than it was. Every time I thought we were there, then I discovered that we weren't.

The first year of trans parenting was undoubtedly one of the hardest years of my life, first getting over my own shock at, entirely unexpectedly, having a trans child and then helping Angus and Stirling overcome their shock. Mostly, though, the hardest thing for me has been accompanying Liv through her traumatic gender-dysphoric storm. This journey has been tough in ways that we, Angus and I, could never have imagined. And, as in the dream, there have been times when we have felt that we would never reach a quiet place to rest.

I cannot even begin to envisage what it must have been like for Liv to feel that the person that she sees in the mirror and in the shower is not her in some very profound ways, indeed that that person is the opposite of how she feels yourself to be. And to know that she has years to go before she can have the surgery that creates an external her that she feels will represent the internal her. Whenever I feel weighed down or impatient with Liv, I try to imagine what it must be like to live with this terrible dissonance. I know that I can never succeed in understanding what it really feels like for her but just trying to imagine it allows me to reconnect with my empathic self.

I have no idea how our journey is going to progress from here: every moment thus far has come as a surprise to us. There has been no overview map or GPS to consult so that we can plot the way. We have had some truly, lovely, competent professionals supporting us along the way and that has made a significant difference. And my daily interaction with the online trans parents' group has been a mainstay for me through the storms. My close friends and my sisters have been enormously supportive. Still, though, it has been quite a lonely experience, most often just me and Liv, me struggling with Liv, Liv struggling with herself, me wondering what the right response should be to so many conundrums. I have never felt so inadequate, so unclear, so uncertain, so desperately lost in my parenting journey as I have during this first year as a trans parent. This book is about the struggle to find some light and clarity, some framework to understand what we are all going through.

Right now, Stirling is doing much better emotionally and psychologically than he has since before Liv came out to him. He seems settled about having a sister. Indeed, his recent emotional troubles have centred not on Liv and her transitioning or any transitional storms, but on a bust-up with his closest friend which took months to resolve. I know that he is more settled internally because he is happier to go to school and more engaged in his classes. And, importantly too, Liv and Stirling are getting along well. As I sit here typing, I can hear them playing a computer game and laughing together. There can be no happier sound for a mother. Stirling has decided, with us, that he will be joining Liv at the International Grammar School from Year 9. It is a school much more in keeping with all of our values than the school he was at (which was the school that was not comfortable to have Liv transitioning).

I am working with a therapist who is helping me to slowly work through my psychodynamics and hopefully one effect of that will be that I will learn to parent my children as cleanly as possible, limiting, where I can, interference from my troubled childhood.

Emigration and trans parenting are the most defining features of my adult life and I realise that both of these massive transformation processes have been manageable largely because of the love and connection between Angus and me. Sometimes when things have been really tough at home, Angus and I have taken the dogs out for a long walk along the Balmain harbour, and found, in those moments together, a kind of contentment and connection that has given us the strength to return to the fray of adolescence and trans parenting with renewed empathy, energy and patience. This connection may well have been our children's saving grace too. Our parent therapist likes to paraphrase the famous psychoanalyst-author Donald Winnicott, who writes about how a positive and loving connection between parents is vital for the healthy emotional development of the adolescent.

We are now settled in Balmain, and our new house and neighbourhood feel like home. I am so relieved that we don't have to contend with living near the Balmain Bruiser any more, that Liv can walk the dogs down to the harbour park near our house and I don't have to worry that she will be bullied by anyone. Well, I hope not – I have learnt that one should never say never! It does feel much quieter and safer here, however.

I can't say that politically things feel safe for Liv under the current Prime Minister Scott Morrison, whose diatribe about gender whisperers in schools making children trans only serves to foster the erroneous and dangerous view that trans kids have some kind of choice about being trans. I wish I could get Liv to write to him and tell him her story, to tell him how she wouldn't choose to be trans, but that she just is, and how her coming out has, in so many ways, saved her. In general, there seems to be a worrying international shift to the political right which threatens the safe space that has been carved out for LGBTIQA people.

I have to remind myself regularly that there are many protective and insulating forces in Liv's life: there is us, her family who are loving her and supporting her through her transitioning, and there is her incredible school where it's OK to be trans and where she has been able to forge lovely connections and relationships. And then there is all the support that we as a family get from our friends and family and the Gender Centre and the trans parents' online page.

And, much to our very great surprise, for the first time, Liv has begun dating someone, a student at her school. The two of them spend hours chatting online and hanging out together at Broadway Mall after school and on weekends. Of course, I worry like crazy that if and when this relationship ends, Liv will be devastated and depressed and we will struggle to get her to go to school. But I also know that this relationship is developmentally appropriate and normal, and I love how happy it makes her.

Liv told me about a dream she had recently. 'My brother was being a bum and so I took Archi and Serena out for a walk and we bumped into Naomi and Jinty [Liv's cousin and her mum] walking KitKat [their cat] and we had such a lovely long walk. Archi was walking slowly and weirdly, plodding along, and people were starting at him but he didn't care. We walked down and up a very steep hill and we came to a coffee shop where we talked about books and libraries and Naomi and I talked about our dream school which had a library with three floors.'

Such a very ordinary dream in some ways but also a dream about some of what really matters to Liv. Interestingly, none of it is about trans matters – it is just about the things that move her. That's what I wish for her, because that's what she wishes for herself. Of course, I do wonder if, in her dream, Liv is represented by her precious dog, Archimedes, because she, like him in the dream, is noticeably different. But, hopefully, she, like Archi, doesn't care all that much about being different. From birth Liv has been an unconventional youngster. And she continues to be. She is not going to be a conventional girl and she never could have been. And we cannot expect it of her, nor should we. She is fiercely and uniquely herself, not willing or able to be categorised or stereotyped and that's the way we would choose her to be. Her cousin Naomi is, like Liv, an unconventional child – hence the walking of the cat perhaps – and I guess that's why Naomi is in the dream: they are both unconventional kids, and yet here they are doing the most ordinary activity: walking their precious pets.

Liv's view that she does not want being transgender as central to her identity is a commonly held perspective amongst the younger generations. The other day on ABC Radio National I heard an interview with Juno Dawson, a famous young adult writer from the UK, in which she was talking about her recent novel called *Clean*. *Clean* is about a drug rehabilitation centre for teens and one of the characters in the centre, Kendall, is a trans teen who is in there because she has an eating disorder. Dawson, herself transgender, spoke in the interview about how it was important to her to represent Kendall's core issue as her eating disorder and not as her being transgender. Dawson spoke about how much she wants her own trans status to be just one singular aspect of her identity, as important as her red hair and freckles, and not something that dominates how she sees herself or how others see her. Hopefully, this will increasingly become the dominant experience for young trans people. It will suit Liv very well.

It seems to me that Juno Dawson, Liv and others are part of a new generation that is just emerging, a generation in which there is fluidity about who one is, so much fluidity perhaps that it is superfluous to even decide whether one is a girl or a boy, gay or not gay. It seems that there is less clarity and certainty around gender and sexual identities than there has ever been. I thought about this the other night when I was in Bunnings with Liv, who I had just fetched her from her ballet class. She was standing in the tools section, in her ballet gear, intensely interested in all the electric tools, explaining to me in great detail the function of each tool. And, all the while that we were in Bunnings and I was listening to her love affair with tools, I reflected on how she absolutely does not conform to female stereotypes and she never will and maybe that helps to contribute towards breaking down gender stereotypes.

Perhaps this generation of trans youth with their open, fluid approach to identity are futurists, human beings ahead of their time, drivers and agents of change, forecasters and predictors living the future long before we have even seen it. This is not an easy role to play in society because usually it entails conflict; just as prophets have been part of human existence forever, so too are those who resist change at all costs, who are determined to maintain the status quo. This struggle between the forces for and against change is, I guess, an ancient battle that has happened throughout our evolution as human beings.

On 25 October, it was Angus's birthday. It was also exactly a year since we had known that Liv was a girl and not a boy. The four of us – Angus, Stirling, Liv and I – were celebrating this joint occasion at a local Italian pizzeria when I asked Liv what her thoughts were about the year that had been,

'It has been the hardest and most important year of my life, Mum.' Indeed.

Stirling followed Liv's comment up with a story from the morning. 'When I got onto the bus this morning, a Year 10 boy from my school asked me, "So, who was that chick you were with at the bus stop this morning?" and I told him, "That was my sister," and he said, "OK, cool."'

And our conversation moved on. I sat back with a glass of Shiraz in the noisy restaurant with the heat pumping out at us from the pizza oven, and I thought about what a big year we had all had. I knew, too, that there were still many more big years ahead of us. I watched Angus listening to Liv and Stirling chatting away animatedly, the two of them jumping wildly between discussions about tools, cricket, technology, mates, things that had happened at school that day, what a teacher had said, what they had seen on YouTube, their plans for the next day. I smiled and thought about how truly, madly, deeply I loved these three human beings. I thought too about the question, 'What would love do?' Perhaps the answer is simply another question: 'What wouldn't love do?'

12

A word with Liv

I dreamt that I was staying illegally in someone's holiday house. One morning early, I realised that there were other people in the house too. I saw two very tall, dark-haired, androgynous girls wandering around in their pink pjs, seemingly squatting there as I was. They were complaining about all the noise and then I realised that this noise was coming from another resident, a very noisy French bloke who couldn't speak a language that I could understand, and vice versa. We struggled as we couldn't understand each other at all. The phone rang and we all considered whether we should answer it but worried about doing so as this could expose us as illegal squatters. When we did answer, it was the fire brigade on the phone. I was afraid too that I was going to be in extra trouble because I had breached social etiquette as I had been telling someone's confidential story to someone else.

This dream reveals a difficult question for me about writing this book: whose story is this to tell? Clearly, I did and do feel, at some level, uncomfortable about telling Liv's story. I asked her to read a draft of the book and to give me feedback on it so that I could remove anything she didn't like about it. This is a record of our conversation with me typing up the questions and then typing up her answers as she spoke.

Me: Your dad and your brother have read the draft of this book, Liv, but you don't want to?

Liv: No, not yet. It's mainly because I don't feel ready yet to look back on some of the stuff that has happened this year. I don't feel like reading stuff about my old name and stuff. I definitely will read it sometime, though.

Me: Even though you haven't read it, though, are you OK with me putting the book out into the public domain?

Liv: Yeah, I'm fine with it. I'm fairly openly trans, so that's not a big deal to me. I'm straight with people when they ask if I am trans so having the book out in the open is totally fine. I do feel a bit nervous about it, so maybe it is not totally fine but I do think it's important that it gets out there, as maybe my story can help other trans people and maybe it can educate people about what it means to be trans.

Me: Some of the very hardest aspects of the last year are recorded here, Liv – your depression and trauma, your tears and rages.

Liv: Mum, people have to know that this is an incredibly difficult process, coming out as trans. It's not something anyone does lightly. I want other trans kids not to feel so alone and so confused, and my story might help them with that.

Me: What are the dominant experiences of the year since coming out as trans?

Liv: What immediately comes to mind is definitely the changing of high schools so many times. I've been to a lot of schools but these school changes have been the hardest so far. Normally, anyway, I'm not a person who easily adjusts to change and so that has been a dominant part of the year. Another big thing that jumped out to me when you asked this question was definitely some of the bullying experiences that happened at the beginning of the year. I mean, compared to some people's experiences of being bullied perhaps they weren't the most dramatic experiences, but they still stick with me a lot, and even now I get fearful when I hear some of the words that those bullies used, even if they're not directed towards me. A final dominant experience for the year has been my family – even if sometimes I get angry and moody with my parents, I couldn't ask for anyone better to be with me on my journey. I can't imagine what it must be like to have family that can't accept you're trans. My heart goes out to those people. I definitely feel much closer to my family after this first year is done and dusted.

Me: What advice do you have for the parents of children who come out as trans?

Liv: The most important thing by far is being supportive for your kid, let them know that you're there for them, take them to psychologists and endocrinologists, support them with their journey in whatever way you can. I know it's not easy for the parents of a trans child.

Me: What advice do you have for trans kids?

Liv: Remember that you're not alone. It's really helped me get out of dark places when I remembered that I was not the only trans kid in the world and there were lots of people out there who are trans and if they could get through the hard times, then I could too. Another bit of advice I can give – although really I'm not the master of being trans – is to keep a hold of who you are, don't feel like you have to conform to stereotypes, don't feel like you have to change who you are to fit in. Look inside yourself and know who you are and don't lose sight of that. And remember that even if it's hard, even if you're close to giving up, just remember that there is a future out there and that if you keep pushing through, you'll reach there eventually. Also, having dogs helps as well because they comfort you. This is not serious advice but my dogs have really been there for me!

Me: What advice do you have for siblings of trans kids?

Liv: I love my brother and he has been mostly really supportive but he has sometimes carelessly said things that hurt my feelings that he didn't think were a big deal. The number one piece of advice for trans siblings is to educate yourself and realise that just because your sibling is trans doesn't mean that they're a different person from the person that they were before they came out.

Me: What has helped you the most in the transitioning?

Liv: 50% family, 10% friends and 40% Netflix! Nah, I'm joking. Although the highest percentage of help coming from family is true.

My family have definitely helped keep me together, so have my friends. I think something that's often overlooked for trans kids is the need to do something that you really love doing. Finding your passion can really help to keep you going, can give you drive and fight. Exploring my passions – computers and dance and, to some degree, woodworking – really has given me something to hold onto, an interest, a dream and a distraction. Doing something you love is really important I think, for all people.

Me: What's the been the hardest thing for you about transitioning?

Liv: Unfortunately, I could have a long list of stuff here but if we're going to talk about the hardest thing, I would say definitely it's been my inside thoughts, things such as 'Do I look girly enough?' 'Do I do enough girly things? 'Am I going to pass?' 'I'm so ugly', and some of those thoughts can be really self-destructive. I won't deny that I do still have those thoughts after a year being out as trans and I am not sure I'll ever stop having thoughts along those lines. Finding love for myself has definitely been really hard.

Me: How do you see the next few years panning out for you in your transitioning journey?

Liv: I'm going through the motions of life, hoping to sort out the problems I have taking hormones at the moment. I've really felt the hormones starting to take full effect. And also, I'll be passing the time waiting for the gender reassignment surgery (GRS) which I plan to have in my gap year, if I can save enough money from jobs and if it's all approved by the doctors. I really want to have the GRS as soon as possible and to have it before I go to university, so recovery won't get in the way of my studies and working. We also have to finalise my name changing so I'm all legally Olivia. There's a lot to do still.

Me: What are your dreams for your future, Liv?

Liv: I just want to be who I want to be, who I am. Thanks for writing this book, Mum.

Me: I love you, Livvy. I am so proud of you.

Afterword

I had a dream which seemed to me to be about the many different ways that we could have engaged in this journey with Liv: I dreamt that I was trying to get somewhere on public transport and I was struggling to find my direction. Angus gave me directions but still I couldn't work it out. I didn't feel able to ask people how to find the bus but eventually I did and a man directed me one way towards the bus stop and it wasn't clear what to do when I got round the corner. Eventually, I just got on a bus and headed off in the direction of the city and when I got off the bus – on a street corner which necessitated a clear choice of direction – I still didn't know which way to walk. I just set off in one particular direction and it turns out that either route would have been fine and I was able to find my way. I was so relieved when it became apparent that I was heading in the right direction despite my just having navigated my way rather randomly, just deciding that I had to make some choice about where and how to go, and taking the risk and ultimately it worked out, but, as it turns out, another choice would have worked out just as well.

I do not want to give the impression that, in finishing this book, I believe that everything is all good here, all worked through for us. Quite the contrary, in fact. Liv's transitioning is going to be a long journey – for all of us. This book is simply my record of my experiences of the first year of her transitioning. Writing it has been cathartic for me. I hope that, in some way, our experiences in this unfamiliar territory can be useful to others journeying with kids who are different.

After the afterword

Reading the proofs of this book that I wrote a year ago, I am taken aback by how much has changed in our lives in the last year. Liv has been living her authentic self for more than two years now and so much has settled and sorted itself for her and for all of us. Indeed, Stirling and I were having coffee this morning and chatting about life (as he likes to do) and he said to me, 'It's all good, Lynds.' He has taken to calling me by my first name as he negotiates his individuation process. He continued to explain what he meant. 'Liv isn't a trans girl any more, she's just a girl, and that's good.' And that's how it is for us. When I meet new people these days, I tell them I have twins, a son and a daughter, and when I meet up with friends and they ask, 'How are the kids?' I tell them, 'All good.'

December 2019

Lightning Source UK Ltd.
Milton Keynes UK
UKHW011255020320
359621UK00002B/427

9 781760 418641